ENDORS

"God has sent out a vision of transformation and renewal to the people of Nashville. The calling has been heard from the streets to the State Capital. The message is simply for those 'who have ears to hear.' Since God does not change—the message has not either. 'Follow Me.' Whether we adhere to the calling now or let it pass onto deaf ears— Nashville is soon to be A City on Its Knees. This book sends a loud message to all cities nationwide—Follow Him!"

—JASON ALEXANDER, Councilman 28th District, Nashville

"In the Civil War the battle of Franklin and of Nashville marked the turning point for the victory of freedom in America. And again in this day, Nashville is one of the most greatly contested for cities in America. A battle presently rages over Nashville and it is again a battle for freedom ... for spiritual freedom, and for freedom of worship! The abundance of music and of publishing that is generated and sent out from Nashville has made it a voice that impacts the nations. If Nashville authentically changes and turns to God, so will this nation ... and if America genuinely changes ... so will the nations! The leaders who have contributed to this book are veterans in the battle for Nashville. Their corporate voice and wisdom is well worth listening to—whether you are fighting for this city or an another."

—SCOTT MACLEOD, Pastor, The Fortress Fellowship
President of Provision Inner City Ministries

"Only the Lord could count all of the passionate prayer and sacrifices that have been offered for Nashville. Every prayer, every passionate person stationed in this city for this hour is essential for the Kingdom of God to conquer the Kingdom of a religious life that is casual and self-satisfying. When the day is over, may it be said of us that we accomplished the purpose of God for our city in our generation. And it is my most fervent prayer that history will not say of these days in which you and I live that, 'THEY DID WHAT THEY COULD DO.' But that we will have so lived, and so entreated Him, that like in the Book of Acts, that He was able to do only what He could do. We have heard the saying, "The good becomes the enemy of the best." For us in Nashville, I believe the enemy of the supernatural is the natural."

—DAVID FITZPATRICK, Pastor, Abounding Grace Fellowship

What would Jesus say to Nashville?
"You are living beneath your potential. You are positioned to impact the world, Nashville! Get a clear Kingdom vision and focus, and see how fruitful you could actually be for ME. To whom much is given, much is required. I am requiring of you that you listen for my voice, obey my word, and throw off every hindering distraction. It's your time, Nashville, to rise up and fulfill your destiny!"

—BRAD WATSON, Pastor, Harvest international Church

"It is said that sixty per cent of the population of America is within a days driving distance of Nashville. If we were to consider that Nashville is the heart of center for so many, what is the heart in the body responsible for doing? It is there that impurities are filtered and a fresh flow of life giving blood is sent. God is calling our city (the Bible Belt) to strengthen what remains to be a center of truth to share the gospel of Christ. What an opportunity!"

—PASTOR DAVID ROYALTY, First Baptist Church Joelton

Eagles Landing Publishing
ISBN # 0-9710294-0-7
For Worldwide Distribution
Printed in the U.S.A.

First Printing: May 2001, by Vaughan Printing

This book is available at Christian bookstores and distributors worldwide.

For a U.S. bookstore nearest you, call **1-888-331-5932**.
For more information on foreign distributors call 615-299-8100 or write:
Eagles Landing Publishing
P.O. Box 121
Joelton, TN 37080
Or reach us on the Internet: **http://www.ACityonitsKnees.org**

ACKNOWLEDGMENTS

First and foremost, I thank my awesome God for all He has accomplished in His inspiration to see this project through.

Second, to my wife, Jodi, you are my angel, my companion, and my wisdom on this earth. If heaven were a place, it would be right here with you.

For my two dear children, James and Jacob I will always cherish the joy you both bring to me for letting me be "your daddy."

To all the pastors and ministers who came together for the purpose to bring God's word to the people of the cities. This wouldn't be in the people's hands if it were not for your unity and sacrifice. Angels in heaven are applauding all of you.

To Steven Mansfield for his inspiration from his book "Releasing Destiny." Thank you for the references to strongholds we repent for in, "In One Voice."

To my pastor and shepherd, David Royalty, who has a unique way of bringing scripture to life by being *a living example* of Christ Jesus, himself.

To Cindy Rogers and Pam Baggott for typing, Wayne Flemming for statistical information, Scott Macleod and Pastor Frank Gill for spiritual editing, and Ed Silvolso for inspiration!

And finally, to all people who make up the Body of Christ everywhere—that through this book you will hear the cry of the city, find the pulse of prevailing prayer, catch the heartbeat of worship, live the pursuit of holiness, and become an active participant of love in reaching the lost through Jesus Christ. Come help us. WE NEED YOU! For this *is our* revival—Christ Jesus, revealed to humanity.

> ... *For the winds of change are now blowing!*
> *Lord, give us ears to hear what Your Spirit is saying!*

DEDICATION

This book is gratefully dedicated to "The City" of faithful intercessors who have recognized the famine of God's presence in the land; that is on its knees in fervent prayer; investing in holy hunger; raging with passion through Spirit-birthed obedience; calling upon God for the fire of revival to fall unrestrained on our land. Through declaration, these prayers will not go unanswered in OUR generation.

It is my prayer and desire, along with those of a heavenly host of other God-seeking believers, that all city gates throughout the world would lift up their heads to kiss the Son, Jesus Christ, and let Him in. "Open wide, ye City gates!" May God arise, and demonstrate His power throughout the city that declares His Name!

It is in this breath that as one united chorus we the people of the city of Nashville, Tennessee, celebrate the love of God in proclaiming and dedicating Music City, USA, to be God's anointed "Worship City," USA! HALLELUJAH! Breathe on us Lord!

Lastly, but most importantly, this book is humbly dedicated to my Lord and Savior, Jesus Christ, who came and saved a wretch like me, removing me from the curse of death, so that I could have a seat with the Master of the universe in all eternity. Thank You, Jesus, for knocking on my door, and sending Your Holy Spirit Fire to me. IT'S IS ALL ABOUT JESUS!

NASHVILLE

A

CITY

ON ITS

KNEES

"…but you shall receive power when the Holy Spirit has come upon you; and you shall be my witnesses both in Jerusalem, and in all Judea and Samaria, and even to the remotest part of the earth."
–ACTS 1:8

"See, I am sending my messenger to prepare the way before me, and the Lord whom you seek will suddenly come to His temple. But who can endure the day of His coming, and who can stand when He appears?"
–MALACHI 3:1,2

WARNING!!!!!
READING, STUDYING, AND APPLYING
THE BASIC FUNDAMENTALS IN THIS BOOK
HAVE BEEN KNOWN TO CAUSE SUDDEN....

REVIVAL!!

R E V I V A L: "SUDDEN APPREHENSION BY GOD"

Oh Lord, have mercy.......

Contents and Authors

From Dream to Reality

by Jeffrey M. Richfield

I REMEMBER VIVIDLY the events that brought the dream to reality in producing: Nashville, A City On its Knees.

It was a restless Saturday night. I had felt the grip of God heavily upon me. Tossing and turning left me with little sleep. I sensed a birthing was soon to take place. As I lay there in the darkness I knew He was right there upon me. Like the Song of Solomon, "I had slept, but my heart was awake." In times past, I had chosen to wrestle with God to my undoing, but this time my encounter with Him was in the fullness of His time.

I arose early the next day, Sunday morning, January 21, 2001. With a crystal-clear vision and a sudden determination in my spirit, I was seemingly obsessed to get a message out to the people, specifically the people of the city. Although God had planted seeds in my heart years prior to write a book, the timing and the plan had not taken root. It wasn't until I got out of the way and made room that the seed could be watered from heavenly places upon fertile soil. In His time I now had a release from God in compiling a book portraying unity, reformation, revival, forgiveness, and love. This Kingdom vision is not only for the city of Nashville, but as a labor of love for all cities that hold these values to be true.

In this labor of love, I have chosen to leave clarity subject to the Author's own voices and have kept their signatures and writing styles true to their heart. If any "grammar expert" argues the integrity of sentence structure/edits please allow some grace. Read in this mindset and you will be touched with the weight of their cries bearing upon your soul.

"For we know only in part, and we prophesy only in part; but when the complete comes, the partial will come to an end."
-1 Corinthians 13:9-10

GOD IS NEVER ON TIME, BUT HE IS NEVER TOO LATE

ONE SUNDAY MORNING

THAT SUNDAY MORNING, on the way out the door to church, in a matter of ten minutes I wrote out on my laptop the title, cover template, themes, authors, and chapter titles. I remember saying to myself, "These aren't my fingers stroking the keys," as they sped out the book's content. As my wife and I hurried off to church, I remember telling her in excitement the vision I had had during the night.

There was remarkable ease in putting the manuscript together. It was a unified effort. All the authors had a sincere desire to get their message out to the people. I was not surprised as many of them had already felt called by God to write the chapters God had picked for them. The cover outlay and design fell right in place as I happened upon a dear friend, Travis Foster, who helped me network and find the right team in graphics and printing. As the chapters kept pouring in, David Prentice, from Vaughn Printing, was so patient with me by allowing for three extensions. As it was, the road had been cleared all the way through to the very end. All I had to do was get out of the way, get the wax out of my ears, be still, and obey His voice.

I remember one testing experience in the beginning as I got the word out to pastors on the book's vision of unity in co-authorship. There was a waiting period of about two weeks that seemed like a lifetime in which I had not received one response. I began to question God's word to me at the "burning bush" and thought, "Maybe I'm not the guy for the task. You see, Lord, I'm not so eloquent with words, and "Maybe I'm supposed to write it all, and I'm backing out by asking other pastors to help write it." I decided to pray that day to receive a word. The very next day affirmative responses came to me from pastors asserting they were on board. I was ecstatic! I felt this was definitely the hand of God.

MANY PRAYERS; MANY THANKS

IN LIEU OF space for this introduction, I will not bring forth my family's testimony as it is still in the birthing process. I will say that God has been faithful in providing my family's way through many valleys. I feel we need to capture more of our testimony's glories in a later book entitled, *"Testimonies."* This first work is expressed from the people of God to the people of the city.

My family and I made a decision from the start to give the first fruits of this book financially to the wonderful ministries in this book. It is my family's sincere prayer and expectation for almighty God to honor His challenge in Malachi 3:10 by providing such a bountiful blessing from you, the reader, that these ministries will have avalanches of wealth fall upon them as the Lord knows their need. He promised we can test Him in this: *"Bring the full tithe into the storehouse......and see if I will not open the doors of heaven for you and pour down for you an overflowing blessing"* (Mal: 3:10).

In reading, my hope is that you are left with this challenge: never cease in supplication for Jesus' impartation of revival in our lifetime! All arms to bear in prayer! To sum it up these pastors and ministers have written the material herein to strengthen your resolve, help secure your desire, and perhaps come alongside you as a spiritual spotter to let you know, "We are right here with you all the way!" I pray that as you read the messages, proclamations, and heart-cries in this book that you will feel its words come to life, opening the eyes of your heart, bringing conviction to your soul, moving your spirit to become heavy for prevailing prayer, and literally transform your walk with God. That it will help take us many steps closer toward revival in the throne room of Jesus Himself, so that this city, may literally become...a city on its knees.

I have never been so excited about the message of this book as it captures so much of the heart of God through its diversity. This project has strengthened the realization that we are a mere handbreadth away from true revival. I feel we are so close to piercing a heavenly veil which when ruptured will pour out God's manifold grace immeasurably and with it the greatest release of the revival generations.

I am now careful to extend all glory to God for whatever He does through this book. May it ignite a holy fire in your life. As we enter into His gates, let's pray: Lord God Almighty, As I read this book I ask You to speak to me personally by Your Spirit. May its words give me a clear message and draw me closer in intimacy to Christ and my community. As I read open my eyes to see Your desire for my life, my family, and my city. Lord, give me a directive, a purpose, and a plan to join You in Your work. I thank You in advance for changing my life by Your message in this book. AMEN.

FIRE FALLS WHERE IT IS LIKELY TO CATCH
AND SPREAD. WILL WE PROVIDE
THE NECESSARY TINDER?

INTERSECTIONS WITH GOD

When the time has finally come
by Don Finto

DID YOU KNOW that over half the believers in all of history are alive today? This is possible since it is only in recent times that the population of the world reached a billion people, that number rapidly swelling to over six billion today.

Did you know that seventy percent of all who have ever come to faith in Jesus have come since 1900? That seventy percent of those have come since 1950, and seventy percent of those Christians since 1990.

Strangely enough, in the last forty years, hundreds of thousands of Jewish people have come to believe that Yeshua (Jesus) is the Promised Messiah of whom the prophets spoke. This has not happened since the first century. These newly resurrected believers have formed hundreds of synagogues of Jesus-believers in Israel, the United States, the former Soviet Union and other nations throughout the world.

At the turn of the 20th century, there were only about one million Christians in China. Today that number has increased to eighty million or more, with an additional 1200 per hour coming to faith, according to a recent report. The African Christian population grew from 3 percent to over 50 percent during the 20th century. In that same time frame, South Korea went from 1 percent Christian to almost 40 percent. South America has seen a dramatic increase of born-again believers in the last thirty years. The predominantly Muslim nation of Indonesia is now about 20 percent Christian. There are 103,000,000 Christian believers in India. More Muslims have come to faith in Jesus in the last thirty years than in all of the history of Islam.

Why?

And what does this have to do with "Nashville, A City on Its Knees"?

We are living in a day of world revival. Mission organizations and denominations are uniting to reach the world. We are in the midst of a vast prayer movement. At this moment tens of thousands of Christians are meeting on prayer mountains, in prayer grottos, in church buildings, in homes or even in forests and caves. Daily we are hearing about miracles and healings that are taking place in the name of Jesus. There are reports of unusual phenomena in South America, in India, in Africa, in the United States, and here, in Nashville, Tennessee. People all around the globe are fanning the flame of desire in their hearts—recapturing "Intimacy Lost" with God and His people.

A blind woman in India calls on Jesus for help and awakens with her eyesight restored the next morning. In one evening in a North African village every member of a Muslim community experienced the Presence of the Lord through a vision, a dream, or an angelic visitation. Gold dust and gold teeth began to show up in South America, and here in Hendersonville, Tennessee. Revival would strangely come upon a church in the North America and some would begin to shake or fall under the power of the Holy Spirit.

Why?

WHEN GOD'S PROMISE INTERSECTS WITH HIS TIMING, HE LOOKS FOR THOSE WHO WILL PARTICIPATE WITH HIM TO ACCOMPLISH HIS WORK.

We are living in a day when the promise of God and the timing of God are intersecting. Today He is looking for those who will participate with Him in bringing to the world, to Nashville and Middle Tennessee, its finest hour: "God's Kingdom on Earth."

From the harbor of the inner city to the ports of our own counties these visitations are increasingly more manifest for those with hungry hearts for this hour.

In Nehemiah's day, witnesses that intersected with God in rebuilding the temple were met with much resistance. As we rebuild "The North Gate" in God's redemptive purposes His work requires the combined efforts of all His people. We cannot afford to wait and quake at the threat of resistance, but break through enthusiastically and overtake the enemy.

When Moses saw the burning bush in the desert of Midian, the promise of God and the timing of God were intersecting. God had told Abraham (see Gen. 15:13-16) that his descendants would live as captives in a foreign land for four hundred years before being brought back to Canaan, the land of their inheritance. Four hundred years had now passed. The timing set by God had arrived.

God was offering Moses the opportunity to participate with Him in the fulfillment of His purpose in that day—the deliverance of Israel from the land of enslavement. There could have been no deliverance one hundred years earlier. Not until the "fullness of time" would God bring forth the promised deliverer.

Nor was it a foregone conclusion that Moses would respond favorably to God's initiative. In fact, Moses did not readily accept God's offer. "Why me?" He moaned. "Who shall I say sent me?" "What if they won't listen?" "I have never been eloquent...I am slow of speech and tongue...please send someone else to do it." Finally, reluctantly, Moses accepted the assignment and became God's partner in leading Israel out of Egyptian bondage.

The timing of the promise had come. Abraham's descendants were returning to the land of the covenant. Moses was an empowered participant.

Like Moses we are at another of those intersections ordained of God, and He is calling for our participation. Participation makes for "True Transformations."

The prophet Daniel had one of those promise and timing intersection experiences one day while he was reading the Jeremiah scroll.

Daniel had been captured and brought to Babylon as a youth in the days of King Nebuchadnezzar. During his "imprisonment" he had to deal with "Matters of the Heart." He lived through the reign of five other kings in Babylon before the Medes and Persians came to power. Darius the Mede was now king. Seventy years had passed.

Daniel, now an old man of eighty five to ninety years of age, is reading from the prophecy scrolls when he happens upon the words of Jeremiah. "When seventy years are completed for Babylon, I will come to you and fulfill my gracious promise to bring you back to this place," the Lord had told Jeremiah (29:10).

"Seventy years," Daniel must have mused. "The time has come! God will deliver us back into our land." And so it was that Daniel gave himself to prayer and fasting. He began to confess his own sins and the sins of his people, knowing that God was about to fulfill His word. He became a prayer participant with God in the fulfillment of all God had spoken. Daniel was "A Man with a Mission." Just as Daniel became a vessel to be used of God through faith, we share the blessings of God in seeing the fruit of our labors.

As noted from Daniel, in returning to "A House of Prayer," upon his knees he had found the keys that literally unlocked the gates of heaven.

Hundreds, even thousands, across Nashville and Middle Tennessee have read, and are reading from the "scrolls." There is a "timing of God" upon us. We have seen His intentions and we are "on our knees" until we see His will birthed.

"The Next Generation" of revivalists will not relinquish ground in their call for a great outpouring of His Spirit in their lifetime. These are "The Revolutionists" bent in reshaping our city for Christ in this, the greatest spiritual assault now upon the human race.

Young Mary from Nazareth was caught in one of God's promise and fulfillment intersections when the angel Gabriel visited her.

Four thousand years earlier a promise had been made in a garden. "He (the seed of woman) will crush your head," God had told the devil (Gen. 3:15).

Two thousand years later another promise was given to a childless father on a starlit night. "I will bless you. I will make you into a great nation...all peoples on earth will be blessed through you" (Gen. 12:1-3).

These two seemingly unrelated promises lay dormant for centuries.

"A virgin will be with child," the Lord said through the prophet Isaiah about thirteen hundred years later (7:14). "The ruler will come from you, Bethlehem," was the word through Micah (5:2). He will come "riding on a donkey," added Zechariah (9:9).

Years passed. No virgin bearing a son. No king arriving on a donkey. The blessing to the nations was delayed. The whole world lay captive to the serpent in the garden.

And then centuries of waiting gave way to a single "suddenly" (Mal. 3:1). An angel appeared to the young virgin from Nazareth. "You will be with child...his kingdom will never end."

"The fullness of time," Paul called it (Gal. 4:14).

Promise and timing had intersected. "The time has come," Jesus said as He began His days of personal ministry at thirty years of age (Mark 1:15). "Father, the time has come," He said in prayer on the night before His crucifixion.

Today we are living in another promise/timing-of-God intersection. You may not hear the voice of God from a burning bush or see an angel, but you can read from the scrolls of Isaiah, Jeremiah, Ezekiel, and Daniel. You can hear the revelation and read the vision that came to Luke, Paul and John from promises spoken by Jesus.

"When these things begin to take place," Jesus said, "your redemption is drawing near" (Luke 21:28).

What things? What was to signal the near return of the Lord? In "The End of Days" we are told of signs and wonders accompanied by false teachers that will lead to a great falling away (1 Timothy 4:1).

Another very substantial scriptural evidence of our redemption drawing near would be *when Israel would return to the Promised land! "Israel Redeemed!"*

Israel would again be exiled from her Promised Land, but would return. When the nation is reborn and the city of Jerusalem no longer under the domination of the Gentiles, this would signal the "beginning of the end," Jesus promised (Luke 21:20, 24, 28, 32).

"Is God finished with the nation of Israel?" was Paul's question to the Roman Christians. "By no means!... Not at all!" is his response. In fact, their return, their "fullness," their "acceptance" will be a time of "greater riches," that will be like "life from the dead" for the whole world (see Romans 11:1,11,12,15).

VIII

"The great event of Israel's return to God in Christ, and His to Israel will be the signal and the means of a vast rise of spiritual life in the universal church, and of an unexampled ingathering of regenerate souls from the world," said Bishop Handley C.G. Moule, chaplain to the Queen of England in the late 19th century.[1]

We are experiencing that revival in our day.

Timing and Promise have intersected. "Can I Find a Witness?"

That is the reason for the enormous influx of Jewish believers. This is why revival is sweeping through Asia, Africa, and South America.

And this is why it will yet move like a tidal wave across Nashville, Middle Tennessee, and the United States. In "Catching the Next Wave," we must be spiritually in tune, focusing our eyes on Jesus as we get wet when revival crashes on the Volunteer state coastline!

The stirring you are feeling in your spirit, the desire to know more of His Presence, the heightened joy of worship, the call to holiness, the growing unity of believers that is reaching across every artificial line, the expanding compassion for the poor, the partnership in evangelizing, the call to prayer and fasting, to confession of our own sins and the sins of the generations—all of this relates to *the intersection of promise and timing in our day.* All these are worshipping Him in truth and in spirit.

GOD IS AT WORK! He is calling us to participate with Him. "Open Your Eyes!" He's right at the door!

We are catching hold of God's desires, and like King David, "After God's own Heart," we are holding on to them tenaciously until *His work is fully birthed!*

About the Author

Don Finto was senior pastor of Belmont church for over twenty-five years. He is married to Martha Ann (Graves) Finto. They have three children and seven grandchildren. His current mission: The Caleb Company, Nashville, TN. His current book is *"Your People Shall Be My People."*

[1]Bishop Moule makes this statement in his commentary on "The Epistle of St. Paul to the Romans," *Expositor's Bible, A Complete Exposition of the Bible in Six Volumes with Index,* vol. 5 (Grand Rapids, MI: Wm. B. Eerdmans Publishing Co., 1956), p. 590.

PART I

RECOGNIZING THE NEED

*"A true revival means nothing less than a revolution,
casting out the spirit of worldliness and selfishness,
and making God and His love triumph in the heart and life."*
—Andrew Murray

INTIMACY LOST

Fanning the Flame of Desire Within You
by Jeffrey M. Richfield

TAKE A MOMENT and ask yourself, "What are the inner desires of my heart?" Are you passionate for what you believe in? What are the most significant values and beliefs in your life today? It is true that if we have not desire then we have not belief. For our belief produces what you desire. Therefore, it's only what you believe in—and *do next*—that brings about what you desire.

You and I grapple through a society that forever pushes us to contend for the norm. As human history grinds on, we find ourselves in a competition of fads and cell-phones, so lured into materialism by advertising and the Internet that it's getting increasingly more difficult to see our way clear, just *what are* the inward desires of our hearts?

We live in a world where truths are suspect and falsehoods are routinely justified. As the pace of today's society gains momentum many are disillusioned by the "American dream" and what it has to offer. Day after day we arise to swab off the deck from the grime of debt we continue to dish out to ourselves for a lap of luxury. Our paradigm has shifted. So much is within our grasp yet so much is out of control. This American Dream offers all things to all people at an incredible expense—our families. We're a people ever so busy. We all want a nice home, a nice car, the big screen TV—but what are we *really* doing with our lives?

As biotechnology tampers with Pandora's Box in the next hypo-advancement of cloning humans and political parties jockey to bring global peace, our generation seems to be drifting ever further and further away from what really matters.

When something drifts away you don't see it leave port. You simply continue with what you normally do and, later, when you finally look up, you notice it has left the harbor and traveled somewhere downstream. Overwhelmed, you run to try to get it back, but come to realize it is much too late. It is beyond your grip, and soon it gets far out of your sight.

Today's modern age over-emphasizes business and success more than the love of God and our fellow man. When we "let go" by taking our spiritual eyes off founding principles that draw us toward the heart of God, we then become spiritually adrift. Once clear doctrinal issues blur out of focus.

At this point of crisis, we *must* come to realize a change is needed and adapt to His Truth—*and apply it*—so God will advance in mercy, throwing out His lifeline of redemption, averting judgment.

FROM THE VANTAGE POINT OF ETERNITY
WE LIVE IN A WRINKLE OF TIME...
SOMEWHERE BETWEEN THE PROMISE
AND REDEMPTION OF GOD

The church today is at a key turning point. There seems to be considerable commotion within the Body of Christ. It's as if the church did have a Y2K dilemma but not quite the one we thought it would be.

What's happening?

Our Master is a renovator! Jesus is rearranging the furniture of His house just as He cleansed His temple many years ago. But today's *den of thieves* has turned the house of God into the house of man (self). Not until Jesus overturns the tables and drives out the self-will in His house will the blind and lame (the unsaved) truly be healed (Matt: 21:14). Our Father is a God of Divine order. His Supremacy is simplicity. God has declared that He will have for Himself a spotless bride—it's that simple. He made it perfectly clear that judgment will begin at His house. As all of nature cries out in silent upheaval God Almighty, at His appointed time, is now dropping the plumbline of His word and squaring the corners of His church.

It is here, that we find ourselves kneeling empty-handed beside the apostle Peter, as we shout in merciful confession, "Now Lord, we understand the testing of our faith! A faith that is much more precious than gold that perishes!" (1 Peter 1:6-9).

Not unlike Lot in Sodom, many struggle with the question, "How do I hold onto my cherished goods and my worldly goals while walking holy with God?" The answer is, *a Holy God will not take second place.* Rather, we need to ask ourselves, "How do we individually and collectively recapture what was lost in the Garden of Eden that God may again dwell and walk among us?"

Understand this! Since the curse upon man, God has been reckless with desire to get His family back. Yet, as God's mercy beckons us for intimacy lost, and His Spirit is poured out to a remnant in greater waves in the days ahead, many will become spiritually adrift, tossed to and fro by the waves (cares) of this world (Eph. 4:14). This is *not* Abba Father's desire.

What then is Father's desire? What is God speaking to the city, and where is He today? Can we trust our God to make something holy and inviting out of the inner-city ghettos, where the gates have been abandoned and the poor and unsaved wander the streets? For our answer we must hear and obey God. We must re-establish our covenant with the Creator, and plead for radical revival for our generation.

Individually, and as a city, God desires our whole heart (Joel 2:12). A city resembles the heartbeat of its' people. It's a reflection concerning unity and relational statistics that are viewed every evening on the channel four news at ten PM. More identifiable, a city that reflects the love of God mirrors a heart of peace.

In these pages, you will be driven to divine appointments with God—the city roads less traveled. We will journey through visitations and examinations from God in times past intersecting to the present, culminating to our long awaited eternal destiny on streets of gold yet to be engulfed in Jesus' hands outstretched. From documented real-life transformations through the redeeming resurrecting power of the Holy Spirit, these authors will testify of our need for the light of Jesus Christ to shine in this, *our darkest hour,* and the life all will experience (even the unsaved) from that light (Jn.1:4-5).

It was in Jesus' darkest hour at the cross that God drew His greatest strength from a moment of ultimate weakness. So what might God do with the apparent failures and hardships of a city? In the same way Jesus rode an unbroken donkey bareback into the city of Jerusalem, it is this identical Messianic King who will break the back of the unbridled spirit over this city. Undoubtedly, it is in our weakest and darkest hour that Hosanna will become enthroned in power!

IMPACTING THE LOST IS FIRST CONCEIVED
THROUGH A DESIRE FOR MERCY AND COMPASSION;
THESE ARE THE BIRTHPANGS OF CHANGE FOR A CITY

Insofar as the heavenly realm extends the picture never changes with God. His notoriously loving desire is as intent today as it was yesteryear with Adam: to gather all things together through responsive, *intimate fellowship:*

"Father, I desire that they also whom you gave Me, may be with me where I am, that they may behold My glory which You have given me; for You loved Me before the foundation of the world...."
—JOHN 17:24

3

THE GRAND INTERSECTION

When our hearts' desires unite with the desire of Jesus' heart for His people we will have come to the grand finale of eternity. We will walk in the Garden of Eden again, *beholding Jesus' glory*. Until that appointed time, what then is our part? "To *Hear* and *Obey* in faith," says the Lord. But how can we obey in faith if we are not first a listening people, who spend time to uncover the Lord's ways, and search out His regal desires like hidden treasures for each and every person in our city? How will we have faith if we do not know and abide in Him? If we do not hear His voice how can we respond to it? "To know Me is all," says the Lord. "For it is in knowing and abiding in Me that you will hear My voice, and it is your response to My voice that determines your future."

Our faith is a function of our ability to listen *and* respond to the Master's call in obedience. When God speaks from heaven and we refuse to listen and obey, then we relinquish ground with God and ultimately our lives, and our city does not reflect what God had originally intended. That grieves the heart of God and we then forfeit that moment of God's abundance of time. From the vantage-point of eternity we should be compelled to see this wrinkle of time we live in as extravagant. When we step aside and view our city from God's panorama and see His purposes for the city, we can then discern and extinguish the plans of satan, and his prince over this city (the ultimate covenant breakers), who keep us in bondage and spiritual darkness.

Let's go back in time now to a place where heaven touched earth—a place where passionate prayer collided with the Holy Spirits' unrestrained providence. Come, take a spiritual journey to rekindle the flames of desire in your heart. See what God can do when a city is poised on its knees in prayer. Take a peek from the lens of Gods' picture perfect perspective of revival, renewal, and awakening for the city—*a look from the Eyes of the Beholder.*

REVIVAL FROM THE EYE OF THE BEHOLDER

I remember it well. I'll never forget it. The year was 1857. It was a year of great prosperity, with railroads on the rise and the industrial revolution being birthed. Many saw a connecting together of the Nation. Many saw a future of hope and success. The headlines looked promising. But my eyes saw something quite different. Slavery was at the top of the moral issues as the Supreme Court cast aside a segment of the population which gave way to racism.

It was at that time, at the peak of financial prosperity of my day, that I felt a certain resolute burning and stirring in my spirit. As I gazed upon the spiritual condition if the multitudes around me, I took note they were living life in open carelessness and shameful rebellion against Almighty God, the One who sent His only begotten Son to die for their eternal welfare. I knew things were not aright in the land of the free and the brave. I'll never forget the night I tossed and turned in bed—as if I were wrestling with God Himself. He planted a seed in me that night. When I awoke from the ordeal I had a clear vision and was thus engaged to act according to His will.

From that time forward, it was all that I could do to get the message out: "PRAY! PRAY! PRAY!" That was the clarion call.

I sent invitations to the businessmen for a simple prayer meeting every Wednesday during the lunch hour. I passed out hand-bills that asked, "HOW OFTEN SHOULD YOU PRAY?" We started with only six men crying out to God for a breakthrough, but thereafter the numbers doubled every week. In three months' time some ten thousand men praying were gathering throughout the city at the lunch hour. To my amazement this work of the power of God speedily took over the northern cities, which eventually led to a nationwide revival. By God Almighty it came! Lord knows it came!

By the mercies of God, I now take to heart and put all my hope in scriptures such as, *The prayers of a righteous man availeth much.* Please do not mistake God's word. It was not because of me but rather in spite of me that God sovereignly poured out His Spirit. For I did nothing on my own accord, but He had chosen me to do a good work for His eternal purposes. He launched the intercessory Spirit in me. God alone was responsible in uniting the masses and giving them a valiant spirit of extraordinary prayer.

Looking back, I see that the foundation was laid with layer of prevailing prayer among men, which led to conviction and repentance with restitution, and sudden unspeakable joy among those who cried out "Jesus!" During the same year there came upon our city a sudden financial collapse and despair unlike any other in my day that was horrendous for many to bear. I knew of persons financially secure one day jumping out of buildings the next. Thank God He had prepared a remnant for the worst. They who had gotten their finances in order before the collapse and were able to minister to those who were caught off guard. When the opportunity came for ministry we seized it with a great zeal.

I now realize the epitome of those who tragically perished were the same ones who had not obeyed the voice of mighty Holy Ghost: "Make yourself ready and prepare to get in the Ark of God." Those who had only gone "halfway" with God suffered enormously, even sevenfold! As you know in the book of Revelation, Jesus "will vomit out the lukewarm"—those who think they are safe but are really not. Those who have dead works, those who are stuck in neutral, half-way in the Ark.

Looking ahead now, if I had one simple word of warning for the last generation, I would ever so implore to you to STOP!! Take a good, hard look in the mirror. What do you see with your spiritual eyes. Do you see salt or blandness? Light or darkness? Are you awake or asleep? Are you preparing by making the fine linen dress Jesus talks about in Revelation 19:8? If not, are you now willing to make a change? What's wrong with you healthy man? What are you doing with your life? Yes, for that generation I say to you, "Get in the Ark— the Ark of Jesus Christ!"

In times past, the scriptures show nations usually enjoyed great prosperity before God's judgment fell upon them. I tell you now, if God chooses to bring economic collapse to a nation, and does so to bring in the unsaved, then He is sovereign. So be it! So I say to you, get in the Ark, under the shadow of His wings. By doing that you will find shelter. It is only there that you will find "the Blesser." "For the eyes of the Lord roam about the earth looking for those whose hearts are His that He may strongly support them" (2 Chron. 16:9).

Before I go I can testify, the Lord searches for one who will stand in the gap so He will not have to strike the land with a curse. For your great city's sake, stand up and pray with a fervency! I plead you to stand with wringing hands before God, to kneel on humble knees before our Savior, to cry out for His never ending mercies. Pray, I tell you, pray! But weak man if you cannot stand, as your forefathers did and bled for your freedoms that will surely be a very sad day. If you cannot stand in the gap for your city's lost and unsaved, may God have mercy on your soul. Kneel before God and ask Him to stir up in you a heart of compassion. Yes, begin within yourself. Begin today...as I did.

For without us He won't move a City, and without Him we can't........

In the spirit of Jeremiah Lamphier,
a broken man of like flesh and bone...

HOOKED ON JESUS?...

Jesus declared, "Follow me, and I will make you fishers of men"(Matthew 4:19). Jesus hasn't lost the art of fishing. He just has trouble finding faithful fishermen. While the Father has drawn His hook of redemption, Jesus intercedes for His followers to cast the net upon the lost. As the children of God we are "the bait" of the Father's love that draws men. In our hearing, God grants us time in His mercy to adjust to His divine purposes. It is then in the fullness of *His* time, with our obedience, that God's plan of witnessing is revealed to us. But are we a hearing people? Are we *hooked* on Jesus?

In the pursuit of the desires of our heart, we will first cast back into our spiritual heritage to re-define the desires of God's heart for His Body of believers. Scripture shows repeatedly that God has one chief desire: *Intimacy for the lost.*

In Genesis, Adam had an intimate relationship with God as they walked together "in the cool of the day"(Gen.3:8). But when sin happened he was cut off from the warmth of God's closeness in the Garden of Eden, and so, intimacy now lost, he was sent out to *bear fruit*: "...therefore the Lord God *sent him out* from the garden of Eden, *to cultivate*"(Gen. 3:23). Since then, God has been hot on the trail to get back intimacy lost from the first bite—to gather all things back together again (Mark 13:27) (Luke 19:42).

Through intimacy, Noah walked with God (Genesis 6:9). Having then been chosen, he *was sent* on the ark to become the seed in *bearing fruit* for all nations: "Be fruitful and multiply, and fill the earth" (Gen.9:1).

Abram was chosen by God intimately; Abram believed God intimately; Abram was *taken outside* where God would show his offspring more numerous than the stars in the sky (Gen.15:5). In obedience, Abram *went forth* as the Lord had spoken to him (Gen.12:4).

6

In a search for intimacy, Jacob was sent away by Isaac to Paddan-aram to find his wife, Rachel (Gen. 28).

Through intimate encounters God chose all these, and sent them out to *bear fruit.*

Some find great difficulty in being sent out. Such a man was Joseph—a slave in Egypt. Like Jesus, he learned obedience by the things he suffered. But through interpretation of dreams he became Pharaoh's "chosen" and was thereby given power blessing a nation during famine. Another of these was Jonah, who later came to his senses after being swallowed by a fish!

Later, God sought out Moses through an intimate encounter, and sent him with power to deliver Israel that led to the Exodus of a nation (Exodus 12:33).

Finally, in the New Covenant, it was Jesus who sent the twelve apostles out to do His bidding with "power" to the remotest parts of the earth: "..but you shall receive power when the holy spirit has come upon you...and you shall be my witnesses.." (Acts 1:8). Time and time again God reveals to us that He is *intimately involved* in the *sending business.*

In sending us, God's grand purposes for this "power" was, and still is given as He has always sought out—to win the souls of people, cities, nations, and continents to Christ. This power is afforded to us at no cost in witnessing (Luke 10). Sometimes we turn God's message around to our benefit by using this 'power' selfishly instead of in witnessing to others.

We serve a God who has been sending out humankind ever since the Garden to win the world over. Do you think it's any different for us today in Nashville, Tennessee?

The human race has always been about a just God in a reckless search for lost intimacy with a lost humanity. In the New Covenant, we are to reflect Christ's own Body in search of that warmth and intimacy with a lost community.

It is through the God of intimacy that He became known as the God of Abraham, Isaac, and Jacob. These here are the initial seeds (the Patriarchs) whom God chose by sending them out to give birth to the countless array of over-comers (the great multitude) clothed in white robes who are eventually eternalized in heaven before Jesus' heavenly throne (Rev.7:9). This will be the culmination of completion of His Great Commission. And time is running short.

Like Father God, Jesus has always been a Harvester, but the laborers have always been few. In Luke chapter 10 verse 2, Jesus tells us to beseech the Lord of the harvest to send out laborers who will cast the net. He sends us out with reassuring words in verse 3, *"Go your ways; behold I send you out as lambs in the midst of wolves."* You may ask, "How can we fight and win against the wolves?" It is in the love of God, not the terror of God that we will draw "the wolves." Next are the four methods Jesus models for us:

1. Make peace with them.
2. Fellowship with them.
3. Meet their needs, and
4. Proclaim the kingdom of God.

A revival that touches the lost is what God desires. Anything short of that is not what He intends. When Jesus told Peter to feed His lambs, He was looking further than the four walls of a church building. It is in this context that I submit to you that the 'intimacy lost' for the church today is not as much with our intimacy with Jesus, but that we have lost intimacy with His chief directive. Satan has effectively "choked" out intimacy with Jesus through "the cares of the world" which has contributed toward the lack of identifying with and intimately caring for the lost. In that, we have lost the true character of Jesus, "a friend of sinners." This in part comes from our believing the lie satan has shifted towards us that says church is for the saved inside four walls.

We can find 'sinners' wherever we see the footprints of satan. Dig deep and you will find the defiled areas where the devil has 'scooped burning coals on lost souls.' Follow the trail of Jesus in asking Him to send you, and the God of power and of peace will bring you to broken homes, to shattered dreams, and to lonely hearts.

In this breath I close by exhorting the congregation of Nashville to become a friend of sinner's by reaffirming their dignity as human beings, removing the pointing of the finger, modeling grace, and by speaking blessing and proclaiming the word of God to them in love. This is our "feeding of the lambs." This is our intimacy. It's our commission! Let the peace of God flow through your prayer's so they feel the draft and good vibration of a loving God—a just God who will love them unconditionally just as they are, but through an intimate encounter will love them enough to desire a better way for them. Sow the seed and let God do the watering. Through finding compassion for the lost we will rediscover passion and intimacy with Jesus. Just follow Jesus—in His steps.

INTIMACY WITH JESUS IS MODELING
JESUS THROUGH FINDING INTIMACY WITH
"THE LOST"

ISRAEL REDEEMED

Hosea 3:4-5
by Michael J. Lax
Messianic Rabbi

ABOUT THIRTY YEARS ago, while in high school, I decided to cut some classes. I didn't realize, until a few weeks ago, how this decision affected my life.

This day in early April was beautiful, a perfect day to go up to the beach and just hang out. There were quite a few other kids that made this choice also, so I wasn't alone.

There under the boardwalk, I met a girl, a girl named Cyndy.

Over the period of time, we shared cokes, pizzas and dreams. Within a year and a half we were married.

Our first years were difficult. We worked hard, had children and tried to build a future. You see, Cyndy and I came from completely different backgrounds. She was Episcopalian, I was Jewish. These differences presented some real challenges; especially raising kids, celebrating Chanukah, Christmas, Passover and Easter became exercises in futility.

One evening, I came home from working a twelve-hour day, climbed into the shower, fell into bed and began to talk to Cyndy about how the day went. She stopped me and said, "You must repent of your sins, accept the Lord Jesus Christ or you will go straight to hell when you die." For a Jewish boy, from a kosher home, this was something I didn't care to hear. I thought it was my punishment for falling in love with someone who wasn't Jewish. My family told me this would happen and they were right.

You see, people from our neighborhood, became friends with Cyndy and over time, they brought her to the Lord.

Her faith made me angry. The day she was baptized, I left her. I moved home to my parents. Living with my parents was not such a great thing. I decided that it would be better to live with my Jesus freak wife then to listen to my Jewish mother kvetch. In my mind, I realized that this was just a phase for her, something like ceramics. It would last for a season maybe, and then everything would be back to normal.

No matter what I did, her belief in Jesus wouldn't go away. I returned to Orthodox Judaism, treated her rude and even kicked her Bible friends out of the house, but still she remained faithful to Jesus.

My anger reached a point where I would not allow her to go to church. It was church or a divorce. That's when Cyndy started to pray for my salvation.

I verbally abused her. She prayed.

I mocked Jesus. She prayed.

I made fun of her faith. She prayed.

I made Saul look like a fairy god-mother. She prayed.

For six years she prayed and then on the anniversary of her baptism, I received Messiah.

Proverbs 31:10 reads, "An excellent wife who can find? For her worth is far above jewels." I found her almost 30 years ago, when I cut school. You see…God uses all things for good, even skipping school.

A few years later, we caught the vision for Messianic Judaism. Eventually, I was ordained as a Messianic Rabbi and started to plant a congregation that lasted for seven years. Four years into this ministry, the Lord, through His Word, made it clear that we were to move here, to Nashville.

I chose not to. My rebellion caused loss of everything except my wife and family. The ministry was gone, friendships were ruined and life as I knew it, was over.

God is the God of second chances. I repented, prayed and rested in the Lord. He sustained us and moved us here three years ago by the power of His mighty hand. If you knew of all the details of this move, you'd be amazed.

Why Nashville? It's simple. Nashville needs a Messianic Jewish Synagogue that will impact the unsaved Jewish community for Messiah Yeshua.

Why me? That's simple too…the gifts and calling of God are irrevocable. My rebellion four years ago did not change God's mind concerning why He called me to plant a Messianic Jewish Synagogue here in Worship City, USA.

We're living in a prophetic time, I believe, the last days. The prophet Hosea spoke about these times and said this; "For the sons of Israel, will remain for many days, without a king or prince, without sacrifice, or sacred pillar, without ephod or teraphim. Afterwards, the sons of Israel will return and seek the Lord their God and David their king and come trembling to the Lord and His goodness in the last days."

It's been over 2,000 years and there hasn't been a sacrifice or any type of temple worship and according to God's Word, His people will begin to look for His goodness and David their king. It's my calling to present the invitation to the unsaved Jewish community to meet their King, the Son of David… Messiah Yeshua.

In the book of Romans, Rabbi Shaul (Paul) expressed how nothing could separate us from the love of God that's in Messiah. He went on to share of his deep desire for the salvation of the Jewish people. With such agony, he announced that his desire was so strong that he would be willing to be separated from God, in other words, if possible, return his salvation…spend eternity in hell, if just some of these people would accept Messiah.

I understand his feelings. As the work progresses, I find myself in tears traveling past the synagogues in the West End. I get locked into prayer repenting for the sins of my people asking for grace and more time. But, I know that the time is short, that the day of salvation is now.

I think of the elderly and the sick, these people are getting closer to the end of their lives and the knowledge of them leaving here without Messiah overwhelms me. There are three real important reasons to reach the Jewish community:

1) Primacy-the Jewish people hold the primary position in God's kingdom. Some people confuse primacy with superiority and that's just sad. We all know that the ground at the cross is level and that there is no difference between Jewish and Gentile people. We're all sinners saved by grace.

   Rabbi Shaul (Paul) taught that the Good News went to the Jew first, and according to the book of Acts, he practiced what he taught. Israel and the Jewish people in the diaspora, are still the primary focus of God's eye toward this earth.

2) Resuscitation-according to Scripture, Israel's rejection of Messiah was reconciliation for the world. Acceptance of Messiah by the Jewish people would be 'life from the dead.' No matter how 'on fire' your church might be, it's really just a 'brush fire'. When the Jewish people start coming into faith, there will be a revolution in the Body of Messiah. You'll see the Ruach Ha'Kodesh (Holy Spirit) move mightily throughout the world. Signs. Wonders. Power. Glory. These things have always hung around us. Remember the amazing things that the Lord worked through Elijah, Moses, Joshua, Peter, John...all Jewish boys, smack in the center of God's will. How much more will God do when hundreds of thousands of Jewish people are in Messiah, the real center of God's will for their lives.

   Remember Peter, at Shavuot (Pentecost)? All he needed was a little help from the Ruach HaKodesh and a five-minute message. The result...3,000 Jewish people came to faith.

   Pray for the Jewish community. Pray for a move of God's Spirit. Pray for a five-minute message that will move thousands of Jewish people to trust their Messiah.

   Help resuscitate the corporate body of Messiah by praying Jewish people into faith.

3) Gentile salvation-one of the most important aspects of a Messianic Jewish Synagogue is to maintain a Jewish heritage and culture. It's important because this inheritance comes from the Lord.

In Revelations 22:16, Yeshua in His resurrected body, affirms this heritage by saying "...I am the root and offspring of David..." If this heritage is important to Him, it should be important to every Jewish believer.

In my opinion, Jewish believers do harm to the unsaved Jewish and non-Jewish people by assimilating into Gentile churches. They harm the Jewish community simply by casting away an identity that has survived atrocities like the holocaust. The harm that is done to the unsaved Gentile's is by hindering performance of the Scripture in Zechariah 8:23 that says; 'Thus says the Lord of hosts, "In those days ten men from all the nations will grasp onto the garment of a Jew saying, "Let us go with you, for we have heard that God is with you."

As Jewish believers, we need to maintain our heritage so that both the Gentile and Jewish communities can believe in Messiah Yeshua.

The work to plant a Messianic Jewish Synagogue takes a great amount of prayer. I'm hoping that this chapter will burden you to pray for the unsaved Jewish people here in Nashville and around the world. This job can't be done without prayer.

About the Author

Michael is originally from Southern New Jersey where he served Congregation El Shaddai, as the Messianic Rabbi, for seven years. Currently, Michael is preparing to plant a congregation in the West End of Nashville. He is working with a core group of people that have a desire to reach the unsaved Jewish community. They've been meeting for one year in and around the Franklin, TN area. In addition, Rabbi Lax is on the executive and steering committees of the International Federation of Messianic Jews (IFMJ). The IFMJ, located in Tampa, Florida has Messianic Jewish Synagogues in Europe, Canada, the United States and South America. His marriage to Cyndy has produced six beautiful children. Cyndy and Michael have three gorgeous grandchildren.

ADVANCING GOD'S KINGDOM IN NASHVILLE

by Pastor Brad Watson

Jesus taught us to pray like this: *"Let your kingdom come, your will be done ON THE EARTH as it is in heaven."* (Matt. 6:10).

ONE OF THE biggest paradigm shifts that is happening in the church today is the concept that we are to represent, usher in, and establish God's Kingdom reign on the earth. We are not simply waiting to die, or killing time until the rapture, but we are forcefully advancing the kingdom of Christ with real Kingdom authority. This is not to deny the necessity of Christ's return, or to insinuate that we can do the job without Him. There will be a day when He puts His foot on the Mount of Olives, and physically returns to fully establish His Kingdom (Zech. 14; Rev. 19).

But in the meantime, we are given the task of "occupying until He returns."

How do we occupy? How do we advance and expand His Kingdom? Well, the obvious simple answer is that we get people saved. Evangelism should always be at the core of everything we do. As Evangelist Reinhardt Bonnke says, "We plunder hell to populate heaven!" Recently Evangelist Ed Silvoso was in Nashville and said, "Any doctrine that is attempted to be understood separate from, or apart from the great commission will be misunderstood, or at least not understood fully." As Paul said, "we are ambassadors of Christ as though God were making His appeal through us!" (2 Cor. 5:20).

But what comes next? Is our commission from God broader than just witnessing to individuals? Jesus seemed to think so. In Matthew's account of the Great Commission, according to the original Greek, Jesus actually commanded us to *"disciple the nations"* (Matt: 28:19). In Matthew's account of the judgment of nations, Jesus indicated some nations would be like goats (discarded and judged), while others would be like sheep (included in His Kingdom). Notice these are not just individuals being discussed, but NATIONS! Jesus indicated that there would be entire nations that come to know Him in the end times. Even His beloved Israel will come back to Him in mass with national repentance (Zech. 12:10-chapter 13; Rom. 11).

Obviously, we have our work cut out for us in spreading the Kingdom. But it is tremendously exciting and encouraging knowing that Jesus actually believes His church is going to get the job done! Many look with fear and discouragement to the increase of evil in our time. But remember Jesus prophetically said that in mankind's history evil and good would mature together until the end. The wheat and the weeds (chaff) BOTH GROW AND MATURE until the end (Matt 13). So what is the point? Many cities and nations are hanging in the balance. Will they be wheat or weeds? Will they accept the Kingdom or reject it? In the end will they be goats or sheep?

Cities and nations ARE BEING TAKEN for the Kingdom of God. Christians are trusting God at His word when He said, "Greater is the one in you than the one in the world" (I JN 4:4). Some believers are becoming convinced that Jesus WILL continue to "build His church and that the gates of hell WILL NOT PREVAIL against it (Matt. 18)!

To take cities for Christ (like Nashville), the body of Christ must reclaim strategic centers of culture. May God give us grace and shrewd strategy to take over the arts, the business community, the educational system, financial centers, the music industry, the sports and entertainment industry, the political arena, and more! Each of these foundational elements of our culture represents a stronghold. We must tear down the enemy's strongholds and build strongholds of righteousness in their place! The Lord is even now raising up Christians with Kingdom vision, strategy, and resources to invade the darkness in each of these arenas and turn on the light of life! He is giving us divine appointments and divine favor to change the course of our city by invading its very heart with the love, truth, power, and light of God!

We must begin to see that revival or awakening must happen not only inside, but also outside our church walls for anything to change in our world. God is opening the eyes of our hearts and giving us Kingdom vision to see that we really can change things by His power (Eph. 1:18). We CAN transform the atmosphere of our city - change its spiritual climate. CS Lewis once surmised that Christianity is like a virus - it's contagious! We must move the Kingdom forward to infect Nashville as we infiltrate every culture, stronghold, and "gate" of our city.

Believers must become convinced that the answer to everything lives inside of us (Jesus!). He will use us, in spite of our weaknesses, to touch hurting humanity with His eternal life. For the world to really see God, however, they must see Him show up in their world. This is the incarnation principal. "The Word became flesh and dwelt among us. And we beheld His glory..." (John 1:14). Jesus wants to walk into *their* world—in the marketplace, through the movie screen, in the music, etc., and show them His glory. We must remember that we are His hands, His voice, and His feet. His resurrection power is even stored inside of us (Eph 1: 19)! We are fully equipped by the Spirit of God to represent the person of Christ and the authority of His Kingdom. It's time that we step out of the boat—leave our comfort zones; throw off our unbelief; look at the world through eyes of love and faith and begin to believe that anything is possible. Our commander in chief Himself said, "Anything is possible for he who believes" (Mk 9:23)!

Nashville thinks they know the church, but I've got news for them—"They ain't seen nothing yet!!" The church is about to break out of the box of predictability. We are truly on a mission from God! Real life, real joy, real peace, real promise, real answers are the treasures that live inside every believer. The light will not be hid behind a bush any longer. It's time that we "come out of the closet" and let the world see the awesome life of God available to anyone who believes. As St. Augustine said, "The glory of God is man truly alive!"

Dear Father God—We declare the Nashville is YOUR CITY. We say, may Your Kingdom come, Your will be done on the earth as it is in heaven! Thank you that we will be MORE THAN CONQUERORS through Christ. Lead us Lord, that we may permeate every stronghold of this city, walk through every gate, and claim every soul for Christ. Give us a fresh look and a fresh sound, Oh Lord. Let Nashville look up and take notice. Let your people be good "poster kids" for the Kingdom of God! Let us represent You well in everything that we do, in every place that we go. Let our light shine forth, Oh Lord. Give us Your love for the people of this city, and your faith to believe that the city can truly be WON to you! Raise up Spirit-filled people to represent you in business, the arts, sports, technology, education, politics, medicine, music, and more. May every Christian marriage be a Kingdom marriage, a bright light broadcasting your love to others, and drawing them to You! May every Christian church be filled with fresh hope for tomorrow, with Kingdom vision and Kingdom authority. We prophetically declare that Nashville belongs to Christ! Nashville is an outpost for the kingdom of God! We thank you Lord for raising us up for such a time as this! May you be glorified in and through your people. In the Name of our Glorious King Jesus, AMEN!!!

About the Author

Pastor Brad shepherds Harvest International Church in Hermitage, TN. He has three beautiful daughters and originally hails from Texas—where everything is big! He has a big heart for God's presence to fall over Nashville, TN., the whole state, the nation, the continent, and the world! *Nothin's* too big for God!

PREPARING A CITY

by Sandy Powell

"Who may ascend the hill of the Lord? Who may stand in his holy place? He who has clean hands and a pure heart, who does not lift up his soul to an idol or swear by what is false. He will receive blessing from the Lord and vindication from God his Savior. Such is the generation of those who seek him, who seek your face, O God of Jacob."
—PSALM 24:3-6

THERE IS INCREASED activity in the heavenlies as the body of Christ is assembled to ascend the Holy Hill of the Lord. Attaining this higher level of positioning will require clean hands and a pure heart.

The Lord is blowing a shofar over Nashville breaking the enemy's back for a smoother course ahead. The sound of the shofar reminds us to pray for Israel as a combination of the outpouring of God's Grace and His redemptive purposes. For us individually and corporately, these are being released with great acceleration. It's important that God's people catch this coming move of the Holy Spirit in order to be prepared. The watchmen have been stationed at the city gates.

"Lift up your heads, O you gates; be lifted up, you ancient doors, that the King of glory may come in."
—PSALM 24:7

Prayer, Unity, and Worship are primary keys for advancing Nashville into its Kingdom destiny despite the enemy's schemes in the opposite spirits of distraction, division, and idolatry. Rest assured that the Lord will take what the devil intends for our harm and use it for the good of those who love the Lord and have been called according to His purposes. We WILL be transformed into the pure and spotless bride (a pure heart and clean hands) because the plans of the Lord stand firm forever and the purposes of his heart remain through all generations.

History repeatedly tells us a minority with God can become a victorious majority. There are many factors that can contribute to the victories, but ultimately, it's when a people understand and put into action God's purposes for the land, or a specific area through their lives. Mightier accomplishments can then be achieved out of response to obedience. Such was the case when the scaled down army of Gideon was set apart to achieve a seemingly impossible victory...With God nothing is impossible. Such is the case with a remnant of assembled troops in Nashville, Tennessee.

PRAYER

With this coming move of the Lord, signs and wonders will be released in dramatic portion. The prerequisite is a hunger for more of the Lord. He must increase and we must decrease. We see this in effect as organized prayer for our families, churches, city, nation(s) and the peace of Jerusalem has come to the forefront. In my own life I was given a divine opportunity to give a prophetic word to the Minister of Music for the Bush campaign. I shared the necessity for organized prayer within their camp despite how good the campaign numbers looked at the forefront. This seemed like foolishness at the time as the prophetic word was given prior to the debates and any hint of the forthcoming decline of Bush's support.

God will use the prophetic voice that is being released across the land and through his church to sound an alarm. He'll back up his people with signs and wonders. He'll confound the wise with even foolish things like feathers, gold teeth, gold dust, and more. Nashville is in a season of first miracles. The enemy to prayer is distraction—to be pulled away or diverted from the task at hand. Maintaining our position as watchmen is crucial for the coming wave of the Lord to run its course. If Satan could keep us from victory, his target would be to distract us from prayer.

UNITY

Because it is true that we are at the threshold of a greater unity that bridges dividing walls than ever before, I'm hesitant to bring forth the details of a parallel move that will simultaneously create separation in the church today. The ultimate purpose is to make strong the weak and to separate the true believers from the false.

As lukewarmness has invaded church society today through the subtle compromise of dealing with the world, complacency has rooted itself in the bowels of the body. Church leaders around the land have faithfully carried out their responsibility to protect the sheep, resulting in many sheep not being prepared for what's coming. A spirit of offense crouches at the door. Satan will attempt to distort the outpouring of the Holy Spirit by releasing a condemning pharisaic spirit to stop the River of Life. For man does not live on bread alone, but by the Spirit of the Lord.

A remnant in the body of Christ will come forth that is smaller in size but stronger in power as the Glory of the Lord will be revealed through His manifested presence. This Gideon army will rise seemingly out of nowhere made up of new radical believers and old soldiers who will rise up with wings like eagles able to do a greater work than what they perceived through their failures in the past. The acceleration of the release through the David's that are after God's own heart will astound even the David's themselves. They will initiate the rebuilding of the temple.

Separation always comes when light reveals what is in darkness. When we are truly unified as a church body, then we will have nothing to fear, as there will be nothing to separate. Mindsets, doctrines, and philosophies of man will be challenged and crumble to the ground as the Lord reveals Himself to all. Forgiveness will be a key element in ascending this Holy Hill of the Lord.

Recently I experienced a prophetic dream where my family was gathered together in a room visiting with one another. My family represented the church today. My deceased grandmother entered the room and I began gently ministering to her. I laid my hand on her forehead and she was slain in the Spirit. A few minutes later she started to get up from the floor and after she was about half way up, I stretched my hands toward her and blew and she was slain again. A family member from the room (I could not see who, but this represents a church member) got up and said under their breath as they were leaving, "I've had about all of this I can stand." My grandmother was unaffected by the statement as the Holy Spirit was bringing her back to life. But some of the family members (body of Christ) were very uncomfortable and there was a tendency to take sides as it was discussed what was appropriate and what was not appropriate at family gatherings (church). Instead of celebrating the victory of my grandmother's resurrection and renewal, our time together was robbed by division. I personally was held responsible for the confusion.

Through this dream the Lord is saying there is a coming move of the Holy Spirit for life and renewal. The spiritually dead will come back to life, as the captives are set free. But persecution will come from within and all around us as an anti-Christ spirit rises up to create chaos and division within the body of Christ. Our church family as well as our families in the natural won't be left unaffected. Jesus didn't come to take sides. He came to take over. He said that we were either with Him or against Him.

We are getting ready to see a move of the Lord's hand like we've never experienced. It will surpass even the great stories of the forerunners before us. Just as the pharisaical spirit accused and condemned the work of Jesus Christ, so those that walk with an authority in the things of the spiritual realm will be extremely attacked. Specifically apostles and prophets. Families will split and churches will divide as the enemy plays on the religious mindset of man. But to him that overcomes and continues to strain ahead, Jesus will give the keys to the Kingdom. "Strain" means violent effort to stretch. The prayer to combat this warning would be to:

"...demolish arguments and every pretension that sets itself up against the knowledge of God, and to take captive every thought to make it obedient to Christ."
—2 CORINTHIANS 10: 4 &5

WORSHIP

Freedom and Intimacy in Worship will produce miraculous healings and deliverance. It won't look like what the church has been trained for. The greatest performance for the King of Kings has begun. Those that have come to be entertained will be uncomfortable with the holiness birthed from intimacy with the Lord. Others will speak unjustly just as Mical spoke against her husband for his weakness to dance...before the Lord with all his might.

There will be opportunity for Satan to slip in and take things out of order but God will override the attempts to sabotage the purpose for which music was intended...worship.

In the story of the tower of Babel the Lord went down to earth and confused the people speaking the same language. Music has been called a universal language. In Nashville, Tennessee, the Lord has begun to still the world's language of music and establish His sound. The man-made empire of the Music industry has created altars of idolatry impacting our world with a dynamic that exalts itself against the knowledge of God. Unhealthy competitive spirits combined with a sense of producing something in our own strength initiated a spirit of pride to dwell over Music City. But this territorial stronghold is weakening as we see Nashville's country music sales at an all time low.

"This is what they will get in return for their pride, for insulting and mocking the people of the Lord Almighty. The Lord will be awesome to them when he destroys all the gods of the land. The nations on every shore will worship him, every one in its own land.
—ZEPHANIAH 2:10&11.

With numerous record labels having closed their doors, God is closing this window to release His sound and the true song of freedom.

"...do not make for yourselves an idol in the form of anything the Lord your God has forbidden. For the Lord your God is a consuming fire, a jealous God."
—DEUTERONOMY 4:23 & 24

God is going to take the sound of Praise; spilling it over into the streets to turn the hearts of the lost toward the Father. Spiritual fathers and men of Godly authority are being reinstated within the city marketplace.

The Lord's redemptive purposes have begun. The song of the Lord will affect secular music, as musical warriors after the heart of God will be recruited to plunder the enemy's camp. It is the solidifying of the praise warriors combined with the prayer warriors that will produce a newfound unity in the doorway of revival.

The judgment of the Lord has fallen on the country music business industry leaving only a small remnant of survivors to establish the true things that cannot be shaken. This same judgment has produced much brokeness, which will bring forth the fruit of justice. God will have His way, as Music City becomes Worship City—a city known for its sound of praise.

"Yet a time is coming and has now come when the true worshippers will worship the Father in spirit and truth, for they are the kind of worshippers the Father seeks."
—JOHN 4:23

FUTURE CONCERNS

On March 10, 2001 I experienced a 90-minute open vision at the North Gate of Nashville. I saw a rider on a white horse whose name is Faithful and True. This Rider and his army were on call as the saints released the prayers to fill the prayer bowls and come back to earth as answered prayers on behalf of our city. I also saw a black horse whose rider was death and destruction. There was a strategy of the enemy to kill, steal and destroy beyond distraction, division, and idolatry.

Natural disasters of great proportion are coming. I was reminded that in 1999 I had publicly and in published form given a prophetic word that an east wind would eventually blow in bringing war with it. I saw famine. Economic decline. And finally a major earthquake running its course through the state of Tennessee.

It is known that man will turn to God in a time of crisis.

"This is what the Lord Almighty says: In a little while I will once more shake the heavens and the earth, the sea and the dry land. I will shake all nations, and the desired of all nations will come, and I will fill this house with glory, says the Lord Almighty."
—HAGGAI 2: 6&7

I continue to see things that concern me but that no one could deny there is a war raging in the spiritual realm. Unexplainable fireballs will stream through the sky and showers of electricity spears will fall on the earth.

PREPARING THE WAY

There is a season for every activity under heaven. God has called Nashville to ascend the Holy Hill of the Lord. We must have a pure heart and clean hands and put no other Gods before him. Unity is essential, as God desires Nashville to be dressed in the garments of heaven and not the world. While governments try to divide the land of Israel, so too is God drawing his lines of separation. Either we are with Him or against Him.

Once we ascend the Holy Hill of the Lord, when Nashville comes into her true destiny, then what?

> *"Blow the trumpet in Zion; sound the alarm on my holy hill. Let all who live in the land tremble, for the day of the Lord is coming. It is close at hand."*
> —JOEL 2:1

There is great favor and Grace on this season and this generation of the assembled troops in the body of Christ. It is the empowering presence of the Lord that will enable us to be the people He has called us to be and to do the things He has called us to do.

> *"The one who calls you is faithful and he will do it."*
> —I THESSALONIANS 5:24

Prophetic Evangelist Sandy Powell

The tranquillity of a Tennessee hilltop is worlds away from the non-stop bustle of a touring country music entertainer. But that is the journey the Lord has called Sandy Powell to take. After surviving a mid-air plane collision in the early 80's, a new course began in 1985 with a clear voice from the Lord. The journey has not been easy; the sacrifices, many. But blessed with a gift of prophecy, a heart to worship, and an unflagging spirit of optimism, Sandy has persevered, sharing her ministry with Believers in all places who hunger for more of the Lord.

Sandy is the founder of PowerHouse Ministries and an associate minister with the Indiana Company of the Prophetic giving personal and corporate revelation to churches and leaders throughout the country. She is ordained through World Bible Way Fellowship in Irving, Texas. Together, she and her husband, Prater, operate a Prophetic Ministry Retreat and Provision Center at the North Gate of Nashville Tennessee and come under the covering of Belmont Church in Nashville.

For more info on PowerHouse Ministries
Ph (615) 726-1780
Fax (615) 726-1632
Email: SPPowerHouse@Mindspring.com
Website: www.sandypowell.com

THE REVOLUTIONISTS

by Dave Simmerman
Youth Pastor

THE AMERICAN REVOLUTION was a historical struggle by which the Thirteen Colonies that were to become the United States of America won independence from Britain. By the middle of the 18th century, differences in life, thought, religion and economic interests had formed between the colonies and the Mother country. Acts such as the Stamp Act and the Townsend Act, roused a violent colonial outcry and spurred on such acts of violence as the Boston Massacre and the Boston Tea Party. The colonists convened the Continental Congress and petitioned the king to address their grievances. Fighting erupted on Apr. 19, 1775, at Lexington and Concord, and was followed by the battle of Bunker Hill.

The colonist then chose General George Washington to command the Continental army and, on July 4, 1776, what was to be the United States of America adopted the Declaration of Independence. After several other battles between the colonists and those who remained pro-British Loyalists, Gen. Cornwallis surrendered at the close of the Yorktown Campaign ending the fighting, and the Treaty of Paris recognized the U.S. as a nation. The American Revolution was a success and now the U.S. is the most powerful nation in the world.

But now in the year 2001, a new revolution has permeated this nation founded on the principals of God. This revolution, led by satan himself, is destroying the moral and ethical values of our society. This revolution has changed the way most think, act and react. It has introduced a loose interpretation of sin and its consequences. This revolution says pre-martial sex is the norm. This revolution says drink all the alcohol you want, just don't drive. This revolution says kill unborn babies and let homosexuals have their rights. This revolution has been successful within the governmental system by taking prayer out of schools and pushing the teaching of evolution and other hypocrisy. This revolution preaches tolerance for other sinful lifestyles. This revolution has resulted in students killing their peers in school with semiautomatic machine guns and pipe bombs. This revolution has resulted in a rise of sexually transmitted disease. This revolution has resulted in broken homes, child abuse and violence.

ITS TIME FOR A CHANGE! ITS TIME FOR A RADICAL TRANSFORMATION OF THE WAY WE LOOK AT OUR SOVEREIGN GOD. ITS TIME THAT WE AS A GENERATION OF YOUNG PEOPLE STOP BEING CONFORMED TO THIS WORLD AND FOR US TO BE TRANSFORMED BY THE RENEWING OF OUR MINDS. ITS TIME THAT THIS GENERATION REALIZES THE POWER OF THE LORD GOD ALMIGHTY IN OUR LIVES AND LIVE A LIFE WORTHY OF HIM. ITS TIME THAT WE GRASP THE ULTIMATE SOVEREIGNTY OF THE POWERFUL GOD AND LET HIM USE US TO CHANGE, SHAPE, MOLD, AND TRANSFORM A NATION BACK TO GOD.

ITS TIME FOR A REVOLUTION!

THE QUESTION IS...

Do you want a revolution!? That is the question! What is a revolution!? A revolution is a forcible, pervasive and often violent change of a social or political order by a sizable segment of a country's population.

The American Revolution spoken of earlier was one such revolution.

The country of Romania also had one such revolution back in the late 1980's. Under the powerful dictatorship of Nicolae Ceausescu, the people of Romania revolted against his tyranny and stormed the capital city of Bucharest. Ceausescu fled, but was caught by the rebellion. Ceausescu and is wife were both executed and Romania became a free democratic governmental system. That's extreme!

You see Revolution is the most extreme option of a nonconforming group. It is a course taken generally when more moderate and legal attempts to achieve recognition or reform have failed. Such revolutions usually reflect a general climate of discontent and displeasure. Whether occurring spontaneously or through careful planning, revolutions depend for their success on crucial timing and popular support.

Are you tired of conforming to this world?

Are you displeased with the lack of Godliness in this world?

Are you tired of our government passing laws that make ungodly things legal?

DO YOU WANT A REVOLUTION?

Revelations 7:16-17 says, *"They will hunger no more, and thirst no more; the sun will not strike them, nor any scorching heat; for the Lamb at the center of the throne will be their Shepherd, and He will guide them to springs of water of life, and God will wipe away every tear from their eyes."*

A song by Kirk Franklin entitled, "Revolution" is described by Rev. Chris Hill from "The Potter's House" in Dallas, Texas, as being a "rhythmic resolution, for a radical revision in the way we realize religion in the modern Christian church." In this song Kirk Franklin is contrasting the healing power of the LAMB OF GOD, the TRUE SHEPHERD, Jesus the Christ with the anemic and often pseudo-pharisaic religious practices which too often are the norm within most churches.

In this scripture, John the revelator, had an extraordinary opportunity to peer through prophecy, into a day where Christian believer's needs are met within the throne room of God. John had the experience of seeing what the results of this revolution that this song talked about would be. Think about it!

A true revolution such as this will occur when the Christian church of today begins to meet the needs of the people of the community (others).

A true revolution will come when all of our own secret pains and unspoken needs are brought to the foot of Jesus in this place we call church (personal).

A true revolution will come when we start saying no the world and start saying yes to a mighty sovereign God (revival).

GENERATION seX

We all need a revolution and Christ is calling us to a revolution! Do you want a revolution in this CITY?! I say do you want a revolution? Let's begin a revolution with the greatest temptation for our youth today: SEX.

I could fill endless pages with the latest polls and surveys that show how promiscuous our teens have become. Instead I will sum it up by saying that in the twelve years I have been working with young people, the issue of sex is the number one sin that teens struggle to overcome. Oh, did I just call sex a sin? Can this God-created, pleasurable, yet controversial act truly be called a sin? This is a question that confuses many but is obvious to others. I truly believe it is our responsibility as a church to restore the sacredness of sex by discussing it in the context of a biblical value system and not referring to it as a sin. Some of you may be asking, but should the church be talking about sex? Should we, as Christians, talk about something that generations past have only whispered about in the privacy of their own homes? I believe the answer is a resounding yes. Talking frankly about sex does not violate its sacredness. God's holy word has a great deal to say about sex (just read the Song of Solomon) and we all need to be aware of God's perspective on this issue. The truth is that the church's response to adolescent sexual attitudes and behaviors is more critical now than it has ever been.

THE HOT TOPIC

It is clear that sex is prevalent in our world. Sex is talked about on TV, at school, the workplace, on the ball field, and at home. Sex is permeated in advertisements for products such as perfume, clothes and even shaving cream. It is obvious that sex is a topic that is not only being expressed in many different ways but also misunderstood, misused and polluted.

1 A five-year-old says to his friend, "I found a condom on the patio." His friend asks, "What's a patio?"
2 A college-aged couple visits their youth worker. The girl is pregnant, they are not married, and both are very upset. They are not upset because she is pregnant—they cannot understand why she is pregnant. They asked God to keep her from getting pregnant every time they had sex.
3 A study compared the sexual behavior of high school young people with no church affiliation to high school people who attend church regularly. There was no difference.
4 And finally, as if you have not gotten the point, when told that their high school daughter was sexually promiscuous, the parents replied, "Frankly, we'd rather not know because we don't want to deal with it!

Folks, it's about time we deal with it! Many churches have long held that the less adolescents know about sex, the less likely they are to engage in sexual activity. I can sympathize with that point of view, but the fact is our kids are getting a sex education. If a five-year old knows what a condom is, it tells us that our kids know much more about sex than we may think. You see, silence does not protect young people, but it only makes them more vulnerable to the sources of modern sex education such as MTV, movies, magazines, and the Internet. I for one question the authority of these impious sources.

The good news is that there has been a nationwide push towards encouraging teens to stay sexually abstinent. One such campaign is called, "True Love Waits". Started in 1992, this campaign has challenged literally millions of teens to sign a card, put on a ring, or log in on the Internet and make the following promise:

Believing that true love waits, I make a commitment to God, myself, my family, my friends, my future mate, and my future children to be sexually abstinent from this day until the day I enter a biblical marriage relationship.

At last, there is something that is sending a positive Biblical message about sex. At last, there is something that teens can hold on to and commit to. But what exactly is "true love"? Why does God want to keep teens away from something he created? Hey, these aren't my questions; these questions come from teens I meet with everyday. Sure, they will sign a card, put on a ring or log on to a commitment via the Internet, but these are the questions they really want to know answers to. Don't get me wrong, I believe in the True Love Waits campaign. It has been a joy for me to watch many of the young people in my youth ministry make that commitment, but we can't stop there with these impending questions coming from our teenagers.

WHAT'S LOVE GOT TO DO WITH IT?

When we say "true love", what exactly does that mean? Love is a word we have distorted so much that it may have lost its meaning. We overuse the word "love" more than any other word in the English language. "I love Pizza", "I love football", "I love you Mom", "Hey baby, I love you", or yes, even at church, "I love you brother!" We use the word "love" for everything! We obviously do not love pizza like we love our mother and I don't think any of you love sister Mildred at your church the same way you love your spouse.

The Greeks looked at love in a different way. They had several different words for love: *eros, phileo, storge* and *agape. Eros* came from the name of Latin god of love. *Eros* has to do with the sensual kind of love. For example one might say "I *eros* pizza" or "I *eros* kissing my boyfriend". *Phileo* and *storge* were used to describe the brotherly love we have for each other or love for one's family. For example on might say "I *storge* my grandmother" or 'I *phileo* my buddy from high school".

And then there is *agape* love! *Agape* love is a deliberate love. *Agape* love is not based on pleasure, the senses, or a warm fuzzy relationship you have with someone of the opposite sex. *Agape* love is unconditional, much like the love that God wants us to have for him.

I have all of these types of love for my wife. I *eros* her because of the way she makes me feel and because of the way she looks. I *phileo* her because she is my wife and the mother of our child. Finally, I have *agape* love for her because I have made a commitment to her in marriage that said I would love her unconditionally for the rest of my life.

True love has all of these aspects and to settle for anything less would be a tragedy. I have had so many young people over the years, say " But, I love him" "He makes me so happy" "We are going to get married when we are out of school, so why wait for sex until then."

God's word is very specific about saving sexual activity until marriage:

Finally, brothers, we instructed you how to live in order to please God, as in fact you are living. Now we ask you and urge you in the Lord Jesus to do this more and more. For you know what instructions we gave you by the authority of the Lord Jesus. It is God's will that you

should be sanctified: that you should avoid sexual immorality; that each of you should learn to control his own body in a way that is holy and honorable, not in passionate lust like the heathen, who do not know God; and that in this matter no one should wrong his brother or take advantage of him. The Lord will punish men for all such sins, as we have already told you and warned you. For God did not call us to be impure, but to live a holy life. Therefore, he who rejects this instruction does not reject man but God, who gives you his Holy Spirit.
—I THESSALONIANS 4:1-8, NIV

The Thessalonians had a reputation for being sexually promiscuous. Paul gave them three motivations in this scripture for a lifestyle of holiness and purity.

1. It is the will of God (verse 3).
2. It is honoring the gift of your future mate (verse 4).
3. It avoids sin against your friends and family (verse 6).

Sex and commitment cannot be separated, that is the way God intended it. Sex is a gift of God, but He only wishes people to enjoy this gift in the bonds of marriage. Yes, marriage is much more than just a piece of paper signed by an official that says you are married. It is a divine covenant, a divine commitment; a vow made to God and your partner. It is a strong, enduring bond that unites two into one. Ephesians 5:31 says, *"For this reason a man will leave his father and mother and be united to his wife, and the two will become one flesh."*

HOW WE DOIN' WITH THIS MAN JESUS?

This generation of young people learn about sex through a lifelong process that begins with discovering they are a boy or a girl. They then start to recognize the main differences in boys and girls by the way they dress, act and react with others. I have not even mentioned the major influences in their life of TV, friends, magazines, slumber party talks, sex education at school, their own experience and sometimes their own mistakes. I even heard one of my student's say that they were getting the clean sex information from parents and the dirty version from other kids at school. And what about the statistics! By the time a student graduates from high school, 7 out of 10 girls and 8 out of 10 boys will have had sexual intercourse. Recent studies have shown that by the time students reach their freshman year in college 90% of them have engaged in some form of sexual activity.

It is clear that teen's need to be taught that God's guidelines for sex does not result from some divine desire to take all of the fun out of life. God has good reasons for condemning sexual immorality, and those reasons flow from His perfect love. God does not want to keep teens *from* sex but keep teens *for* sex.

NOT OF THIS WORLD

Why does this world we live in have such a negative image of sex? It is clear in the Bible where the first negative images of sex began. We can look at Genesis to see where some of these distorted views of sexuality might have begun:

The Lord God said, "It is not good for the man to be alone. I will make a helper suitable for him." Now the Lord God had formed out of the ground all the beasts of the field and all the birds of the air. He brought them to the man to see what he would name them; and whatever the man called each living creature, that was its name. So the man gave names to all the livestock, the birds of the air and all the beasts of the field. But for Adam no suitable helper was found. So the Lord God caused the man to fall into a deep sleep; and while he was sleeping, he took one of the man's ribs and closed up the place with flesh. Then the Lord God made a woman from the rib he had taken out of the man, and he brought her to the man. The man said, "This is now bone of my bones and flesh of my flesh; she shall be called 'woman,' for she was taken out of man." For this reason a man will leave his father and mother and be united to his wife, and they will become one flesh. The man and his wife were both naked, and they felt no shame.
—GENESIS 2:18-25, NIV

Yes, there was a time when there was an absence of any negative understanding of sexuality. God made Adam and Eve in his exact image and gave them the ability to be sexually active. This passage says that Adam and Eve had no shame about being naked. Just imagine living in a perfect sexual world with no shame and to be able to have sex the exact way God intended to be. This was God's original design, that there be nothing negative about sex between man and woman.

The point here is that God's design has not changed...WE HAVE! What happened next in Paradise?

Now the serpent was more crafty than any of the wild animals the Lord God had made. He said to the woman, "did God really say, 'You must not eat from any tree in the garden'?" The woman said to the serpent, "We may eat fruit from the trees in the garden, but God did say, 'You must not eat fruit from the tree that is in the middle of the garden, and you must not touch it, or you will die.'" "You will not surely die," the serpent said to the woman. "For God knows that when you eat of it your eyes will be opened, and you will be like God, knowing good and evil." When the woman saw that the fruit of the tree was good for food and pleasing to the eye, and also desirable for gaining wisdom, she took some and ate it. She also gave some to her husband, who was with her, and ate it. Then the eyes of both of them were opened, and they

realized they were naked; so they sewed fig leaves together and made coverings for themselves.
Then the man and his wife heard the sound of the Lord God as he was walking in the garden in
the cool of the day, and they hid from the Lord God among the trees of the garden.
—Genesis 3:1-8 NIV

A big change happened between chapter two and chapter three.
Adam and Eve viewed their body differently. Adam and Eve disobeyed God
and their sexuality changed! It seems that many of the negative messages we
face today come from the same type of rebellion and poor choices. One
thing is very clear, sex was created by God and it is a great thing. No, it is
not a sin or some terrible curse that all unmarried people are to stay clear
from. But instead sex is a wonderful gift God has given us to look forward
to and engage in within the boundaries He has set for us. As a married
man, I am thankful to God for the gift of sex.

FIGHT TO WIN!

My prayer for teenagers who struggle with the temptation of sex is
that they can absorb more of God's view of sexuality. It is no easy thing to
absorb more of God's view about sex than the distorted ones that surround
us. Hard core pornography is simply a click away, and soft-core
pornography is on many cable stations every night. Hollywood and other
media have made it seem like it is socially acceptable to be sexually active
early in your teenage years. This temptation is without a doubt one of the
hardest things teens have to face in their Christian walk. The right view of
sexuality, the positive view of sexuality, God's view of sexuality is possible to
obtain when you have a right relationship with God—the one who created
sex in the first place.

The following are some passages from the Song of Solomon.
Listen to how much the Bible says about romance, love and sex:

1. Let him kiss me with the kisses of his mouth—for your love is
   more delightful than wine. (Song of Songs 1:2 NIV)
2. How handsome you are, my lover! Oh, how charming!
   (Song of Songs 1:16 NIV)
3. Your two breasts are like two fawns, like twin fawns of a gazelle
   that browse among the lilies. (Song of Songs 4:5 NIV)
4. I belong to my lover; and his desire is for me.
   (Song of Songs 7:10 NIV)

You see the Bible is not silent about important issues like
romance, love and dating. Many traditionalists may gloss over these

passages in the Bible and pretend they are not there. Believing the Bible is the inerrant word of God and that every word is there for our benefit, I believe that God is really concerned about giving us positive sexual messages through these scriptures.

OK, so the Bible says sex is a great thing...so the Bible actually does talk about romance and love. But what about the question kids most often ask about sex! The question goes something like this: "Hey I've signed my True Love Waits card and I know I'm not supposed to have sex. But how far can I go? Can I get all the way to third base as long as I don't score?"

Well, if sex were a game, that would be an interesting question. But sex is not a game. Then the next question comes: "Ok fine, but I just wanna fool around a little. How far can I go without going all the way?"

It's a fair question! The trouble is God doesn't get very detailed about the answer. There's no mention in the Bible about fooling around and nothing about making out in the back seat of a chariot. Then the next question comes: "Look, I'm just trying to get me "some" without having God all mad at me! So, for crying out loud, will you please just tell me, how far can I go?"

Well, OK! But you might not like the answer because the Bible does not really talk about love sex and dating in any modern sense. What the Bible does talk about—quite a bit actually- is lust! So here is your answer: You may go as far as you wish as long as you stop before lust. Lust is a serious fixation on something that's not yours to have: it is a deep focused, inappropriate craving. The Bible has a great deal to say about longing for experiences that are NOT rightly yours, and breaking boundaries to get them. Boundaries are limits on behavior—what you will and will not accept and what you will and will not do!

THE WORD SAYS...

I Corinthians 6:12 says: *"'Everything is permissible for me' - but not everything is beneficial. 'Everything is permissible for me'—but I will not be mastered by anything."*

Back in the day when this was written, a popular saying in Corinth was, "everything is permissible for me" These people had taken Paul's message of grace—that it does not matter what we do, God loves anyway— and turned it into an excuse to do whatever they wanted.

Paul gets bold and says, "Sure, God might not stop loving you, but that does not mean that everything benefits you!"

Teens today are much like the people of Corinth. I truly believe that many teens have taken the message of True Love Waits and said "As long as I don't have sexual intercourse, I can do anything up to that point and that's OK!"

Well, let me get bold and say: "The Bible is very clear on what your body is meant for!" Verse 13 of 1 Corinthians chapter 6 says, *"'Food for the stomach and the stomach for food'—but God will destroy them both. The body is not meant for sexual immorality, but for the Lord, and the Lord for the body."* Sexual immorality is something we read about in the Bible and hear a lot about in Church but in modern terms we do not have a good definition of it, which is exactly what Satan wants. Sexual immorality, according to many teens today is simply having sexual intercourse. As long as they do not "go all the way", everything else is fair game. Allow me to quote Adrian Rogers when he says, "I hear young people talking today about 'going all the way.' Well, that's the one thing they don't do! They don't go all the way. They don't make that last commitment and experience the fulfillment and joy of a monogamous marriage. Oh, there is such ravishing love that comes from one man committed to one woman until death do them part!" This is a point well taken and exactly what we need to relate to our teens today.

I love the commercial on television that advertises brakes for an automobile. There is a man in a lab coat standing in the middle of a raceway in the front of your TV screen. In the background you see a car racing toward the man telling you about the wonderful brakes he sells. At the last moment, the car comes to a screeching halt inches behind the man who is still talking about the brakes without so much as a flinch. The last slogan you hear is, "We don't just stand behind our brakes, we stand in front of them."

It's a great commercial but we humans are not designed with that kind of control—or those kind of brakes when it comes to sexual expression. Many teens today think they can aim their dating at sexual intercourse and then come to screeching halt just before they go to far. Unfortunately they discover that their brakes fail and they smash into the wall of reality. Crash—pregnancy! Crash—sexually transmitted disease! Crash—emotional scars! Crash—betrayal!

ARE YOU ASKING THE RIGHT QUESTIONS?

So what is that safe distance? How far is too far? Let us first look at the purpose of sexual expression? Is it a thank you for a date or a meal? Is it something you simply do on a date? Is it "making love"? The Answer is No, No and especially No! SEXUAL CONTACT EXPRESSES LOVE, IT NEVER MAKES LOVE. So sexual contact should never go farther than the love itself. Not many teens I know are ready to get married and have a married lifestyle within the next year so they need to decide now where their braking point is.

Let me clarify that we are not answering the question of, "How far can I go!" If you are asking this question, you have already sinned against

God! Asking this question already indicates that you want to seek your own pleasures as long as it does not interfere with God's plan. The real question is, "How far should I go?"

There is a simple principal of design that helps us clue in on that safe distance. The principal of design says that sex was designed by God to culminate in intercourse. So anytime a person starts with a form of sexual expression, that is exactly where it wants to end up. There are no brakes. The principle here is that sex is fulfilled only in intercourse. If you don't control your body, it will control you. When sex controls you, you have gone too far.

I have realized time and time again that because of our own sins, the sins of this world and Satan's influence, many of us have crossed that line. We have crossed that boundary! We have made a mistake and we need forgiveness, our brakes have failed and we have crashed and we need a do-over! I'm sure you have all learned about do-overs as a child. As a child we all use to play games with our neighbors and friends! I remember as a 7th grader that we used to have some quite serious and intense wiffle ball games in my back yard. Tensions were high and the competition was tight. We all took it very seriously and the main objective was to win. And every once and a while there would be a play that would present a huge controversy! The entire batting team would think the player was safe and the entire team in the field would think, "He's OUT!

A DO–OVER

Of course this small back yard wiffle ball game could not afford trained officials and umpires so a decision had to be made. And as a favor a "DO-OVER" would be granted. A Do-over was a second chance when someone made a mistake…it was a gift between friends. A Do-over was a favor, an act of Grace! So for those of you who have crossed those boundaries and need a do-over, this section is for you! For some of you teens or adults who have crossed that line of what your body was meant for, this section is for you. For some of you parents out there who have not paid close attention to your son and daughter and they are in desperate need of a Do-over, this section is for you. And lastly, just to be certain I have said it, maybe there are those of you who have been victims of sexualized violence and are in need of a do-over by no fault of your own, this section is for you also.

John 8:1-11 is a great example of what a do-over is all about! Jesus was just hanging out one day when these religious folks decided to test Him. They brought to him a woman in desperate need of a do-over. She had been caught in the midst of having sex with a married man and the law demanded this woman be killed for her sinful act.

How many of us have been caught doing something you knew deserved immediate punishment? What was the outcome? Was mercy granted or did you receive punishment to the full extent of the law?

IF JESUS IS FOR US...

In this story Jesus does a really interesting thing after this woman's accusers challenge him for an immediate verdict on this trial. He bends down and just starts writing in the sand. Wouldn't you love to know what he was writing? Some say that He was writing the names of all the women the Pharisees and teachers of the law had slept with in the past. Maybe that's why, one by one, the Pharisees leave the scene after Jesus challenged them with the words, "Anyone here without sin can cast the first stone."

THE FACT IS JESUS WAS THE ONLY ONE IN THE CROWD WHO HAD THE RIGHT TO CAST THAT STONE. But he didn't. No the God of grace, and the God of mercy gave her an undeserved do-over. So after reading this scripture, this begs the questions, "Can a 16 year-old boy or girl who has already engaged in premarital sex get a do-over? Can a 25-year-old that is dealing with pornography over the Internet get a do-over? Can a 45-year-old who has had an extra-martial affair, get a do-over? Can a teen that has crossed over boundaries in their dating relationship get a do-over!? The answer depends on how we answer another question—Is God for us or against us? If God is against us, it's game over; there won't be any do-overs. We'll die guilty. And don't say God didn't warn us. If, on the other hand God is for us, there's hope. We still must contend with the natural consequences of our behavior, but there's supernatural hope. There is a transformation!

"If God be for us who can be against us?" This is what the Bible says! God's forgiveness covers every kind of wrong. Because God is gracious, people can get a chance to begin again, starting right where we are, even though it's not where we're supposed to be.

So now you say, well that's easy! "No matter what I do, God still loves me! And He will forgive me." NO IT'S NOT THAT EASY! You see we sometimes take forgiveness lightly and it becomes easy to say "It's no big deal," and forgiveness simply becomes something you sprinkle on your past and you move on.

Forgiveness is free...but it's also hard! The last thing that Jesus said to this woman in this scripture is, "Go now and leave your life of sin." Forgiveness and a do-over were offered to her on a plate. It was free of charge and available to her. All she had to do was receive it. But Jesus goes on to say, "Hey, stop sleeping around." It seems that part of a do-over is the chance to get it right. Or in her case, to stop getting it wrong.

But what about those people who take do-overs for granted and continue to make mistakes over and over again. For you I offer this! Jesus didn't die on the cross to take away your feelings. He died to take away your sins. If you confess your sins he is faithful and just to forgive us our sins and purify you from all unrighteousness (1 John 1:8-9). Cleansed of sin, you can work on transforming your feelings into a useful tool for God's service. Your feelings won't lead you downward! They will be transformed, giving you compassion for the pain of others and they will give you deep determination not to go wrong again—to go and sin no more.

RESTORE US, OH GOD!

I am a firm believer that today's youth are not the church of tomorrow, but instead, a very active part of the church of today. The church is mandated to shine a light into a darkened world and we have failed to take our light into this sexually promiscuous culture that surrounds and oftentimes engulfs our young people. Psalm 80:3 says, Restore us, Oh God; make your face shine upon us, that we may be saved. (NIV) Now more than ever, we need that restoration, that salvation in this generation! We must rise up and lead this generation into a walk with Christ that defeats the worldview. We must restore a Biblical perspective of sex that revolutionizes our teens. This must be our vision; this must be our goal! REVOLUTION!!

We must pray as the psalmist David cried out, after committing adultery with Bathsheba, "Create in me a pure heart, O God, and renew a steadfast spirit with in me. Do not cast me from your presence or take your Holy Spirit from me. Restore to me the joy of your salvation and grant me a willing spirit, to sustain me. "

Dear God I pray that you will create a pure heart in this generation of young people. That You will begin a "revolution of abstinence" in our youth! That you can restore to them the eternal joy of your gift of salvation.

My challenge to you today has three parts:
1. If you have not been revolutionized in your own life and you need the transforming power of Jesus Christ in your life, I challenge you and urge you to make that decision now. I know there must be someone reading this book that has never proclaimed Jesus as your Lord. I don't know the reason for that. But I know that today you can have a revolution in your life by accepting Jesus as your Lord and Savior.

2. My second challenge is for some of you to overlook the selfish needs and ambitions in your own life, and to identify two people that you know who need what this scripture (Rev.7:16-17) says is the living water of ministry. I challenge you to take that living water to them in some tangible way.

3. My last challenge to you is that those Christians who have secret pains or unspoken needs in your life that you will simply bring those to the foot of Jesus and experience a revolution in those areas of your life...that you simply start today to say No to the world and yes to a mighty God who can revolutionize your life.

About The Author

David Howard Simmerman lives near Nashville, TN., and is married to his wife LeAnn. They have a 4 year old son named Alex. He is currently the Student Minister at First Baptist Church of Joelton, TN., and is chairman of the Nashville Baptist Association Youth Council. David has been a youth pastor for over 10 years in the State of Tennessee and has previously worked eight years for the Upward Bound Program at East Tennessee State University. David has a passion for teenagers and views youth ministry as a life-long calling. David truly believes that youth are not the church of tomorrow, but instead a very important part of the church of today.

PASS THE TORCH

Lay Hold the Mantle
by Raphael Giglio

DURING THE RECORD hot summer of 1984, I embarked on what has to this day been one of the most ambitious Evangelistic outreaches I have ever been a part of. Fifteen of us, young people from all over the country, took part in "Torch Run America '84" (a coast to coast run where we relayed a torch across the USA from Plymouth Rock, Massachusetts to Los Angeles, California in time for the 1984 Summer Olympics). Most of us were not marathon runners, especially me. We were all in our early twenties and had a desire to evangelize every city we passed through claiming it for our Lord by prayer, intercession and outreach. We were to oversee thousands of young people in youth groups who would each run a mile of the 3000-mile stretch.

I remember being recruited as the Musician of the crew and was told I would mostly be performing concerts and leading worship in all the cities along the way. The planning team had lined up hundreds of Youth Groups to run the torch through their particular area and pass it on to the youth from the next town. As the time of the run approached, a terrible disappointment took place. Most of the youth groups dropped out and there was very little participation from the youth groups that did show up. Our little team of 15 sore and blistered YWAM-ers, ran over 80% of the country by ourselves.

I learned a deep lesson on the back roads of this great country as I ran with the torch through what seemed like endless hills, dales, cow pastures, corn and wheat fields and highway shoulders. I learned what it meant to "pass a torch." Most of the time for the first few weeks when I would run my particular segment of the relay, I found myself gasping my last breath, forcing my over-fatigued body to fight the pain and weariness long enough to see one of my fresh and ready team mates holding out their hand behind them awaiting the torch. In the beginning it was a welcomed sight, I was always ready to let someone else carry the burden for a while. It was great to be a small part of a big day of running and contribute to the 100 or so miles that we accomplished each day in order to cover the 3000 or so miles necessary to complete our journey in about a month. As time went by, we began to enjoy the run. We were a team—peers and compadres with an important mission and the pride that comes with it. We'd wake up early and go to bed late gloating over the distance we covered and the fact that we were actually doing it ourselves, regardless of the fact that the youth groups dropped out. We were still making it across the country in grand fashion.

Somewhere during the middle of our run, perhaps in America's Heartland, or the mid-western prairies, some of the kids began to show up. Not the spectators who were there to cheer us on, Not the crowds of young people who gathered at our nightly outreaches, but the few and far between youth groups who were there to honor their commitment of running "the torch" through their town. They were excited for their friends, families, and neighbors to see them carry this great torch that came all the way from Massachusetts on its way to the Olympic in Los Angeles. They held it proudly as they sprinted down Main Street, waved to their friends, stopped for the local newspaper photographer to snap a picture, and at the end of the day hand it back to us. We would usually need to run it several hundred miles before the next group was willing to participate and take it through a similar display.

At first we were all delighted to see in small ways what we hoped to see all along. We smiled and were thrilled to pass the torch to the locals and pick it back up for the long stretches in between. But as time went on, and we had more and more of our blood, sweat, shoe rubber, and more sweat invested in this trip, we began to resent the newcomers. Who were they to parade OUR torch through their little town only to give it back at the end of the day and have us carry it hundreds of miles before we found more willing runners? They could not possibly conceive of the effort it took for us to leave home for three months to plan and run this mission. Where were they during the dangerous Pennsylvania hailstorms, the weeklong Indiana flood-rains or the Oklahoma heat wave? What did they know of the hours and hours of prayer and intercession that we spent as a group in spiritual warfare over each city or the faith it took for each of us to cover the finances for this trip? As resentment built, passing the torch became a more and more difficult task each and every day.

Eventually it got to the point where we were such good runners, and in such good shape that the paltry 40 or 50 miles that the youth groups offered to run was not only an insult, but also a disruption of our regimen. Still we passed the torch to them. It was not always easy and took all the humility meekness and faith we could muster. I struggled with pride and resentment each time I handed a young man MY torch and watched him carry it through the parade stands or cheering local crowds—after all, I was a better runner. I often knew more about their State and its terrain than they did. I was a professional torch-runner with lots of experience now and they were simply amateurs, and in many cases they didn't even hold it right.

To this day I look back and realize that there was a valuable lesson to be learned in the passing of the torch, and I discover more and more about that lesson all the time.

1963 was what is considered 'a pinnacle year' for America on many levels. It was the year that The Supreme Court banned state-sponsored reciting of the Lord's Prayer, and reading of the Bible as part of devotional exercises in public schools. It was the year that John F. Kennedy was shot and killed in Dallas Texas, and among many other things it was the final year of the post-WWII baby boom. Baby-boomers were like no other generation before. To this day they have accelerated technology, commerce, the arts and freethinking like no other generation in modern history. Baby-boomer pastors and leaders who grew up on rock and roll, radical pop-culture, and sitcom TV populate many of today's churches. They have taken the church from a place where cultural relevance was not ever regarded with any level of importance, to a whole new era of church growth and effectiveness.

Modern worship and music has been the spearhead of the contemporary church movement, as well as innovative inter-denominational teaching and progressive multi-media in TV, Radio, and the Internet. We no longer have widespread rejection of using contemporary instruments in our church services and have for a long time welcomed casually dressed spirit-filled participants in most of the major denominations and movements. As we entered this new millennium, most of us felt more than prepared to facilitate the astronomically increasing percentage of Americans who have either become Christians or joined a church for the first time in the last 10 years. We have everything: great music, excellent teaching, and years of contemporary experience to offer these new believers and the young people who happen to be coming of age in the new millennium. We have held the torch high for decades and have all the fortitude and momentum to continue holding it for years to come. But unlike the Statue of Liberty we are not called to be stationary torch-wielding monuments of freedom. I can tell you from experience that if you stand still holding the torch too long, the wax or burnt oil from the flame drips down your arm and it is very painful. The key is to carry it in such a way that you can run fast and strong; create a path of light in your wake; and then pass it on to someone else.

I was born in 1964. I am among the first of the post-baby-boomer generation, known as Generation "X". Because of this and the fact that I grew up in a family where nine of my eleven siblings are baby-boomers, I can see and draw experience from both generations:

Did you know anyone who graduated High School in 1999 or later, was born AFTER MTV came along?

Most of the kids that will be getting their driver's license this year are YOUNGER than Microsoft Windows.

Even within the church, a youth who may have been taught a 'modern' favorite praise song like, "Lord I lift Your Name on High" in kindergarten, can still sing it this year as he or she is graduating High school!

...and it would not be the least bit unusual for teen-agers who sang songs like "Pass It On," and "For Those Tears I Died," in youth groups to become grandparents in the next few years.

This is a new day, a brand new millennium and a completely different generation than any that has gone before, including ours. Some of the things that we still consider "New Wine" are regarded as "Old Manna" by the younger generation. I believe it is time to "Pass the torch and take hold of the mantle." The generation who ushered the church out of the former millennium made great strides in many important areas. The generation that will carry us into the first few decades of the 21st century has the potential to take it a quantum leap further. We took worship to new heights with our contemporary songs and city-wide praise gatherings. We saw laws changed and babies saved as we marched on Washington hundreds of times over the last few decades to appeal for godly legislation. We have seen the Gospel go forth tremendously around the globe through radio, TV, Bible translators and youth missionary organizations. I believe there will be many occasions for the Lord to say unto the people of our generation, "Well done thou good and faithful servants," especially as we embrace the adult responsibilities of church leadership, mentoring, discipleship and most importantly, positive parenthood.

We have given the younger generation of this new millennium a great gift. They have a legacy and foundation to build on, but there is a challenge that comes with it. I am already delighted to see them 'besting' us in many areas:

While we thought it radical to bring electric guitars and drums into the church sanctuary to make a loud and joyful noise to the Lord,...They will bring worship out into the streets where they will sing the songs of Zion even in a foreign land.

While we welcomed Messianic Judaism, it's music and some of it's culture into Christianity, ...They will respect the eternal promises of the God of Abraham to His people, Israel, and understand that gentiles are "grafted into" a pre-existing vine and given the "spirit of adoptio."

Where we fought tirelessly for the rights of the unborn and to try to overturn "Roe vs. Wade"...They will fight to protect the entire "Sanctity of Life", whether it be in the womb, the old age homes or on Death Row.

Where we made it clear to the homosexual community that their sin is wrong and grieves the Lord...They will communicate to gays and lesbians that God loves them and that His kindness will lead them to repentance.

My prayer is that we will have the grace and humility to know when we are to relinquish the torch that we have carried through many hard years and for many long miles—to relay it into the hands of young men and women who may be eagerly waiting to run it through THEIR chosen time and given generation. May our hands not cling to the torch in fear, pride or mistrust. And may our same hands lay hold of the mantle of responsibility and willingness to grant the roles of leadership that we thought belonged only to the "elders" of the former generation.

About the Author

Raphael Giglio serves as a Pastor along side Michael W. Smith, Bill Todd, Gary Sadler and Lance Hickerson of New River Fellowship in Franklin, TN. He was born and raised in North Brunswick, New Jersey. He is the youngest of six sons, in an Italian/Jewish family of twelve children. He continues to record and tour internationally as a Singer/Songwriter. Michael W. Smith started New River Fellowship in 1999 as a prayer meeting in his barn.

THE NEXT GENERATION

What's Next?
by Shawn Stutz
Youth Minister

IT WAS LIKE a scene straight from the movie *Hoosiers*. Eight seconds was all that remained on the game clock. The opposing team's one point advantage glared down on us all. As the hometown boys in-bounded the ball, we all stood in anticipation of what would happen next.

Seconds seemed like hours as the guard pushed the ball down the court. Silence descended over the crowd as everyone held their breath in hopes of victory. The echo of the ball and the random squeak of a rubber-soled shoe were all that could be heard. "What's next, what's going to happen?" seemed to be the phrase racing through our minds.

The star player drove the lane and with confidence passed the ball to the left wing where the wide-open, free throw expert of the team shot a fifteen-foot jumper. There it went. The final shot, the last chance for triumph was sailing its way to the basket.

With great ease that amazing orange sphere, the focus of every eye in the arena, made its way through the red iron circle, graced the last inch of the nylon net, and fell quickly to the floor. The buzzer sounded, the crowd erupted, and the game was over. My high school's basketball team clinched the Illinois State Championship game and I was there to see it. "What's next?" Well that day we all found out.

That day seems so far away, but lately I have been pondering that same question. It has not been about a game, but about life. What's next on the horizon of God's work in this new century? More specifically, what's next for our youth culture.

As a history fan, I have enjoyed studying the great spiritual leaders of the past. There were people like Polycarp, a martyr burned at the stake, and Martin Luther, the bold reformer. There was also John Wesley, the great Methodist evangelist, and D.L. Moody, the great man of God who spurred spiritual renewal in urban Chicago.

Today we admire mature Christian leaders such as Billy Graham, Beth Moore, Louie Giglio, Max Lucado, and John Piper. All of these people have made strong impacts for the kingdom of God during their lifetime.

And so comes the question again, "What's next?" Or better yet, "Who's next?" Who will stand up and represent the Lord at the dawn of this new century? I strongly believe that there are thousands of students here in Nashville that will stand, as Isaiah did, and say, "Here am I Lord, send me!" Many sociologists have labeled our present day youth culture as Generation Y or the Lost Generation. However, I like to call them the "next" generation. These thousands of young people will make up the generation that leads all generations to spiritual awakening.

Many people have asked me why I believe the way I do. My answer is that I see something different about this new generation verses those in the past. Today's youth now seem to crave for something real and genuine. They want real answers and real hope. Quick fixes and phony charades won't cut it any longer. Those coming next want something real to pour their lives into.

But the question, "Who's next?" needs to be followed quickly with the questions, "What will these young people be like?" or "What will they need to be like to see true revival in our cities and nations?" From what I have seen in my years as a Christian and a youth minister, I can strongly say that this next generation needs a (1) humble heart, (2) genuine sorrow over their sin, (3) and a renewed sense of Christ's Lordship.

A HUMBLE HEART

Students of this "next" generation will need a good dose of humility. Throughout the ages, Satan has deceived the people of God into building their own fame and their own kingdoms. Power, position, and pride have dominated the game of life for far to long. And heaven forbid that we tarnish our image by admitting any faults. Even elementary school years are spent trying to develop and protect the key to worldly success, a reputation. Who are we to the world? Are we important enough? Yet Jesus' life stands in stark contrast to this human way of thinking.

Philippians 2:7 states that Christ *made Himself nothing.* The King James Version translates that verse *"He made Himself of no reputation."* He sought not to bring glory to Himself, but as a humble servant He brought glory to God the Father only. In verse five, Paul challenges us to have the "same attitude as that of Christ." The longing of our heart should not be to "make it big" or achieve a title of fame, but to bring glory to the name of God.

During a small group Bible study one night, a student in my ministry shared that she felt led to lay down her reputation to see her friends come to know Christ. She was willing to cast off one of the world's crowning achievements of personal gain and fame to take up the basin and the towel to be a servant in her school.

Her attitude and mindset ought to bring conviction to every Christian heart. How quick are we to deny ourselves as the scripture beckons us to do? How willing are we to be the servant of all. Today's student culture must be willing to adopt this mindset if they hope to become the much-needed spark of spiritual awakening within our cities and nation.

This attitude of humility is not only personal, but corporate as well. There can be great joy in sharing positive experiences that occur at church, but the church does not deserve nor receive the credit for any reward or harvest. It is a collection of laborers only. When the church capitalizes on its community reputation by aligning itself with harvest rewards, then it takes for itself the glory that belongs to God. Isaiah 48:11 states that God will not yield His glory to any other person or institution. The joy of the church must revolve around humbling itself before the Lord and glorifying Him alone.

True humility also requires total dependence on the Holy Spirit. This "next" generation will have to learn to trust wholly in God. They could sit around tables and devise spiritually ambitious plans to reach the world for Christ and never rely on Holy Spirit. They could create a church that meets every "felt" need of a specific community, and never rely on Holy Spirit. Generation Next will quickly learn that it is not the plans of men, but the power of God that opens the doors of spiritual renewal in our society. To pridefully ignore the power and plans of God would mean never achieving true spiritual humility. Mankind's plans and ideas will never compare to the supremely powerful accomplishments of God.

Being humble is not a single act. It is a lifestyle. The desire of this young generation should be that God receives the glory for the work He has done through lives yielded totally to Him not just once, but day after day.

SORROW OVER SIN

Humbleness is not the only characteristic needed for the youth of the future. They must also adopt an attitude of brokenness. Sorrow and brokenness are often viewed as negative feelings. As a result, these aspects of spiritual maturity are unfortunately over-looked or often forgotten.

There is a positive example of brokenness found in the story of the apostle Peter and his denial. Luke writes of this event in chapter 22 of his gospel. Peter followed Christ for three years and he faithfully and boldly made stands for Christ day after day. And yet, in accordance with Christ's prophesy, around a small campfire a servant girl turns Peter into a cursing betrayer. Luke relates the end of the story by saying that as the rooster crowed, Jesus looked at Peter from across the courtyard. Can you just imagine what anguish Peter must have felt staring deep into the eyes of Jesus knowing that He had denied His Lord?

For me, the key to this passage is found in verse 62. It reads, *"and Peter went outside and wept bitterly."* He was broken physically, emotionally, and spiritually. His soul was weary and His heart was heavy. When faced with the true weight of his personal iniquity, all he could do was weep.

Consider also the story of Mary Magdalene, a woman with an unfavorable reputation. According to scripture, in sorrow over her sins, she emptied a whole jar of expensive perfume while anointing the feet of Jesus. The brokenness she experienced on account of her sin was displayed in her act of great love.

Of course the religious leaders scoffed at her by high-lighting her offensive lifestyle. They even diminished her act of humility. Here she was pouring her heart out to Jesus as tears rolled off of her face. Her body shook from the sobbing. Her hair was wet from cleaning Jesus' road weary feet. And the Pharisees sat questioning her motives and her "uncleanness." Yet Jesus, who clearly saw the condition of her heart, comforted her by saying, *"He who has been forgiven little, loves little, but He who has been forgiven much, loves much"* (Luke 7:47). Those who are truly pierced with Holy Spirit conviction will respond with great sorrow over their sin and great love for their Lord.

Let us examine our hearts. How often do we find ourselves broken before the Lord because of our sin? When was the last time that we wept bitterly in reaction to the knowledge of our wretched state? If we are honest, we might admit that we often downplay our sin in light of God's grace, mercy, and unfailing forgiveness. If we are real honest, we might also admit that we causally confess our sin out of obligation or as a prelude to petitioning the Lord. The psalmist writes in Psalm 51:17 that God loves a broken Spirit. *"A broken and contrite heart, O God, you will not despise."* How broken are we? How often do fall before the throne of grace in humble confession and heartfelt repentance of our sins?

I am becoming more and more convinced that we have not seen a true revival or awakening of God's Spirit because we are not truly repenting of our sins. II Chronicles 7:14 teaches that *"if my people, who are called by my name, will humble themselves and pray, and seek my face, and turn from their wicked ways, then I will from heaven, and will forgive their sins and will heal their land."* God's desire is to forgive our sins and heal our land. But this must be our desire. Generation Next will need a pure understanding of brokenness and repentance, the act of leaving our lives of sin and clinging to God, before they lead out in true revival.

We have seen that the next generation needs a humble heart and a genuine sorrow concerning sin. The final character trait that is essential for this rising student generation is that of Lordship. Simply put, students must allow God to rule and transform their lives.

JESUS IS LORD

Isn't it amazing how we have such a hard time with the concept of obedience? This spiritual handicap seems to develop at such an early age. My two-year old daughter knows that she is not supposed to say "no" when asked to do something. However, I can remember the time that I had to drag her out of the toy store as she screamed, "No daddy, I can't! I don't want to go home!" Of course everyone in the checkout line gave me the "you're a horrible father" stare.

You may laugh, but how many times do we find ourselves acting the same way. We know the commands and desires of God for our life, but we often choose our own. Before long we are caught in a web of consequences or are experiencing the discipline of the Lord. There is really no excuse other than deliberate disobedience.

In John 14:15, Jesus says that, *"If you love me, you will obey what I command."* The essence of obedience is then amplified in the next chapter. It is here that Jesus makes the statement that He is the vine and that we are the branches. We remain in and have fellowship with God as an act of obedience and love. This new generation will see that daily acts of obedience and Christ-like living are the beginnings of transformation. The more that they yield to the work of God's Spirit in their lives, the more they will experience true transformation.

The exciting news is that transformation was God's plan from the start. I remember growing up and playing with toys called *Transformers*. They were multi-colored robots that could change their identity and become a car, truck, or plane. Once their properties had been rearranged, they served a whole new purpose.

The same is true with us as Christians. Generation Next must understand that once they give their lives to Christ, He has the right to rearranges their every priority. They will then become vessels of God's purposes and plans. Self-fulfillment is no longer an option, because the desire to conform to Christ in every way replaces it.

For example, I consider it a joy to work for the Lord as a minister of students. But it hasn't always been that way. First, God had to change my heart and open my eyes. I still remember the day that I responded to God's call on me for youth ministry. Sitting on a bench in the open yard of my college campus, I began to tell my wife-to-be that I no longer felt like becoming a lawyer. It was like the river of political ambition and law practice desire had dried up within me. Simply stated, my passion had changed.

I looked at her and began to share that God wanted me to work for Him and His kingdom. I felt as though I needed to surrender my life to serve the "next" generation of young people. With Christ as my Lord, I could not resist the calling, and so I said to her, "Michelle, I think I'm supposed to be a youth minister."

Without surprise or hesitation she softly said, "I know." It was as if God had confirmed His call for my life. He knew, she knew—and as a strange peace flooded over me—I knew. From that point on, I have not questioned for a minute that I was called by God to work with Generation Next.

Once one's relationship with Christ becomes a top priority, lives, families, cities, and nations are changed forever. Christ-like people see obedience as an opportunity to show their love for God. Their hearts break for those lost in sin and the salvation of a nation becomes their burden. Their tongue becomes a tool for worship and edification, not destruction. Sacrificial ministry and giving are seen as ways to serve the Lord with gladness. When Christ is allowed to truly be the Lord of a believer, transformation and awakening will be the result. It is my prayer that this young generation will join with all generations by embracing the Lordship of Jesus Christ.

THE VISION OF TRANSFORMATION

Can you just envision a city surrendered to the Lord? Can you imagine a generation of young people sold out to Jesus? Can you picture the potential? There would be prayer meetings at every middle and high school. These meetings would be filled with students praying that God would send revival to their school. Christian Clubs by practice and not just name would pop up around campus. The number of lost youth giving their lives to Christ would be staggering. Schools would begin to see percentages of their student population become followers of Christ.

Young believers setting the example in faith and action would challenge adults to press on in their walk. As a result, parents and youth leaders would unite to pray for students to have the boldness to preach the gospel. Churches wouldn't know what to do with the overflow of young people. Youth ministers would be scrambling to baptize and disciple the students that God had recently placed in their ministry.

The schools and the churches would just be the beginning. Theaters would see a decrease in ticket sales because the Christian majority had consecrated their minds for God's work. Youth from all over the city would be found meeting together on the weekends to worship. Missionary youth would be sent out to the wild weekend "parties" to proclaim the peace of God to their lost friends.

Are you still with me? It gets better. Styles would change as well. Retail clothing stores would have to adjust the sizes of their clothing because of their loss in sales. The new catalogs would demonstrate the trend by switching to a more modest clothing line.

48

Young men would unite to form fraternities or cell groups of purity. These groups would be zealous (not self-righteous) in their efforts to fight the battle against lust and pornography. Each young man would know that a phone call to a supportive Christian brother was his escape from a temptation to sin by lusting. As a result of these purity-hungry accountability groups, adult bookstores across the city would be crippled to the point of closing. Play that out to the next generation and study the effect that passionate purity, and integrity has on marriage statistics and I guarantee it will be startling!

The great news is that some of this dream is already taking place. First Priority, a strategically evangelistic school club, has taken high school and middle school campuses by storm. Hundreds of students are being saved each month nationwide. Prayer teams are even meeting before school daily as a result of *See You at the Pole.* Also, look at the rise in worship concerts and music labels geared to draw students to encounter God in prayer and even fasting. The DC/LA youth event sponsored by Youth for Christ saw almost 20,000 students flock to the nation's capital last summer to pray for revival. In addition to that, thousands of sexual-purity commitments are being made each year as a result of the *True Love Waits* movement.

It is amazing what God *could* and *is* doing! The truly exciting part is that this is just a portion of my dream of youth-led transformation. What would God's dream look like? Oh the possibilities! In John 14:12, Jesus says *"I tell you the truth, anyone who has faith in me will do what I have been doing. He will do even greater things that these!"* I am ready for greater things. How about you, are you ready? The encouraging fact is that it will only take *one* student, completely sold out to Christ, to spark the flames of revival and a generation of students to fan that flame into nation-wide spiritual awakening.

A WORD OF CAUTION

I would love to conclude with these words of hope, but there must also be a word of caution. This youth culture must not neglect the wisdom of the generations that have gone before us. This next generation must also really crave true revival before God will send revival. I do not say that to suggest that we can in any way manipulate the plans of God. My intention is to stress the Christian's role in revival. God is eager to send His Spirit, but before He rends the heavens and comes down, we must fulfill the covenant promise of II Chronicles 7:14. Let's review.

First of all, we must encourage this student generation towards humility before the Lord. Our ways are not His. Our plans are not enough. Our programs will not succeed. We must bow down and glorify the Lamb before He will reveal His glory to us.

Secondly, this young generation must truly come to a place when they realize the devastating impact of sin. There must be a sorrow for sin, a genuine brokenness that leads to sacrificial service once God's forgiveness has been experienced.

And finally, when this next generation leads out in Lordship obedience, the pathway of revival and awakening will be made clear. Transformation will only occur when we let God rearrange our priorities and purpose for living.

Revival will come, but until it comes this young generation will be on its knees in prayer.

About the Author

Shawn Stutz is a minister to students in Fairview, Tennessee. He is a father of two blessed gifts from God and the husband to his greatest friend. He is convinced that Jesus is the true way to life and that God's desire is to bring an authentic Awakening to His church and His people. Shawn is a graduate of Union University in Jackson, Tennessee with a degree in Youth Ministry. He is currently pursuing a Masters of Divinity and enjoys speaking and proclaiming a message of genuine revival to the church.

PART 2

REPENT AND BE SET FREE

*"We cannot justly expect sinners to be saved,
and our places of worship to be filled by those from the outside until
we ourselves get right with God; and this can only be done
by absolute surrender of our whole lives to Jesus Christ as King in repentance,
and a faith acceptance of the Holy Spirit to be set free."*
—Wales Revival 1904

IN ONE VOICE

Father Forgive Us
by Jeffrey M. Richfield

GOD CALLS HIS church to be first in repentance. "Bend the church and save the world," was the motto from the Wales' revival. The end result of exposing sin is not to bring condemnation and shame to the church but to bring godly sorrow producing repentance, leading to a true change of heart. Our nakedness is covered in full by Jesus' all saving, all encompassing, all redeeming blood. But we must appropriate it! In a proclamation from the heart we exchange our blood stained rags and put on His redemptive white robes. It is through intimacy re-established that Father God then pulls us up close in His tender loving-kindness and whispers, "Now may I tell you about a few things I've noticed that hurt my heart."

Even with the vastness of today's cities it is not impossible for Almighty God to communicate to all of the people of the church as He did through Nehemiah, and other God fearing men, in a public display of repentance. We have the luxury of email, TV, radio, newspapers, telephone and the Postal Service to reach not only the church, but also the lost. If our own Postal Service can reach all 1 million people in Nashville in three days or less, what then can we do with the help of an omniscient omnipotent God? I plead each of you to recite these sins individually and/or corporately, reflecting upon God's willingness to forgive even a whole city through those who are willing to stand in the gap in confession. Take the personal revival quiz at the back of this book. God works in the world when His people are right with Him. The success of the Gospel in the case of the unsaved is conditioned by its success in the case of the saved. We need to have a holy jealousy for our God and weep sorely because of the fact that satan is loose in our city. Ask God for a heart of compassion. Plead the blood for the love of our city...

"Son of man, describe the temple to the house of Israel (Nashville), that they may be ashamed of their inequities; and let them measure the pattern."
—EZEKIEL 43:10

A CALL TO REPENTANCE

"Return, faithless *Nashville*,
   Says the Lord.
I will not look on you in anger, for I am merciful,
   Says the Lord;
I will not be angry forever. Only acknowledge your guilt,
   That you have rebelled against the Lord your God,
And scattered your favors among strangers under every green tree,
And have not obeyed my voice,
   Says the Lord.
Return, O faithless children,
   Says the Lord,
For I am your Master; I will take you, one from a city
and two from a family, and I will bring you to Zion."
—JEREMIAH 3:12-14 *(Italics added)*

...And so Lord, we come to You, O Lord God Almighty, Maker of heaven and earth—Jesus, we come humbly without condemnation on behalf of Your city of refuge, Nashville Tennessee, as *a city on its knees* individually and corporately. Lord, we are cut to the heart. Our hearts lie broken before You. We come too ashamed and disgraced even to lift our faces to you. Open the heart (eyes) of Your church to the horror of our sin. We have been at ease, a people of pleasure and comfort sitting on our blessed assurance-not bringing the good news to the poor and unsaved to change the spiritual climate of this city. We cry Holy, Holy, Holy, art thou, O Lord—Your loving kindness lasts forever! We lie down broken—with anguish of heart. Our tears fill the cup of Your hands, over the brim. For we have forsaken the greatest commandment, "To love the Lord our God with all our heart, and with all our soul, and with all our mind." And the second, "You shall love your neighbor as yourself" (Matt. 22:38-40). Lord, we have failed in not caring for the needs of the lost. "I go on and God loves me, while everyone goes to hell around me." The church has to happen in the city not in four walls. Forgive and restore us O Lord!

FOR OUR HISTORICAL SINS...

As we approach your Holy Mountain, for the city of Nashville and the state of Tennessee, oh great One, we implore Your mercy and forgiveness. We cry mercy, Lord, Oh Lord, have mercy! In your wrath, remember mercy! For the sins of this people (Your church) in this city have reached up higher than our heads, and our guilt has reached to the heavens. For we say we are rich, but we are really blind because we don't care enough for the poor and naked. We have replaced fellowship with religious bigotry in a full display of a self-righteous Pharisee. Our guilt is great, oh Lord. For we have each gone astray—each to our own way. Now consider we are all Your people. Your city has become like a barren wilderness, so we make mourning as for an only child.

Lord, You are correct in asking, "Is this not the state who commingled with racism through the KKK? Who made the trail of tears, and slain innocent Indians? Is this not the people who called their city, the "Athens of the South," and embraced idolatry and Greek thinking? And so we replied in tears, covering our face, "Yes Lord, we are that people. That is us. We are defiled. That is why we come this day in one accord to seek forgiveness for our abominations and our transgressions. As we approach Your perfect love, will You please forgive us? Please, Lord, have mercy, have mercy over Tennessee, our state, and Nashville, our city."

FOR OUR DIVISION AND OUR TRADITIONS...

Our hearts, Lord, You say, "Our hearts are divided," and we admit this to be true. Your Body lies broken before You, Lord. So many religious denominations lie before You, Father, in the streets of Nashville. "The Buckle of the Bible Belt" lies open, unfastened and lacking strength with nation raging against nation. Because our division is a mile high, we have become a powerless church body. We fragmented and torn to pieces each with our own doctrine of beliefs. We have forgotten the "March for Jesus!" with Your children singing in the streets of which You were greatly honored. Pride puffed us up! Restore it, oh Lord! Our traditions and religious spirits have constricted and rendered the Word of God useless like salt without flavor. We pull down self-centeredness and put on Christ-centeredness. In compromise, we have offered "designer services" in Your house to appease the people. We have made the church house no more than a social club. Your ruptured Body is in need of repair. God forgive us. We are One Bride. Lord, take away our indifference, selfishness, and grant unity!

FOR OUR COMPLACENCY IN PRAYER AND FALSE RELIGION...

We have wasted time on teaching and programs, more study, more meetings rather than building a house of prayer for all nations, Lord. We have become a people ever learning but never doing. We have failed You, Lord. In prayer, we have failed miserably. Forgive us for spinning our wheels instead of changing the spiritual climate of our city. Overturn the tables in Your house, Lord! We have sought the approval of man more than the fear of the Lord, and so You have stricken our land with a curse of fatherlessness. Lord, we are a city "fat on worship." We have created worship celebrities and "pop stars." We have sought our own reputation even though You said no flesh will glory in Your presence. We are a city of performance, forever on stage. But all our righteous deeds are like a filthy cloth before You, almighty God. Please have mercy.

FOR OUR LACK OF FEAR OF THE LORD...

We lack fear for Your great name but fear the names of men. We fear mans rejection instead of fearing Your rejection. We have become people pleasers and have lost the ancient way. Some say, "Because there are no signs from heaven, there is no fear of heaven" (Josh.4:24). Lord, if You are willing, show the people a sign that we might again fear Your great name. Forgive us, mighty God, for sensationalizing people and events more than honoring You. For You have left us to our passions and lustful desires and delivered us into the hand of iniquity. We confess we are sick of the fact that little or no significant difference is seen amongst believers and the lost. Holy One of Israel, we have not honored and celebrated Your feasts but have embraced pagan holidays, and so have largely ignored the importance of remembering our spiritual roots. As Your Body, Lord, we declare we will stand in the gap. Have mercy on us, O God of compassion for we are but clay, and You are the Potter; we are the work of Your hand. Lord of compassion, forgive us.

FOR OUR SEXUAL IMMORALITY AND IDOLATRY...

Lord, we have come very low in depravity and have brought sexual immorality into Your temple. We have compromised with Your word in exchange for the love and pursuit of this world. We declare an increased pursuit of holiness Lord. Our apostasies have convicted us. The reverence of You is in severe lack. In this city we have been wrapped in the clutches of lust, pornography, and prostitution, in our city streets, and, worse yet, we have allowed it into Your church! In a city called to Christian publishing, Nashville boasts the world's largest adult bookstore. Massage parlors and strip joints are within our city's gates. Our city is lackadaisical towards these as they operate unhindered by local law enforcement. This is an appalling demise degrading to our city's moral and honor, and a direct reflection of the churches apathetic view and poinzy stance on it.

We have allowed this abomination in our homes and allowed our children to be subject to our depravity. The whoredom and idolatry we have allowed in Your house have reached Your ears and so has been released into our city streets. Change our hearts, O God.

This city has been polluted with false gods such as Athena and structures dedicated through the power of deception in free masonry and mythology. Forgive us for these "high places" of idolatry. God, hear our cry, please forgive this city.

FOR BEING LUKEWARM AND NOT TITHING...

We have been spoiled through materialism and entertainment. Self-control and discipline are far from us, seemingly out of reach. Surely, we have slung a noose around our necks ready to be drawn. Our city is at ease, and her church lukewarm because we have allowed the "American dream" to take precedence over an intimate relationship with You. We have become very, very busy but not obedient. The weeds of success have choked out the word of God to the unsaved. We have hoarded Your word for ourselves and have eaten its delicacies. Through our lack of kindness, patience and arrogance we have ridiculed sinners to keep things "business as usual." We have not brought the whole tithe into Your storehouse and so have not obeyed You. We have burdened our shepherds with worldly cares and have abused Your full blessings. Lord, have mercy.

FOR OUR NEGLECT OF THE POOR AND FOR MURDER...

We have lost our way of discernment, Lord, and even now are considering gambling as a cure for our irresponsible expenditures. We have neglected the poor and needy and rewarded laziness and called it welfare. We have been deceived! The blood of the innocent runs through the streets. We void the anger and rage in our streets and replace it with hope and love.

We have been a people of unclean lips. We have used our words carelessly against Your own Body, and so we have brought judgment upon ourselves. Gossip, grumbling and complaining, distrust, suspicion and unforgiveness have crept into the house of God. We must not let its' leaven spoil the dough. Lord, circumcise our hearts! Fear and worry have crept into the Body. Cancer, heart problems, and ailments have manifested themselves in Your Body and they are not what You intended for us! Remove it, O Lord. Your people are in great pain.

We have killed our unborn and called it freedom of choice. We have been a selfish generation and have sacrificed our unborn before they have been given a chance to live. We plead the Blood of Jesus over all murders and killings in our State and ask Your forgiveness over these evil practices.

Change our hearts, O Lord. Forgive us for the 250,000+ babies killed since 1973 alone as documented by our state records! Lord, we have forgotten that it is better to obey rather than sacrifice. Restore us, oh Lord.

FOR OUR PRIDE AND REBELLION...

The pride of our hearts has deceived us. Covenants are broken in Your house. Our land is polluted with unfaithfulness. Divorce has entangled us and separated your Holy people. Bitterness has taken its deadly root. We declare this must change for the sake of our city. O God, have mercy! We lie broken before You! We realize, mighty God, that You sent Nashville a whirlwind as a warning and in Your mercy only one was taken. But, Oh Lord, we have turned our face from You in greed and played the harlot! Restore us, God of compassion, from our witchcraft. We implore You! Our sins lie before You. My Father, You are the friend of our youth; will You be angry forever? Only You can forgive Lord. You are a God of love. If You do not forgive us then others who do not know you will say, "Look, their God is not a gracious God for He did not hear their cry in distress and forgive." For Your great Names' sake forgive, and heal us, O Lord.

NASHVILLE STATISTICS

The 'Stats' are in for Nashville. How are we doing with this Man called Jesus?

Attached find a table giving the number of Tennessee residents that had abortions in Tennessee for the years 1975 throughout 1999 and year 2000 statistics.

YEAR 2000 STATISTICS		YEAR	ABORTIONS	YEAR	ABORTIONS
MURDERS	- 74	1999	15,286	1986	18,128
RAPES	- 456	1998	15,650	1985	17,432
ROBBERY	-2,357	1997	16,557	1984	17,295
ASSAULT	-6,330	1996	16,153	1983	16,892
BURGLARY	-7,700	1995	16,582	1982	16,847
LARCENY	-27,339	1994	15,668	1981	17,744
AUTO THEFT	-5,535	1993	17,210	1980	19,066
		1992	17,821	1979	18,713
		1991	19,200	1978	15,015
		1990	17,464	1977	13,257
		1989	17,126	1976	13,582
		1988	17,748	1975	9,283
		1987	17,641		

May God in heaven please forgive his church for not praying enough, caring enough or coming alongside those who have been bruised, battered, beaten and murdered. Please help the church to open Her eyes to the foul atrocities in our city that pollute the land. Forgive us, holy God, and now send us out to make restitution with these who you care for and love so much that You sent Your only Son to die for them that they would live eternally. Oh God, heal our land.

REMOVE THE CURSE OF BLOODSHED IN OUR CITY, IN JESUS NAME!

WITH GOD THERE IS HOPE...

But now for a brief moment in time Lord, You have been gracious in leaving us a remnant and giving us a firm place in Your sanctuary and so You give us light to our eyes and a little relief in our bondage. Though we have each gone astray You have not deserted us. You have shown this city mercy and great loving kindness. You have granted us new life to rebuild the house of our God and repair the ruins of greed, lust, rebellion, pride, idolatry, and witchcraft by giving us a wall of protection through Your grace. But some have accepted Your grace in vain and have trodden down the power of the Gospel by treating the holy things of God as common. Forgive us, merciful Lord.

But now, oh God, what can we say? For we have disregarded the commands you gave through your servants. To the same degree our city has been degraded we have polluted ourselves with all these evils by mingling with the world and have defied Your command, *"Be ye holy, for I am holy"* (1Peter 1:14). We suffer the results of our evil deeds and great guilt, yet, our God, You have punished us *less* than we deserve and have given us a remnant. Shall we again break your commands?

Oh Lord, God of Israel, you are righteous! Here we are before You in guilt, oh God, but because of Your Son's atoning blood we can stand in Your presence. Your Holy Spirit admonished us, yet we paid no attention but now we hear and obey. We rebuke the lies the devil has planted and bewitched us with that says the church is inside four walls. That's a lie! We move from church secrecy to public display in radiant love. All city parks must have jubilant worship! Teach us to celebrate Your love openly, Lord. You warned us time and time again to obey You and be a faithful people, but we sinned against Your ordinances and disobeyed Your commands. We have not as a people sought forgiveness and righteousness. And so a curse is upon us. But we now implore Your righteousness and blessings over Nashville!

"Yet in spite of all these things you say, 'I am innocent; surely His anger has turned from me.' Now be warned, I will bring judgment for saying, 'I have not sinned.'"
—JEREMIAH 2:35

OH LORD, HEAR OUR CRY; GRANT US VICTORY

"Thus it is written...that repentance for forgiveness of sins should be proclaimed in His name to all the Nations, beginning from Jerusalem. You are witnesses of these things."
—LUKE 24:47-48

Now, if we have found favor with You Lord, may You bend Your head and ear earthward toward Jerusalem and Nashville as we proclaim repentance and forgiveness of sin. We cry mercy! Mercy! We stand at the crossroads of Your mercy seat, and make confession to the Lord, Jesus Christ, and commit to do His will in prayer for Israel. Bless Jerusalem Lord! From every street corner to every rooftop may all people proclaim Yeshua saying , "Blessed is he who comes in the name of the Lord!" O God, strengthen the defenders of the Holy Land; grant them salvation and crown them with victory. Establish peace in the Land and everlasting joy for its inhabitants!

We return to You Lord with our *whole* heart as a lasting possession to the Lord through holiness and active participation in reaching people for Christ. We declare that this city fears God and keeps his commands; for this is man's all! Let us now make a covenant in Your presence to cease from sin, cleanse ourselves, and turn from our wicked ways. We separate ourselves from the world and all defilement of the flesh. Then, O Lord God, by Your great mercy and compassion, hear from heaven, forgive our sin, and heal our land. Bring in lost souls. Purify us, O Lord! Hear our lament!

Now, great God, we have confessed our sins unto You and to each other. We seek Your Redemptive purposes for this, Your city, is to be a refuge in which people from all Nations are sheltered, discipled, trained, and commissioned, to proclaim the Gospel throughout the world. May the shed blood of Jesus Christ of Nazareth remove the blood-guilt of these sins and their root causes. Remove these sins, transgressions, and iniquities as far from this city as the east is from the west! Make us a spotless bride, Lord! Oh, that You would tear open the heavens and come down, so this city would quake by Your presence and its people tremble at Your word.

We implore You, Lord, will You not revive us again, that we may know Your pure loving kindness? Will You prolong Your anger for yet another generation? Will You not forgive us, that we may see your wonderful enduring mercy in action displayed for *our* generation. Oh Lord, for the sake of our children have mercy. Oh sovereign Lord, will you on the behalf of those interceding and pleading right now spring up new wells of deep spiritual maturity in your church and remove the stumbling blocks the devil has laid in our midst? Expose the footprints of satan so we can "sack" him and scatter his demons out of the city. Mighty God, rip off the old well caps of revival and spring up rivers of refreshing, holy reverence, and *sheer* Christian joy, with a Spirit of prevailing prayer hung over the city of Nashville. We plead and implore You majestic King, for a continual wave of *pure Pentecost* upon us birthed from Calvary.

Restore Joshua's Warrior Spirit over the people who bear Your name in the city of Nashville. We lift up our political leaders, judges, and officers which You appropriated as our leaders over the city. We stand in the gap for these in ambient intercession. We pronounce blessings over Mayor Bill Purcell. We ask for his forgiveness as we have not been a true reflection of love in caring for his unmet needs as he diligently serves the people of this great city. Lord, grant him Godly wisdom and divine protection right now in Jesus' name. Father we declare, that any problem which needs a miracle in the Mayor's office would be met by our prayer teams. May we lock hand in hand, arm to arm, in a concerted effort to win this city to Jesus Christ. Lord, open doors of favor between the church and the Mayors office.

We lift up our police Chief Emmet Turner, and ask for forgiveness from him for not being at his side in prayer. His officers face the most grueling and dangerous circumstances. We, the Body of Christ, are sorry, sir. Please forgive us for our apathy and lack of showing our appreciation of the security you afford us. We declare your officers will get prayed for as we 'adopt a cop' in prayer. We declare no more bloodshed in the streets!

Lord, give wisdom to Governor Sundquist and Senator Frist. May they use their God given authority in serving justice. Give them wisdom and discernment regarding Capital Punishment! Mighty God, we declare as one church of Nashville, blessings and prosperity over all branches of our Government and civil agencies.

Thank You for giving us shepherd's after Your own heart who will feed us with knowledge and understanding. We lift up their arms and ask You to send forth Your Word to them. Breathe life anew, and give Your peace blessing over these who have given so much and received so very little from us.

Breathe upon us afresh Lord. Grant an anointing so thick that students in school drop under conviction of sin and businessmen throughout the city close their doors at noon for an hour of prayer. Let justice reign in the judges' chambers and in the city streets! Lord, blow the trumpet through the land and raise a standard of godliness toward Nashville. Give us the joining of the revival generations!

By the blood of the Lamb and the power of the cross, we smash and demolish every mythological occult and free masonry seal, rites, and curse that have been given authority over Nashville. We renounce any demonic Masonic activity, as You are worthy, Oh lord, to open the seals (Rev.5:9-10). Jesus, we ask You, the chief cornerstone, to replace the cornerstone set in place by free masons in the wall of our state capitol. Reseal it, Lord, with Your Blood. With Your authority Lord, and Jesus' blood, we smash and refute all false worship relating to Athena, the false goddess, and all occultic strongholds over Nashville.

We ask You, heavenly Father, for no fewer than three to five church services daily—many into the dawning hours as the sun rises over the city gates of Nashville saving souls. We ask for churches so full that preachers and ministers must go out into the streets for open air preaching, and may their voices be heard a mile away with no microphones! Send the pains of hell upon the people as they feel convicted by the Holy Spirit. Let strong men literally weep in the streets of the city crying out for salvation, running to You, Lord, in total dependence on Your Grace and mercy.

May the children of 10 and 12 years cry out in agreement for souls—as their elected prayer's fire with precision far superior to learned ministers. May the blessings of revival begin through our youth as You said to come forth as children. May wringing of hands, streams of tears, and unutterable anguish grip us as we uninhibitedly confess our sins in tones of unmistakable sincerity, and appeal to the Lord for mercy with piercing cries. Lord Jesus, have mercy on our sinful souls; Lord Jesus, come to our burning hearts; Lord, pardon our sins; Oh come, and lift us from these flames of hell!

Thank you, Holy Ghost! Thank you, Jesus, thank you, Father, for the widespread outpouring of Your Spirit and bringing these things to pass. May Nashville be called "a throne of the Lord," and all nations gather to it. Vindicate Your name. Lord, may Your fame be spread by Your compassion towards us. As Your great name is vindicated pardon us according to Your word so that the whole city of Nashville is filled with your glory! We declare to the church, "Stand up and walk! Reach out to the unsaved!" We go now, Lord, we go because our feet are shod and because we love You.

Jesus, You said You have put all things under Your feet. You said You are the head of all the churches of Nashville, which is Your Body, the fullness of Him who fills all in all. Lord, there is only one church in this city. Fill us with Your love and mercy. Gather all things together into the Holy of Holies according to the working of Your mighty power for Your eternal glory in the heavenly realm! Oh Lord, Jesus Christ, will You hear our cry for revival and make this the hour of Your visitation? Pardon dear Lord, if we neglected to confess any hidden sins from Your all seeing eyes. As we meet in concerted, united prayer to do battle in the heavenlies in the coming days, anticipating a New Prayer Wave with *CRUSHING* force and precision inconceivable to our minds toppling over the realm and grip of the anti-Christ over Nashville, may we remember one thing...IT WAS PURE GOD!!

We celebrate the unity of our great city. In faith we drive a stake in the ground of Nashville's heart signifying PEACE, LOVE, UNITY, AND RECONCILIATION to all one million plus people to GOD through Jesus Christ. Save us Lord. By Your grace, save us now! We humbly submit our plea through Jesus Christ, our Lord. AMEN.

Now we sing a beautiful new song over Nashville to Jesus Christ, our Lord, in one accord:

Oh Nashville, how beautiful are your dwelling places! The Lord longs and even yearns for the courts of Nashville. The heart of Nashville and its' flesh sing for joy to the living God. For even the smallest has found a home, a dwelling place to lay their head at night, by the altars of God. How blessed are those who live in Nashville! They are ever praising Thee. Tourists passing through Nashville receive the springs of life, and they are covered in showers of blessings. Every person in Nashville goes from strength to strength, from glory to glory in God. O Lord, hear our prayer. Verily I say, the courts of Nashville are as the courts of God! Behold, the shield of Nashville, is our God, our bullwork, and our covering. For the Lord is the sun and our shield; the Lord gives grace and glory; no good thing does He withhold from Nashville because we walk uprightly! How blessed is Nashville, Tennessee!

May this cry begin with you! Blessed be the peacemakers.

"Then we, the people of Nashville, saw the holy city, New Nashville, Coming down out of heaven from God, prepared as a bride adorned for her husband."
—REVELATION 21:2 (names substituted)

"Now to Him who by the power at work within us is able to accomplish abundantly far more than all we can ask or imagine, to Him be the glory in the church and in Christ Jesus to all generations, forever and ever. Amen."
—EPHESIANS 3:20-21

We declare Jesus as King on our billboards!!

We declare blessings over the homeless...

We cover the nakedness of our city with a garment of praise!

"And they will repair the ruined cities..." Is. 61:4

The Lord has sent me to proclaim liberty to the captives...Is. 58

We pronounce blessing in our streets!

We give a garland of beauty instead of ashes.

We remove the 'porn' in the house of God…

There's a river of God running through our streets…

We bless Nashville's architecture in Jesus' name…

We name Jesus as King over Nashville!!

Jesus is our *V*ictory!!

The glory of the Lord will be your rear guard…

Lord, remember Nashville as Worship City USA!!

New Wine Fresh Manna

by Pastor Gerald Prior

ALMIGHTY GOD, TO whom all praise, belongs. You alone, O Lord, are righteous and holy. Today we approach your throne of grace that we may obtain mercy and find grace to help in time of need. Humbly and gladly we cry out to you in the lovely name of Your Son Jesus for Nashville and Middle Tennessee.

May we enter your gates with thanksgiving, with every blessing from your hand. Mighty God, had it not been for your goodness and mercy we would still be in darkness without hope. Your great love to us causes us to come with jubilant praise and worship into your courts. Truly, You, O Precious Father, are the only one worthy of worship. So with hearts of gratitude and lips of praise, we shout out "WE LOVE YOU, WE ADORE YOU."

Dear God, passionately we seek your face and desire to turn from our wicked ways. Please forgive us for going our own ways, doing our own thing, and putting ourselves as #1. Before we ask you for the great things for our city, may we first be cleansed and rid of pride. Yes, Lord, as a people of God who should know you better, we have walked in pride and self-righteousness. We ask you today O Lord for forgiveness of not recognizing and honoring your body. When parts of your body have been different from us, we have shunned them, talked evil of them, and judged them. This is sin against you as head of the body of Christ. Have Mercy on Us. Mighty God we ask you to open our eyes to these places of darkness that hold our city in chains. We pray for judgement to begin in the house of God and leaders to weep, leading the way to repentance and humility. Thank you for grace that leads to brokeness.

Thank you for sending us new wine and fresh manna to help prepare the way for REVIVAL. Truly, it is your mercy that sends the spirit of Elijah the Prophet to turn the hearts of the people and prepare the way of the Lord. So, Father, we cry for you to send to our land these last day Elijahs that speak the truth and are filled with love. Allow this generation to see your Glory cover the earth. As we are cleansed from pride, may we then be filled with Your Glory. Please break the curse with your blessing.

COME ALMIGHTY GOD AND SAVE US.

About the Author
Pastor Gerald shepherds New Life Community Church in Joelton, TN. He is married with two children. Gerald ministers to the prisoners and the sick to set the captives free, and to heal broken hearts. He also has a gift of laying the mortar of prayer.

MATTERS OF THE HEART

by Ken Carpenter

Jesus speaking:
"Behold, I come quickly: hold that fast which thou hast, that no man take thy crown."
—REV. 3:11

"Not every one that saith unto me, 'Lord, Lord' shall enter into the Kingdom of Heaven; but he that doeth the will of my Father which is in heaven."
—MATT. 7:21

MANY TODAY WALK around in religious circles wearing many hats or faces, one for church, one at work, one at home, and one for their worldly friends. If you take a bulldog that wants to tear the pants off the mailman, and you put a muzzle on him, he still wants to attack, but can't because of the muzzle. That is what "Religion" does. The outward man quits drinking, chewing, cursing and chasing, but in the heart he still wants to do these things.

Religion fills his heart with pride and he becomes "Self Righteous", always right, insensitive, conceited, and controlling with selfish ambition. Then greed moves in and he becomes a lover of money. He is possessive, a lover of power, stingy, hoarding and discontented. On Sunday, he will go to church and act holy and blameless on the surface...while in his heart, he lusts toward someone in the choir. When he leaves church, he puts on a different face and treats the waitress with rudeness, then leaves her a Bible Tract, and a measly quarter for a tip.

On Monday, he tells one of the guys at work about Jesus and the others off color jokes to others. Wednesday, he slanders an acquaintance of his, then asks others to go to church with him. Friday, he is stingy with his worker's wages. Finally at week end, he grumbles at home, and is critical of his wife and children.

If this sounds like you, and you know something is not right—that you used to have a fervor and love for Jesus, and you know that in your heart you have lost your first love...then the following three short stories will expose where you have fallen.

THE POWER OF FORGIVENESS

As an air conditioning contractor in Hendersonville, Tennessee, I installed a heating and cooling system for the Mayor's brother.

One Friday morning I received a telephone call from the Mayor's brother asking me to send a service man to start his new heating and cooling unit in order for him to be able to move into his new home. The electric power had been turned on the same morning the concrete had been poured for the new driveway. My service man arrived, and did not realize the concrete was wet, and drove down the new driveway. My service man, stepping out of the truck said, "Oops!."

That afternoon I received a phone call from the owner who explained to me he had two tire tracks down his driveway about a half-inch deep. He informed me that the concrete man had examined the damage, and said the only thing he could do was to saw the drive at the end of the tire prints and jack-hammer the damaged concrete out and re-pour at my expense.

After I hung up the phone I became enraged at the serviceman. As I was venting my anger, a minister friend of mine, Charles Green, who happened to be in my place of business said, "Let's go to your office and talk." As we shut the door he said plainly to me, "You know, as a Christian, you are going to have to forgive this man." This calmed me down.

We prayed together, and I said, "Lord, I choose to forgive this man for his mistake. Lord, you will have to handle the concrete."

Monday rolled around and the owner didn't call. Tuesday, about lunchtime, as the serviceman drove by the owner's house, he called in on the two-way radio in excitement, and said, "A miracle has occurred. The concrete is picture perfect!"

I knew in my heart that if I hadn't forgiven the serviceman, I would have been spending a large sum of money to fix the driveway. As a young Christian, ignorant of a mighty God and His ways, I started studying about forgiveness and what would motivate the Lord to do such a miracle. I knew faith wasn't the issue. When we prayed and asked the Lord to handle the problem, I never dreamed He would simply fix the concrete. I figured I would have peace, that things would go well with the insurance company and the owner, which is I suppose, a form of faith.

I knew that if we forgive others, the Heavenly Father will also forgive us (Matt. 6:14). In Matthew 18:21-35, Peter asked Jesus, *"Lord, how often shall my brother sin against me and I forgive him, up seven times?"* Jesus answered and said, *"I say not unto thee, until seven times: but until seventy times seven."* Which means, don't ever quit forgiving. Then Jesus told a parable about a man forgiven of a tremendous debt of ten thousand talents. This was a sum of money he couldn't live long enough to pay back, but he was forgiven the debt.

Is this not a picture of salvation? But this man that was forgiven went out and found a fellow brother who owed him a small debt, and wouldn't forgive him, but kept him in bondage to the debt. When his lord found out about it, he was angry with him, and turned this man over to the tormentors. Jesus says in Matthew 18:35, *"So likewise shall my Heavenly Father do also unto you, if ye from your hearts forgive not every one his brother their trespasses."*

WE CAN'T AFFORD BITTERNESS

A little later, I was moving my place of business to a smaller building to reduce my expenses from $850.00 a month to $500.00 a month. Before I could move in I had to remodel the new office. I was on a close timetable, so I hired a Christian friend (I will call Jim) to trim the office. He kept telling me he would come the next day, but he never showed up. My time was running out. I was going to have to pay rent on two places because of this man.

One Saturday morning I stopped at his house and asked, "Are you coming or not?" He said, "I'll be there by noon." So, I went to work doing some wiring. Noon came—no John. One o'clock, two o'clock—still no John! I really got angry. A voice spoke to me, "All you have done for John, and look what he did to you!" My flesh wanted to hear these words, so I received them and agreed with the devil. At this time I did not realize I had agreed with the devil.

The next morning as I awoke an urge came over me to run. My peace was gone and worry was filling my mind. All at once I realized the devil was moving into my life because I had agreed with him. I knew better than to do that but I was deceived. So, I repented and said, "Lord, I choose to forgive John and I will confront him in love." Suddenly, peace like a river came upon me.

The next day, Monday, John arrived early to begin working. He told me it would take him three days to trim out the office. As he worked during the days, I would try to get an opportunity to confront him, but he was getting so much work done, that I started thinking that maybe I would not have to do what I told the Lord I would do. About four o'clock, John asked, "Will you pray for me? I have been sick all day."

Before I could think, out of my mouth I blurted, "It won't do any good." Then I said, "Brother, I've judged you. Will you forgive me?" John said, "Ken, I haven't done right either. Will you forgive me?" So, we prayed and the Spirit of God filled the place and John was healed. I learned a valuable lesson. I couldn't afford bitterness. My Heavenly Father, who loves me, would turn me over to the tormentors until I repented.

To find out what was happening in the situation we will turn to the Old Testament. In I Samuel chapter 17, David has killed the giant Goliath and is coming back to town. In I Samuel 18:7, David is the hero and everybody is joyful except King Saul. King Saul is angry in verse eight, and he is jealous and suspicious of David. I ask you, did Saul forgive David? What did Jesus say would happen to Saul or anyone who didn't forgive in Matthew 18:34-35? Jesus said they would be turned over to the torturers, which is torment by the Heavenly Father.

Now, let's see what happened to Saul in I Samuel 18:10-15. In verse 10, an evil spirit (a tormentor) from God came mightily upon Saul and he raved (he was in a rage). In verse 11, Saul hurled a spear at David and tried to kill (murder) him. Verse 12 tells us that Saul was afraid of David. Verse 13 tells us that Saul did not want David in his presence, and verse 15 tells us that Saul dreaded him. That is, David's presence depressed Saul.

Now, if you will, do a personal inventory of your life. When someone hurts or disappoints you and you don't forgive them, does this describe what happens to you? *Anger* rises up, *jealousy* moves in, and then *suspicion*, then you get your feelings hurt easily, and then you can't open your mouth without being critical of yourself, the system, and especially others. The anger turns to *rage*; then *hate* and *murder* move in also. Next, comes *fear, anxiety, worry* and *dread* become a way of life with no peace. Then, when the pressure is on, the urge to run away comes to you or you want to remove the person that you have not forgiven, from you presence. You can see that person in a store and turn your head from them acting like you don't see them because you dread to face them. Depression moves in next along with hopelessness. Eventually, "Mr. Suicide" begins to talk to you saying, "nobody cares about you; just end it all." If these symptoms from a root of bitterness are left in your thoughts long enough, *diseases* move into your body. Over the years you go from one sickness to another.

Nothing can release you from these tormentors except the finished work of Calvary. Jesus Christ shed His blood for your sins! Come to the cross of Jesus and repent. Choose to forgive those that have offended you. Then in James 5:16, you confess your sins to one another that you may be healed. Call your Pastor, an Elder, or a Christian friend that you can trust, and confess your unforgiveness.

The peace of God will then fill your heart. Afterwards, call or write that person, if you can, and ask them to forgive you for judging them and forgive their trespass against you. Then get ready to be tested. Remember it's about fifty miles from your head to your heart! Situations will present themselves to you again where you will have to forgive. When these circumstances happen again, in the fear of the Lord, you choose to die to yourself, and agree with the Lord Jesus, who will fight your battles for you. Come to the cross of Jesus Christ to be forgiven and healed.

POINTING OF THE FINGER

As a child, I remember standing at the back fence with my mother, as she was talking to our next-door neighbor, Mrs. Andrews. I listened as they discussed what happened the day before to Mrs. Summers—a "friend" of theirs. She had fallen on her back steps and had broken her right arm. Mrs. Andrews made a derogatory remark about the incident. About a week later Mrs. Andrews fell on her back steps and broke her right arm. Later, I asked my mother about the significance of what Mrs. Andrews had said against Mrs. Summers. Mama quoted what Jesus said in Matthew 7:2, "Do not judge lest you be judged; and by your standard of measure, it will be measured to you." WOW!

Looking back in my life, and what I have seen happen to others, I understood that my mouth had gotten me into a lot of trouble. The Word of God talks about the tongue being like a rudder on a ship in James 3:1-12. It guides us through life by our standard of measure. James goes on to say in James 5:9, *"Do not complain, brethren, against one another, that you yourselves, may not be judged; behold, the judge is standing right at the door."*

One evening I received a call from a youth pastor asking me to go with him to pray with a lady in his church that had Chronic Fatigue Syndrome. She had to stay in bed most of the time. She had gone to doctor after doctor, with no relief. As I was sitting there with this lady, I discerned it had something to do with her mother. So, I asked her to pray for her mother. As she prayed she said, "Mama, you were always so tired, you never had time for me." As she prayed, Matthew 7-12 came to my mind, *"by your standard of measure, it is measure to you."* I quoted this to her, her mouth flew open, and she said, "I judged my mother!" We prayed together, and she repented of judging her parents. Right in the middle of the prayer, she was healed—and will stay healed, unless she goes back to judging others!

In John 20:23, Jesus said, *"Whosoever sins ye remit, they are remitted unto them; and whosoever sins ye retain, they are retained."* When you forgive, you release the sin. When you judge your parents for their sins (by your standard of measure) that sin will be retained by you. The lady that had Chronic Fatigue Syndrome had judged her mother when she was a young lady. Without a daddy at home, her mother was working two jobs trying to provide for her children. The young lady would ask her mother to go shopping with her and she would decline because she was so tired from working two jobs. So, she judged her mother for being tired all the time, and not being able to spend time with her. Then when she was 38 years old, the disease of tiredness came upon her. Which was simply good measure pressed down; shaken and running over. She was judged by her standard of measure she had placed on her mother. If you love, you will get love back in good measure; if you give hate, you will get hate back in good measure.

Later, I preached a message called, "Pointing The Finger", in a church in Clarksville, Tennessee. When the altar call was given, a man came up for prayer and confession of sin. He told me, twenty-three years earlier that he had judged his former wife. While he was in Vietnam, she started running around on him, and gambled away their savings. When he returned home they got a divorce. He could not forgive her for what she had done —especially the gambling. He had become her judge twenty-three years later; at the time he was a remodeling contractor. He was paid $1,200.00 cash for a job. He sat down at his kitchen table, got his deposit ready, and then made out his bills. The next morning, he drove by the Post Office and mailed his bills on the way to the bank. At the back, he discovered he had lost his deposit. He searched for it for hours by going back to the Post Office, searching in the mailbox, going back home and looking, but still could not find the money. Then, in desperation, he stopped at a bar, gambled and won $150. He thought that this was the way the Lord would give him his money back!

The Friday before the Sunday I preached, he received a notice from the bank for $1,500.00 in bad checks, and $1,000.00 in bank charges for the bad checks. It took twenty-three years for his standard of measure to come back to him. Paul, in his letter to the Romans said, *"Therefore thou art inexcusable, O man, whosoever thou art that judgest: for wherein thou judgest another, thou condemnest thyself; for thou that judgest doest the same things."* Romans 2:1

HAS THE HOLY SPIRIT SPOKEN TO YOU? DO YOU KNOW WHAT TO DO?

- First, examine yourself. Have you been the judge of someone, like your parents, your friends, your business associates? Have you judged God? Have you ever felt He is appointed you?

- Second, let's ask the Holy Spirit to reveal those you have judged.

- Third, James 5:16 says to confess your sins to one another, and pray for one another, so that you may be healed. Get with your pastor, or a Christian friend you can trust and confess judging.

- Fourth, repent of judging. That does not mean to say the words, and go out and do it again! It means to turn from the sin and stop doing it.

- Fifth, make restitution if you can, by calling, writing, or just looking at them eyeball to eyeball, and ask them to forgive you for judging them. (*Note) I know these people have hurt you, done you wrong, beaten you out of money, but I'm concerned about your heart before the Lord! You will be surprised how humbling yourself allows the Holy Spirit to convict those who have offended you by bringing them to repentance.

Now, let's pray. Lord Jesus, I come to Your Throne of mercy, asking for Your forgiveness for my sin of judging (name) _____ Lord. I repent, and plead Your precious blood on my sin. I confess that You are the Judge of the whole earth- not me. Please create in me a clean heart to walk in love, because love does not take into account a wrong suffered! Lord, I ask You to remove every sickness, disease, and every unclean spirit that came into me as a result of my sin of judging others. In Jesus Name, I pray. Amen.

THE AWFUL SIN OF COMPLAINING

In Paul's letter to the Corinthians, in the tenth chapter, he listed five sins that brought the wrath of God on the children of Israel. With whom was He angry for forty years? Was it not with those who sinned- whose bodies fell in the wilderness (Hebrews 3:17)?

The last sin Paul listed, and likely the worst, is complaining. I Corinthians 10:10-11 says, "Now these things happened as an example, and they were written for our instruction, upon whom the ends of the ages have come." Paul, quoting from the book of Exodus, tells the church of Corinth, "Then Moses led Israel from the Red Sea (a great miracle) and they went out into the wilderness of Shur; and they went three days in the wilderness and found no water (a dry place), and when they had come to Marah (a bitter place, hard to accept, galling, offensive, grievous), they could not drink the waters of Marah (bitter). So the people grumbled at Moses saying, "what shall we drink?" Then he cried out to the Lord, and the Lord showed him a tree (cross) and he threw it into the waters, and the water's became SWEET (gratifying, pleasing, delightful). There he made them a statute and regulation, and he tested them" (Exodus 15:22-25).

Each time they entered a new trial the Lord was testing their hearts. So, today trials come to expose our hearts. When we get squeezed under pressure, what comes out of our mouths is what is really in our hearts. The children of Israel complained against their food, water, their leadership, and living conditions. They didn't know it, but each time they were actually complaining against the Lord!

"And the Lord spoke to Moses and Aaron, saying, 'How long shall I bear with this evil Congregation who are grumbling against Me? I have heard the complaints of the son's of Israel, which they are making against me. Say to them, as I live, says the Lord, just as you have spoken in My hearing, so I will surely do to you.'"
—Numbers 14:26-28

The word "Murmuring", in the Strongs' Concordance is defined as: *to be obstinate, to hold a grudge, to mutter in discontent, ingratitude and envy*—which is a characteristic of depravity. Ingratitude and envy can never be satisfied. If you're always looking at your neighbor's house, career, spouse—looking at their position of possessions with envy or jealousy, that's a sin against God!

"Break up your fallow ground, for it is time to seek the Lord until He comes to rain righteousness on you."
—Hosea 10:12.

Fallow ground is ground, which has once been tilled, but has gotten hard and now lies waste. It needs to be broken up and made soft again. Then it will be ready to receive seed. If you know your walk with Christ is not what it used to be, then you need to break up the hard places of your heart.

Let us first begin with "Self-Examination", which consists of:
• Looking at your life
• Considering your motives and actions
• What kind of fruit they are bearing

Do they bear the Fruit of the Spirit (love, joy, peace, kindness, etc. Galatians 5:22) or are they producing the thorn and thistles of envy, strife, jealousy, gossip and anger?

When grumbling or complaining comes out of your mouth, it exposes your heart. It reveals that the sins of ingratitude (unthankfulness) and envy (spiteful malice and resentment over others' advantage) are in you! This criticism (one given to harsh judgments) exposes unforgiveness toward others, yourself, and even towards the Lord! Thus fear, anxiety, worry and dread become a way of life, with no peace to be found.

Your sins were committed one by one, and must be dealt with one by one. Therefore, it's a good idea to write them down on paper, as the Holy Spirit brings them to your mind. Every person you have borne resentment and unforgiveness toward, are accounts that must be settle before God. Look closely at your relationship with your parents; are they intimate or distant? "Honor thy father and thy mother which is the first commandment with promise:

"That it may be well with thee, and thou mayest live long on the earth."
—EXODUS 20:12.

If things are not going will with you, I would search this area very closely. The Lord didn't say we have to honor their sins, but that we must honor (respect) THEM.

If you find that you have committed a fault against anyone, and that person is within your reach, go and confess it to them- IMMEDIATELY! Get it out of your way! If they are too far, or you cannot settle it face to face, write them a letter ore better yet, call them on the phone. Confessing the injury or judgments, even the unforgivness you may have toward them for their injuries to you. Remember, forgiving is not approval of sin, but obedience to God's commandments.

"But if ye forgive not men their trespasses, neither will your Father forgive your trespasses."
—MATTHEW 6:15

A PRAYER FOR DELIVERANCE

Dear Lord Jesus, I believe You are the Son of God, and You are God manifested in the flesh; that You were born of a virgin; that You died for my sins; that You rose again three days later and that You are returning.

Lord, I ask You to forgive me of all unforgiveness, judgments, and murmuring I have had against You and anybody that has hurt me. I choose to forgive them and bless them now. Lord, I confess anger, hate, gossip, and slander that went out of my mouth which exposed that my heart was full of unforgiveness.

Lord, I murmured against You and Your provisions in my life. That was sin Lord, and I trust Your mercy and Your grace to forgive me now. Lord, I receive Your forgiveness, and ask You to show me where I have left my first love. I repent of that and lift up my hands to You.

Lord, release all that unforgiveness, hate, anger, and murder. I command all those unclean spirits of fear, anxiety, worry, dread, depression, suicide, and sickness to leave me now, in the Name of Jesus Christ, the Son of God. I plead the Blood and the finished work of Calvary over my life.

Lord, I love You with all my heart. I thank You for the truth that is setting me free now, in Jesus' Name. Lord, I know that I will be tested whether I have spoken empty words or spoken from a true desire in my heart to please You. (Every Word of God is tested — Proverbs 30:5). Please give me eyes to see, ears to hear, and a heart to perceive Your unsearchable riches; to hear Your voice, and walk bearing fruit (love, joy, peace, patience, kindness and goodness) and find Your rest. AMEN.

About the Author

Ken Carpenter preaches and teaches to prisoners not only in jail, but in everyday life. He has a prophetic anointing and believes revival will be birthed through a time of purging of the church. Working as a heating and airman, Ken has his hands on the thermostat of God's house. He and his wife, Day, reside in Whitehouse, TN., and attend Jesus Reigns Fellowship. They have two lovely Children, and a Grandbaby!

A Cry for Mercy

by Pastor Scott Dobbins

I BELIEVE THAT it is time for the spiritual leaders of this city to begin to realize that God has not forsaken the City of Nashville. It is the pastors, and those that are to guard the gates, that have forsaken our post. It's time that we pray and lay claim to the city and not give our territory to the enemies of God and His people anymore. We must begin to pray for three things over our city:

1) Repentance
2) Request
3) Resistance

We proclaim: On the basis of the Word of God (Job22:26-30)

We stand today and *repent*, and ask God to forgive us for the sins of this region, state, and this city. We ask for forgiveness of the sins of political corruption, racial prejudice, moral perversions, witchcraft, occult, and idolatry.

We pray that the blood covenant of Jesus will cleanse our hands from the shedding of innocent blood. We ask for forgiveness for the divisions in the Church, pride, arrogance, sins of the tongue, and anything else that would damage or offend the name of Jesus.

We *request* that God's Kingdom would come and be established in us and through us. We ask for the mercy of God to be poured out upon our city. We ask that grace and the fire of God will fall upon our city and consume us (Heb 12:29)...that the Holy Spirit would be released in this city to bring true spiritual revival that would cover the homeless shelters, the communities, and the inner city...that God would cause men, women and children to run to him, seeking his face, turning from wickedness so that God will hear us and bring healing to our land (II Chron 7:14).

We request that the Father would visit our city, our churches, our homes. We declare that this city will fulfill the destiny that God has given us in restoring the foundations of righteousness in the city.

We also resist, on the basis of our submission to the will of God, by faith, we resist the Devil, and all his works, and all the powers that have taken hold of our city (James 4:7).

We *resist* the spiritual wickedness that has established strongholds in our city, the dark places, and the mystery places that the enemy has been setting his camp in.

We call on the name of Jesus that all spiritual strongholds be destroyed, and we declare this day that the authority of the Holy Spirit will now control this city.

We hereby give notice that we are evicting the principalities that have ruled our city in Jesus name. Today we stand in the gap, and build a hedge of protection, and a mercy seat for the City of Nashville.

In the name of Jesus!!

About the Author

Pastor Scott Dobbins shepherds Bellshire Assembly of God. He and his wife Loni have two precious boys and reside in Madison, TN. Scott brings with him a gift of unabashed worship to Nashville.

ON II CHRONICLES 7:14...

by Joyce Green

God began to show me that, instead of simply looking at this scripture corporately for the church or for our nation, we should look at it for our individual lives. It is my heart that God wants to cleanse from all the manifestations of selfishness and self-centeredness. When I am God-centered and my life is centered in loving others, I will understand what it means to walk in humility as a servant like Jesus did. (Phil. 2:5-8) I will walk in personal revival and that revival will spread to those around me.

Next, God took me to Ezra 9, where He was upset with His people because they had not separated themselves from the practices of the other people in the land. When God convicted Ezra's heart of the sin, he responded:

"I arose up from my heaviness; and having rent my garment and my mantle, I fell upon my knees, and spread out my hands unto the Lord my God and said, 'O my God, I am ashamed and blush to lift up my face to Thee, my God: for our iniquities are increased over our head, and our trespass is grown up unto the heavens.'"
—Ezra 9:5-6

Just what were the iniquities that had made God so angry and which made Ezra blush before Him? God said His people were living just like the people of the land. What did He mean? By definition, the names of the other peoples or 'nations' in the land were sin. Their names mean: *rejection* (which usually results from the lust for approval), *fear, unforgiveness and bitterness, defilement, pride* and *worldliness*. Among the abominable people were the Moabites and the Ammonites, descendants of Lot's union with his own daughters. The definitions of their names describe the spirits that cause God's people to want to huddle together (in a cave) because of fear, trying to preserve a seed (message) which has become perverse.

Isn't God's word for us in these scriptures amazing? He is making it clear. He is calling us to repent for all the ways we walk, talk, and act just like the people who don't know him. He wants to make us a sign and wonder in the midst of this crooked and perverse generation so we will shine as lights in the world.

I believe that the city of Nashville and the nation of America can have revival. I encourage you to become one of these who choose humility, the fear of the Lord, and prayers of faith. As you come before Him, seeking His face and not His hand, He will be faithful to reveal to you any wicked way in your heart. When you repent, He will forgive you, bind up your broken heart and will heal your land (your life). As each of us, who are called by His name, come to this place of brokenness, repentance, and wholeness, there will be revival! Like a fire, it will spread and grow, carried by the breath of His Spirit.

About the Author

Joyce Green is the widow of the late Milton Green. A noted minister with a 'John the Baptist' anointing with a call to the church to prepare her robes! She maintains the Lord's ministry, "Be fruitful and multiply," from Palestine, Texas and hails from Cleveland TN.

TENNESSEE REDEMPTIVE PURPOSE STATEMENT

*A Guide to Praying for the State of Tennessee in a new Millenium
by Laura Smith*

10 HISTORICAL FACTS THAT YIELD POINTS OF PRAYER FOR TENNESSEE'S FUTURE

When troublesome history repeats itself in the life of a rebellious individual, we recognize it as a sin pattern. When history repeats itself in the life of a city, state or nation, we refer to these patterns as strongholds, and seek to remove them through prayer, repentance and reconciliation.

"The weapons we fight with are not the weapons of the world. On the contrary, they have divine power to demolish strongholds."
—2COR. 10:4

As you read through these 10 points of prayer for the state of TN, remember that Jesus has given you authority to bind all curses, and more importantly, to then loose the blessings they have been hindering.

"I tell you the truth, whatever you bind on earth will be bound in heaven, and whatever you loose on earth will be loosed in heaven."
—MATT. 18:18

Even more significant than the removal of enemy strongholds from a region is the task of rebuilding God's kingdom within it . Let this first begin in your own life. Often in a region, it is common for those living there to unknowingly be under the swaying influence of its strongholds, such as with the city of Sodom in which God could not find even 10 innocent people. As you encounter these strongholds in yourself, repent, and as you encounter them in others, pray (bind) and walk in the opposite spirit (loose). Our spiritual revelations are never license to condemn those for whom Christ died.

"If I have the gift of prophecy and can fathom all mysteries and all knowledge, and if I have a faith that can move mountains, but have not love, I am nothing".
—1COR. 13:2

"From the time the world was created, people have seen the earth and the sky and all that God made. They can clearly see His invisible qualities – His eternal power and divine nature. So they have no excuse whatsoever for not knowing God."
—ROM. I:20

If Tennessee's fertile soil, temperate climate, vast water supply and abundant minerals make her a state rich in natural resources, then according to this scripture it is a mere picture of the super-natural resources available to all Tennesseans. All around us we have opportunity to see God's invisible qualities. We have "no excuse whatsoever for not knowing God", and yet many of us do not.

" I keep asking that the God of our Lord Jesus Christ, the glorious Father, may give you the Spirit of wisdom and revelation, so that you may know Him better."
—EPH.I:17

BIND: TRADITION · LOOSE: RENEWAL

Across Tennessee's 42,244 square miles of spacious mountains and valleys are over 5 1/2 million people within 95 counties. Major cities include (in order of population) Memphis, Nashville (TN's capitol), Knoxville, Chattanooga, Clarksville, Johnson City, Murfreesboro, Jackson, Kingsport, Oak Ridge, Hendersonville, Bristol, Germantown, East Ridge, Cleveland and Cookeville. Since a state's capitol city greatly influences governmental and cultural decisions made for that state (which in turn has lasting reverberation on its spiritual climate), the far-reaching effects of Nashville on all of Tennessee is easy to understand. Nashville, known as "the buckle of the Bible-belt", emits an air of religious supremacy which permeates the entire state. While dedicated Christians can be found in any district, unfortunately many Tennesseans define their Christianity as church membership, reducing their relationship with Jesus Christ to a once-a-week affair. Despite the fact that Nashville has more churches per capita than any other American city, (between 600-800 churches in the city's 533 square miles) this gains the city its reputation of "a church per mile". It also results in a greater number of smaller churches instead of larger, stronger congregations, unintentionally promoting competition and disunity. History reveals that denominations not only refuse to come together and often mock one other, but that within many individual churches, the pastor's authority is often mocked and disregarded, thus Tennesseans are famed for eating "fried preacher" after church. Tennessee's state bird is the Mockingbird.

"These things indeed have an appearance of wisdom in self-imposed religion, false humility, and neglect of the body, but are of no value against the indulgence of the flesh."
—COL. 2:23

BIND: RELIGION · LOOSE: RELATIONSHIP

Coupled with the "business of Christianity" and its numerous "industries of religion", Tennessee is often regarded as a religious society that "talks the talk but does not walk the walk." Where duty replaces joy, the outcome is lifeless, leaving Tennessee impotent in reflecting the true face of Christ to those watching. Due to the vast numbers of Christian entertainers centered in Nashville, ("Music City USA"), Christianity is always "on stage", the fruit of which is "religious" service that seeks public acceptance rather than God's face. This is especially significant for Nashville's country music industry, which was birthed through Gospel music years ago with songs that gave honor to God. Although Elvis Presley (who's historic home "Graceland" is in Memphis) sold over 1 billion records and had 131 albums and singles certified gold, platinum or multi-platinum, the only Grammy Awards he ever received were for his gospel recordings (1967, 1972, 1974). Nashville, TN is the religious publishing capitol of the U.S., and maybe even the world.

It is home to Gideons International, The Baptist Sunday School Board (word's largest producer of Sunday school material), "The Upper Room" (a Methodist publication and one of the most widely circulated Christian devotionals), Thomas Nelson Publishers (the world's largest Bible producer), and of course, countless denominational headquarters.

"If my people, who are called by my name, will humble themselves and pray and seek my face and turn from their wicked ways, then will I hear from heaven and will forgive their sin and will heal their land."
—2CHR. 7:14

BIND: CONFLICT · LOOSE: COVENANT

Tennessee's history is as futile as it is fertile. Within her soil have been countless battles. Some, between enemies and some, between brothers. All, a picture of what rages in the heavenlies just waiting to be determined by our effectual prayers; all a symbol of the warring in our members. More Civil War battles were fought in Tennessee than in any other state except Virginia. On November 30, 1863 in the victorious Battle of Franklin, more than 8,000 men died within a five hour period, three-fourths of which were Confederate soldiers. Two weeks later in the Battle of Nashville another 5,500 men fell, leaving much of the ground near Hillsboro Road, Harding Pike, Belmont Boulevard, Granny White Pike, Battlefield Drive, Harpeth Hills and Franklin Road saturated in blood. TN earned its nickname, "The Volunteer State" due to its record of soldiers provided in the War of 1812 & the Mexican War.

Before that, Tennessee settlers known as the "Overmountain Men", were key to winning the American Revolutionary War. Tennessee also ranked first among all U.S. states in the total number of Soldiers who fought in the Civil War. TN was the last state to secede from the Union and the first to be readmitted after the war. Divided as a state, East Tennesseans were strongly pro-Union, while Middle and West Tennesseans sided with the Confederacy.

"For we are not fighting against people made of flesh and blood, but against the evil rulers and authorities of the unseen world, against those mighty powers of darkness who rule this world, and against wicked spirits in the heavenly realms"
—EPH. 4:12

BIND: SUPREMACY · LOOSE: HUMILITY
COUNTER CURSE: UNFORGIVENESS · LOOSE: MERCY

While Tennessee has at times past and present held an esteeming place for its African-American community, there has also been a strong spirit of racism present whose aim is to prevent us from fulfilling our election to be a discipling and healing hub to every nation, race and tribe. The Ku Klux Klan was birthed in Pulaski, TN, and held its first national planning session in Nashville in room #10 of the Maxwell House Hotel in April, 1867. Martin Luther King was was shot and killed on April 4th, 1968 in Memphis, Tennessee while supporting a strike of black garbage men. Contrary to all this, a progression towards racial redemption has always attempted to emerge. The first abolitionist publications in America devoted entirely to ending human slavery, the "Emancipator" and "The Manumission Intelligencer", were published in Tennessee's oldest incorporated town of Jonesboro. By the late 1800's black Tennessee businessmen were being elected into local government offices (city council in 1868, and the TN General Assembly in 1872) and then in 1911, James C. Napier, a prominent black TN lawyer, was appointed Registrar of the U.S. Treasury under President Howard Taft. Today, Meharry Medical College (founded in 1876 as the very first medical education program for African Americans in the United States) is now the largest private institution for the schooling of black health care professionals in the United States. Bridging gaps between races only happens in the presence of Him who created them.

Prayerful Tennesseans continue to lift up the name of love, actively tear down the justified whirlwinds of anger and hatred.

> *"May the God who gives endurance and encouragement give you a spirit of unity among yourselves as you follow Christ Jesus, so that with one heart and mouth you may glorify the God and Father of our Lord Jesus Christ."*
> —ROM. 15:5-6

BIND: CONTROL ("Jezebel") · LOOSE: LIBERTY
COUNTER CURSE: REBELLION · LOOSE: SUBMISSION

Native American Indians make up 0.2% of Tennessee's population, a small number considering that Indians once roamed Tennessee's mountains and forests. Looking at the reasons why Indians are so spiritually significant in Tennessee, one gets a sense of why such intense warfare surrounds their Tennessee history. First, many American Indians practiced religions which were undoubtedly occult at their core, unleashing demonic forces which helped form the spiritual atmosphere in our state. Since Indians are known to have cursed the Tennessee ground which was taken from them forcibly, it is critical that those curses be broken through prayer. Secondly, since history records that the first white settlers to Nashville and Tennessee dealt wrongly and even maliciously with the Indians who preceded them, repentance before God for these acts is crucial to our future prosperity as a region. It was on December 29th, 1835 in a "Treaty of Removal" that the Cherokee Indians (by then an official Christian nation) were granted $5 million for lands east of the Mississippi with the agreement that they would move west within two years. When hardly any Indians had done so by 1838, one of the darkest events in our nation's history took place known as "The Trail of Tears", in which nearly 18,000 Cherokee Indians set out by foot (and flatboats) on a trail winding through McMinnville, Murfreesboro, Nashville and Hermitage, TN. Over 4,000 died along the way. It was said the trail passed so closely by the home of renowned Indian contender, President Andrew Jackson, that he actually spoke with them as they passed by. Oddly enough, Jackson is also known for saving the life of an Indian boy named Lincoya and raising him as his son.

> *"He searches the sources of the rivers and brings hidden things to light."*
> —JOB 28:11

BIND: BARRENNESS · LOOSE: FRUITFULNESS

20 major lakes and reservoirs. 19,000 miles of warm and cold water streams. 3,800 documented caves. The Guinness Book of World Records lists the "Lost Sea" in Sweetwater as being the largest underground lake in America. Tennessee is known as "The Big Bend State" because of the sharp turn made in the Tennessee River which causes it to flow through the state twice. In the winter of 1811-12 the worst earthquake in American History took place in northwestern Tennessee, causing a vast land area to drop several feet which forced the Mississippi River to flow backwards. From that was formed Reelfoot Lake, home each winter to the largest population of American Eagles in the eastern U.S. In 1933, Congress created the Tennessee Valley Authority, and power from their dams and steam plants reaches 80,000 square miles of factories, stores, farms, mines and homes within the Tennessee valley which includes parts of TN, KY, VA, NC, GA, AL, and MS. The only South-eastern state to not reach out and touch the vast ocean, Tennessee, with all its countless supplies of water within, is a prophetic picture of the well-equipped body of Christ who must learn to reach far and creatively touch the world for Jesus Christ. *"Whoever believes in me, as the Scripture has said, streams of living water will flow from within him."* (John 7:38)

"Rather, we have renounced secret and shameful ways; we do not use deception, nor do we distort the word of God."
—2 COR. 4:2

BIND: DECEPTION · LOOSE: TRUTH
BIND: SECRECY · LOOSE: OPENNESS

When the dark forces of Freemasonry entered the scene upon Tennessee's founding soil (through TN forefathers such as James Robertson, John Donelson, John Sevier, Timothy Demonbreun), many Tennessee churches were built upon the foundations of brotherhood within the secret lodges instead of brotherhood within Christ alone. Although not every Christian recognizes Freemasonry as a "dark force", their rites and activities are easily traced back in time to Babylonian occultism and ancient Egyptian ceremony which evoked and invited demonic forces. Unaware of the presences and principalities he has given legal right to in his life, a mason may hold fast to his masonic loyalties while being blinded to the subtle but sure losses of passion in his true faith. It is said that the more Masonic a region is, the more its architecture will resemble Greek, Egyptian and Babylonian models. From the Pyramids of Memphis, to Nashville's full scale replica of the Parthenon with its statue of the Greek goddess Athena,

Tennessee is full of masonic influence. In 1845, the cornerstone of the state capitol in Nashville was sealed with full Masonic rites, and the entire building was in fact designed by architect William Strickland, a well-known mason who requested that he be buried inside the capitol. His body is still entombed today within the northeast wall.

"Let us not give up meeting together, as some are in the habit of doing, but let us encourage one another—and all the more as you see the Day approaching."
—HEB. 10:25

BIND: DIVISION · LOOSE: UNITY

Many local and national sources record that Tennessee's name originated from the old Yuchi Indian word, "Tana-see", meaning "The Meeting Place." What a better legacy as we now face a people much in need a meeting place of unity. Divided denominations. Divided races. Divided histories and divided visions for achieving oneness for the future. Consider that Tennessee is not only home to the Tennessee Aquarium, the largest fresh water habitat in the world which preserves the life of over 7,000 animals, but also to Oak Ridge, the "secret city" begun in 1942 that housed the world's first nuclear reactor and was used to produce the first atomic bomb. Such polarities are useful for fulfilling Tennessee's state motto: "Agriculture and Commerce", but are even more useful when looked at as a spiritual symbolism of the people within her borders. Tennessee: a state which is known on the outside for its conservative faith, and yet observed on the inside for its lukewarm liberalities. The world's capitol for the publication of religious educational material, Tennessee is also known for the controversial Scopes Trial of 1925 in which the nation watched as a Tennessee high school teacher named John Scopes was arrested for teaching the theory of evolution, and then freed on a legal technicality. "Choose for yourselves this day whom you will serve" (Joshua 24:15). If our true desire is to meet with God, find fellowship with His Holy Spirit and see Tennessee fulfill the purposes for which He created her, we must have individual "meeting places" with God as well as corporate ones.

"And he did not do many miracles there because of their unbelief."
—MATT. 13:58

"So we see that they were not able to enter, because of their unbelief."
—HEB. 3:19

"Immediately the boy's father cried out and began saying, 'I do believe; help my unbelief!'"
—MARK 9:24

BIND: UNBELIEF · LOOSE: FAITH

How can it be that a people who have the Word of God on every corner, and in some cases on every coffee table, have no room in their lives for the God of the Word? How is it that the spirit-filled life can be proclaimed but not practiced? Furthermore, how can unbelievers visiting the Bible-belt leave unchanged?

"For this people's heart has become calloused; they hardly hear with their ears, and they have closed their eyes. Otherwise they might see with their eyes, hear with their ears, understand with their hearts and turn, and I would heal them."
—ACTS 28:27

The Bible says that without faith it is "impossible to please God" (Heb. 11:6). It also says by faith we can "move mountains" (Matt. 17:20), "receive salvation" (1 Peter 1:9), "heal the sick" (James 2:17), "fight the good fight" (1 Tim. 6:12), "resist the enemy when suffering" (1 Peter 5:9), "conquer kingdoms", "shut the mouths of lions" and "raise the dead" (Heb. 11:33-35). Jesus even said, *"I tell you the truth, anyone who has faith in me will do what I have been doing. He will do even greater things than these, because I am going to the Father"* (John 14:12). With the endless possibilities of miracles that await each believer, and the endless reminders of defeat that await our enemy, Satan, it is no wonder that he works so hard to blind the eyes, deafen the ears, and shut the mouths of Christians.

BINDING THE DEAF AND DUMB SPIRIT

Like the argument of the chicken and the egg, many Christians have various opinions on which comes first -- a spiritual deafness which results in unbelief, or an unbelief which results in spiritual deafness. The Bible seems to support both. For instance, in John 8:43 Jesus said, *"Why is my language not clear to you? Because you are unable to hear what I say"*. Likewise, He spoke of a "god of this age" who *"blinded the minds of unbelievers, so that they cannot see the light of the gospel of the glory of Christ, who is the image of God"* (2Cor. 4:4). On the other hand, at times it seemed that it was a person's unbelief that caused them to become mute and/or deafened and unable to hear God's voice. God told Ezekiel, (12:2) *"son of man, you are living among a rebellious people. They have eyes to see but do not see and ears to hear but do not hear, for they are a rebellious people."* And of course, when Zacharias did not believe that Elizabeth would give birth to a son, God said to him, *"And now you will be silent and not able to speak until the day this happens, because you did not believe my words, which will come true at their proper time"* (Luke 1:20). Obviously both of these strongholds feed each other, and while it may seem impossible to separate them and determine their origin, there is one key in Scripture which at least shows us a place to begin. Romans 10:17 says that *"faith comes by hearing"* (..."and hearing by the Word of God"). While we cannot predict if the absence of unbelief will produce proper hearing, we can definitely conclude from Romans 10: 17 that hearing ears give birth to faith. Moreover, Romans 10:14 reveals the domino effect that hearing has on believing by stating, *"How then shall they call on Him in whom they have not believe And how shall they believe in Him of whom they have not heard?"*

> *"Hear, you deaf; look, you blind, and see!*
> —ISA. 42:18

Isaiah prophesied of a time when *"...the eyes of those who see will no longer be closed, and the ears of those who hear will listen"* (Isa. 32:3). Through Christ, we fulfill that season now because Jesus said, *"The blind receive sight, the lame walk, those who have leprosy are cured, the deaf hear, the dead are raised, and the good news is preached to the poor"* (Luke 7:22). As reports are shared from across the nation, it seems that in regions where there is evidence of a spiritual "deaf and dumbness" amongst its residents, there will be high levels of confusion, memory loss, physical hearing loss, and even Alzheimer's. Other symptoms of the deaf and dumb spirit are a presiding sense of "dead religion" or "staunch tradition" in area churches. Whenever Christians cannot hear God's voice speaking fresh mandates to them, they will inevitably cling to the traditions and instructions He gave in times past. While many intercessors become angry with those who display such tradition and pride and view them as a hindrance to God's plans, it needs to be said that only love and prayer will free them from the sway of such a strong territorial spirit. Since we cannot pry open people's ears to the truth of God's Word, we must instead pray. Jesus said in Mark 9 that the deaf and dumb spirit *"comes out only through much prayer and fasting"*. We see that even Michael the archangel was delayed in reaching Daniel during his fastings and prayers due to a territorial spirit which he called "The prince of the Kingdom of Persia" (Dan. 10:13). As we pray in unity we will see this principality flee from our city, state and nation. Matt 12:29 says that if we bind the strongman we can *"plunder his whole household"*, thus indicating that if the deaf and dumb spirit is indeed a key stronghold over Tennessee. Once he is bound we will see the defeat of other hindrances such as pride, unbelief and religiosity, rebellion, and unforgiveness.

> *"Then he said to me, "Prophesy to these bones and say to them, `Dry bones, hear the word of the LORD!"""*
> —EZEK. 37:4

Excellent scriptures describing spiritual deaf & dumbness :
Jer. 5:21, 2 Tim. 4:3, Mark 8:18, Isa 42:20, Rev. 13:19, Ps. 115 :4-8,
Matt. 13:13-14, Acts 28:26 , Ezek. 40:4

PRAYER TOOLS: CONCLUSIONS

As you pray for Tennessee and for those in governmental seats both politically and spiritually, don't forget to *"Obey your leaders and submit to their authority. They keep watch over you as men who must give an account. Obey them so that their work will be a joy, not a burden, for that would be of no advantage to you"* (Heb 13: 17). Be active daily in prayerfully binding strongholds of religiosity, tradition, conflict (rebellion), supremacy (pride), unforgiveness, control ("jezebel"), barrenness, deception, division, unbelief and the deaf and dumb spirit....remembering also to loose God's blessings of renewal, relationship, covenant, humility, liberty, submission, fruitfulness, truth, unity, faith and opened ears. May we begin with our own lives! *Better is he who rules his own spirit than he who takes a CITY.* Proverbs 16:32

James 5:16 says, "The effectual, fervent prayer of a righteous man availeth much." These key words, when studied in Strong's Greek Concordance, translate: "The heated, zealous, hot and glowing, jealous, active, mighty, powerful prayer of an innocent, holy, just, right and fair man forces much to happen."

The call is out! Many are heralding that we can take the CITY of Nashville, and State of Tennessee for GOD!! Our redemption draweth near!! Guard the CITY gates with prevailing prayer and righteous hunger for Jesus to take His seat and pour out His mercy! In His Great and Mighty name of Jesus we pray!

About the Author

Laura Smith is an Intercessor and the state coordinator for the Tennessee State Prayer Network. Her husband, Chris and her reside in Old Hickory, TN., and attend Harvest International Church. They have three precious boys and three beautiful girls.

THE END OF DAYS

by Pastor David Long

EVERY TIME I SEE a full moon my mind and heart are flooded with thoughts and emotions taking me back to an unforgettable moment in the spring of 1966. The moon hung majestically in the middle-eastern night sky bathing the stone buildings of Jerusalem in soft white light. From my view atop the edge of the Mount of Olives I could see the gleaming silhouettes of the old city of Jerusalem. Above the historic city walls the Temple Mount stood out from the shadows of the sleepy narrow streets. The stillness and quiet were in sharp contrast to the busy, almost frantic marketplace hustle of earlier that afternoon. Bloody sheep carcasses hung in front of shops next to hucksters offering falafel or shiskabob. Raisins, olives, dates and produce of every variety were crammed into little stalls between shops catering to tourists with olive wood bound New Testaments, gold jewelry, archaeological artifacts, and Kodak film. Peanut butter and Colgate toothpaste were available in the crowded corners of other shops. The smell of manure from chickens, donkeys and sheep mixed with the odors of freshly woven baskets, cooking meat, incense, sweat, and hundreds of pungent, mild, and hardly detectable scents - fleeting - constantly moving - coming and going - gave one a sense of the incomprehensible, mysterious yet fascinating life of the place. The chaos was somehow not threatening because there seemed to be some unseen conductor orchestrating his own private market place symphony that would have meter and resolution if given time and heard in the right context.

What a captivating scene the Temple must have been from my vantage point 2000 years ago. Brilliant white stone with a facade of abundant gleaming gold trim would have been almost blinding in bright sunlight. On a night like this, it would have been magnificent to watch moonbeams caught and instantly cast back out over the city, and Judean hills spreading a sparkling reflection of the dwelling place of God.

I knew the Scriptures which clearly explain that when the signs of the end of the age are complete there will be a series of cataclysmic events bringing about the rule of the Messiah over all nations from the Temple Mount in Jerusalem. This is the end of the age of the church as well. Possibly, right where I was sitting Jesus will someday stand, and a great split in the Mount of Olives through a world-shaking earthquake will take place. Through this canyon will flow half of the fountain of living waters conceivably from under the throne of God toward the Dead Sea, creating a

huge fresh water lake, washing the heavy mineral laden brine into the gulf
of Aqubah, at the top of the Red Sea. This is no little stream but might be
something on the order of the volume of water at Niagara Falls. The other
half will flow into the Mediterranean Sea forever solving the water shortage
in Israel. This great earthquake will apparently flatten the hills in the
Promised Land and elevate Jerusalem so it can be seen for miles around.
The new rebuilt Temple will blaze with light. I like to think it will be light
from within and The Glorious Light Of His Presence will radiate through
the walls and illumine the whole landscape.

I felt incredibly lonely there by myself. I wanted to share the
beauty, mystery and sense of being in the flow of cosmic destiny in time
and place with someone who understood. In fact, I wanted to share my
whole life with this reality as central. It was the year before the six-day war
and I was a student at Near Eastern School of Archaeology situated on the
Mount of Olives over looking the Old city of Jerusalem in what was then
Jordan. I clearly knew who that someone was. I had met her on the trip to
the Holy Land and asked her out at the Church of the Nativity in
Bethlehem. We had our first date a few days before in the city glistening in
the moonlight below me. She was now far away in Switzerland studying with
theologian Francis Schaffer at L'bri. A year later we would be married, and
for the first time in over two thousand years the city below me, and the
Mount of Olives where I stood, would be under the rule of Jewish people.

The Scripture is clear that when the Jewish people begin returning
to the land they will also return to their God, and the times of the Gentiles
will be fulfilled. This would initiate a brief time of transition from the age
of the church to the final page of history when the Jewish King Jesus rules
His earth from His throne in His city: Jerusalem. The excitement I felt at
that time has grown over the years to an all-consuming passion. It is the
belief that, "even so you too, when you see all these things, recognize that
He is near, right at the door. *"Truly I say to you, this generation will not pass away until
all these things take place"* (Matt. 24: 33-34). We may be that generation. If we
are not, we are raising our children to be it. In the last century there has
been a great revival in the world, beginning in California at Azusa Street
and sweeping through the third world in the last fifty years. Even so,
according to Jesus, *"only a few are being saved"* (Luke 13:23).

During this time of transition there will be a small but powerful
army of believers who like the sons of Issachar understand the times and
know what to do (I Chron. 12:31). I like to call this group the John the
Baptist generation. They will come before the Lord comes like John with
the voice of Elijah crying in a wilderness of false Christianity for
repentance. They will have a clear understanding of the lies, which Satan has
used to deceive the Church and prevent revival. In a regular weekly prayer
meeting for revival on Monday mornings, we asked God to show us what

issues were blocking revival. We had heard of great revivals in other countries and wondered what was hindering revival here at "the buckle of the Bible Belt". An answer came with confirmation. The problem is with the Church and that problem is our religion which has been corrupted, and is contrary to the teachings of Scripture. In the seven churches of Revelation chapters 3 and 4 the Angel finds faults in five. I agree with many Bible scholars that the church of Laodecia represents each of the seven churches. This is the last church and is typical of the church in the last days, especially in the U.S.A. This is the church which the Lord will spew out of His mouth if they do not repent. Apparently they did not repent, as there is no record of its existence shortly after this warning was written.

The overwhelming reality of the promise of the whole earth being filled with the knowledge of God; the lion lying down with the lamb; the nursing child playing with the Cobra; and nations beating their plow shares into swords is near. For six thousand years the creation has been groaning waiting for this time. The birth pains are upon us. Many today are unaware of the realities of the painful birthing process, which is underway. The issues, which prevent us from experiencing a mighty revival locally, are the same issues that are prevalent in the last day church ushering in the Antichrist and his brief malevolent rule. I have chosen some biblical concepts important for every true believer to understand to endure the last days and see revival. God will choose to bring revival in certain areas where people humble themselves, and pray, and turn from their wicked ways. But whether or not a city gets spiffed up with revival before the worldwide Kingdom of God takes place, be sure that His Kingdom will come and the whole earth will be drastically changed acknowledging Him and dwelling in His presence. In that same Monday morning prayer meeting my good friend and fellow prayer warrior, Frank Gill, used the term spiffed up in thinking of present revivals in comparison to the physical earthly presence and rule of King Jesus. It helped us with perspective. When God's people are in sin and He is about to bring judgment, they do not want to hear about it. In the times of the ancient prophets, the people cried for a "positive message." The false prophets gave them what they asked for saying there would be peace and safety so they could continue in their comfort and deception. It is no different today. Ultimately, this is a positive message. The Kingdom will be born soon and the long awaited worldwide revival will come. *"All mankind will come to bow down before Me,"* says the LORD" (Isaiah 66:23b). Is exhorting a mother to prepare emotionally and physically for the birthing process a negative message? A negative message would be to encourage no prenatal care and to ignore the reality of the trauma of birth.

DISTORTING THE SCRIPTURE

"Dear friends, while you are waiting for these things to happen and for him to come, try hard to live without sinning; and be at peace with everyone so that he will be pleased with you when he returns. 15 And remember why he is waiting. He is giving us time to get his message of salvation out to others. Our wise and beloved brother Paul has talked about these same things in many of his letters. 16 Some of his comments are not easy to understand, and there are people who are deliberately stupid, and always demand some unusual interpretation–they have twisted his letters around to mean something quite different from what he meant, just as they do the other parts of the Scripture–and the result is disaster for them. 17 I am warning you ahead of time, dear brothers, so that you can watch out and not be carried away by the mistakes of these wicked men, lest you yourselves become mixed up too. 18 But grow in spiritual strength and become better acquainted with our Lord and Savior Jesus Christ. To him be all glory and splendid honor, both now and forevermore. Good-bye."
—2 PETER 3:14-18 LIVING BIBLE

Most Christians would agree that it violates Holy Scripture to say that homosexual acts are permissible for those claiming to live according to the teachings of those Scriptures. Nevertheless, there are many today who claim to be Christian while engaging in a homosexual life style. Some ministers claim that the Scriptures condemning these relationships are not for today, but were written for a people in a specific culture and in a different time which make them irrelevant for today. They quickly distort or wrest the Scripture to make it comply with their life style so repentance is not necessary for them to be "Christian." "How terrible," we say! "Wait a minute!" Many when interpreting Scripture regarding the gifts of the Holy Spirit, relegating them to another age, use the same kind of sloppy thinking. Which is worse? Permitting homosexual life styles in the church or resisting the Holy Spirit by not allowing Him to do His work through the means He has chosen for this age to minister repentance and life to His people? "Wait another minute!"

Many who would be willing to die for the issue of releasing all the gifts of the Holy Spirit in the church use the same technique to allow them to follow the world's leading: by the feminists who threw their bras in the Chicago River back in the sixties regarding the role of women. This was an event which became known as the announcement of the sexual revolution symbolic of throwing off all restraint and rejecting millenniums of sexual roles and values. They say the clear teaching of Scripture does not apply since that revolution which began a few decades ago negated 2000 years of Church History. We adapt the Church to the world's standards so we can maintain the world's life style. With surprising rapidity the styles of dress, types of music, movies we watch, and sexual roles we expect have drastically changed. What was unthinkable thirty years ago is commonplace today.

Books that every pastor had on his shelf in the last generation warning of the Antichrist and his system are now out of print. It is not necessary to have gone to graduate school to learn higher criticism, Greek, Hebrew, and hermeneutics to understand the Bible. It can be understood far better by an uneducated humble person depending on the Holy Spirit than by a highly educated, proud intellectual, justifying his own sin by explaining away clear truth.

James tells us that if we are hearers of the word and not doers we deceive ourselves (James 1:22). We are clearly warned that in the last days people will not endure sound doctrine but will have itching ears wanting them to be tickled with fables (2 Timothy 4:3). This is not referring to others in another time and place. It is referring to us here and now. It is talking about religious people holding to a form of godliness but denying its' power.

LOVERS OF SELF

"But realize this, that in the last days difficult times will come. For men will be lovers of self, lovers of money, boastful, arrogant, revilers, disobedient to parents, ungrateful, unholy, unloving, irreconcilable, malicious gossips, without self-control, brutal, haters of good, treacherous, reckless, conceited, lovers of pleasure rather than lovers of God, holding to a form of godliness, although they have denied its power; Avoid such men as these. For among them are those who enter into households and captivate weak women weighed down with sins, led on by various impulse always learning and never able to come to the knowledge of the truth."
—2 TIMOTHY 3:1-7

A healthy self respect, based upon being created by God in His image is what every Godly parent strives to instill in his children. When Christ told us to love our neighbor as our self, He was acknowledging what is natural for every human being which is caring and nurturing one's self. Paul did the same thing when he commanded husbands to love their wives as they love themselves.

What is being discussed here is selfishness resulting in self-worship. Since Satan deceived Eve in the Garden of Eden, the lie that mankind should ultimately worship himself has been gaining momentum. We have been taught that through evolution we created our selves. Through psychology we have been taught to love our self. Democracy has taught us that we can rule our selves. Why not worship our self?

Noah Webster in his 1828 American Dictionary of the English language defined selfishness: "The exclusive regard of a person to his own interest or happiness; or that supreme self-love or self-preference, which leads a person in his actions to direct his purposes to the advancement of his own interest, power or happiness, without regarding the interest of others."

Selfishness, in its worst or unqualified sense, is the very essence of human depravity, and stands in direct opposition to benevolence, which is the essence of the divine character. As God is love, so man, in his natural state is selfishness.

The Biblical mandate is the opposite. In Philippians chapter 2 Paul in giving Christ as an example says:

"Do nothing from selfishness or empty conceit, but with humility of mind regard one another as more important than yourselves; do not merely look out for your own personal interests, but also for the interests of others."

Paul goes on to talk about ministers:

"for they all seek after their own interests, not those of Christ Jesus."

James indicates that this selfish, Godless kind of behavior results in demonic activity:

"But if you have bitter jealousy and selfish ambition in your heart, do not be arrogant and so lie against the truth. 15 This wisdom is not that which comes down from above, but is earthly, natural, demonic. For where jealousy and selfish ambition exist, there is disorder and every evil thing."
—JAMES 3:14-16

He continues:

"What is the source of quarrels and conflicts among you? Is not the source your pleasures that wage war in your members? 2 You lust and do not have; so you commit murder. You are envious and cannot obtain; so you fight and quarrel."

It is no wonder marriages are failing and the idea of committed family relationships is fading into history. Kids are growing up unloved and murdering each other at school. Prisons are overflowing and society is disintegrating. Jesus said three things choke out the Word of God: Riches, Pleasures, and The Cares of this world. The idol of self demands the frenzied pursuit of these. The lie is that self-fulfillment is possible through these avenues and that self-fulfillment will bring meaning and happiness to life. I once saw a sign hanging in an office: "I have gone to find myself. If I get back before I return, please ask me to wait." Trying to find meaning by searching self, instead of searching for the Creator only makes the same kind of nonsense as that sign. Only in surrender and intimacy with The God of Creation can the created find fulfillment and meaning in life. We find Him by looking outside of our self to God and then to others.

A dear Christian worker shared with me how she a struggled with thought of suicide all her life. Only her deep faith and fear of the Lord had prevented her from succumbing to this persistent temptation. She explained to me how it was a battle with self-love. Suicide would be a self-indulgent escape from the pain. This shows the ultimate self-destructiveness of being a lover of self rather than lovers of God.

WITCHCRAFT

"For rebellion is as the sin of witchcraft, and stubbornness is as iniquity and idolatry."
—I SAMUEL 15:23 KJB

I am treating the subjects of rebellion and witchcraft as one in light of the verse above. They are prominent in the last day deception and falling away of the Church. The essence of these two concepts is the same. It is the denial of the distinction between God and His creation. They are fueled by pride. Lies and deception puff up the mix resulting in being given over to debauchery driven by demonic energy. This process is described in Romans 1:18-32. Rebellion is ultimately refusal to be in submission to God and His ordinances. They are summed up in the great commandment to love Him and each other. To ignore Him or his created order is not to love Him. American ideas of rugged individualism, independence, and autonomy all feed our natural inclination to rebel. We are a culture where defiance is honored and rebellion has become virtue. When this rebellion is formalized into a belief in The Great Mother Goddess, and the popular idea that all is one and nature or the earth is part of universal creative feminine circle of life, it takes on spiritual power from demonic forces. This is the ancient pagan belief going all the way back to the four lies Satan offered Eve in the Garden. Webster defines Witchcraft as, "The practices of witches; sorcery; enchantments; intercourse with the devil; power more than natural."

How does this relate to the Church? When we engage in or flirt with rebellion against the authority of parents, husbands, pastors, police, or any God ordained authority figure we enter into this intercourse with the Devil resulting in allowing ourselves to be deceived and vulnerable to demonic bondage. When we accept popular ideas contrary to Scripture regarding God, His gender, our gender, His creation, or His created order, we become vulnerable to the process described in Romans 1. The Church of today (the last day Church) is permeated with this kind of rebellion and deception.

Every one who works with metal and welding is familiar with an acetylene gas-cutting torch. It is a tool, which heats steel or iron with

A City on its Knees

acetylene gas and a little oxygen until it is red-hot and then with a burst of oxygen blasts the molten metal out of the way making an effective cut through the stock. Selfishness and rebellion are like this synergistic effect on the metal. By themselves they are plenty destructive, but together they become an overwhelming blast of evil cutting through everything noble and good. They will not be stopped with human effort. Only Divine intervention will cool the white-hot fury of self, fueled with the demonic energy of rebellion.

APOSTASY

"For if we go on sinning willfully after receiving the knowledge of the truth, there no longer remains a sacrifice for sins, but a terrifying expectation of judgment and THE FURY OF A FIRE WHICH WILL CONSUME THE ADVERSARIES. Anyone who has set aside the Law of Moses dies without mercy on the testimony of two or three witnesses. How much severer punishment do you think he will deserve who has trampled under foot the Son of God, and has regarded as unclean the blood of the covenant by which he was sanctified, and has insulted the Spirit of grace?"
—Hebrews 10:26-29

If we were not already in the midst of the Great Apostasy this concept would strike terrible fear into the hearts of church members. Please do not think this is an attempt to argue for or against the concept of eternal security. Your personal belief in, or denial of this teaching is not what this is about. It is about the reality of the Scriptural teaching that in the last days there will be a massive falling away from the true faith and a continuance of a form of religion but denying the power. Whether this falling away is by people who have never been born again or people who have actually been written in the Lambs book of life and then been blotted out is not the issue here. The point is that the Scripture teaches that before the Antichrist appears and before Jesus Christ annihilates him with the breath of His mouth, the church will largely be a false church. If you believe you will be raptured out before this time and are not concerned for yourself in this regard, please consider your children, family members, church friends, neighbors, coworkers, and acquaintances. I believe there is abundant evidence that this is not a future event, but is already traveling a significant distance on the highway of history.

In Romans 11 we are told that the Jewish people were broken off from the Olive Tree of spiritual life for their unbelief in their long awaited Messiah King Jesus. It also tells us that when the fullness of the Gentiles has come in the Jewish people will be grafted back into the tree. In this same passage Paul warns the Gentiles to not be arrogant toward the Jewish people, but to fear being broken off just as the Jewish people were. If we are honest, we must admit there is not much humility or respect among most Christians for the Jewish people. This process of the Jewish people being grafted back into the Olive Tree is happening with increasing speed. In 1967 there were no Jewish congregations holding to their Jewish customs and traditions who worshipped their Messiah. Today there are hundreds of such congregations. Could it be that this process of breaking off the arrogant Gentile Church and the engrafting in of the Jewish people is already under way? I think so!

During this time of transition from the church age to the Kingdom for which the Church has prayed for 2000 years, several things will happen. The Jewish people will turn to their Messiah, King Jesus saying, "Blessed is He who comes in the Name of the Lord" referring to their acceptance of the Messiah fulfilling one of the main conditions of His return. The believing saints at that time will come under tremendous persecution along with the Jewish people. The remnant of the Church, which is not apostate, will be purified through this and this will allow them to be a pure Bride ready to rule and reign with Christ.

We know that only a few will be saved. *"For the coming of the Son of Man will be just like the days of Noah"* (Matt. 24:37) ; *"in the days of Noah, during the construction of the ark, in which a few, that is, eight persons, were brought safely through the water"* (I Peter 3:20). We are not saying that only eight people will be saved. We are saying that many that assume they are saved may not be. Like in the days of Noah only a few are aware of the wickedness and perverseness of our own culture. The church is often following the world in style of dress, values (the American Dream) and lifestyles. When the disciples asked Jesus if only a few would be saved here was His answer:

"Strive to enter through the narrow door; for many, I tell you, will seek to enter and will not be. Once the head of the house gets up and shuts the door, and you begin to stand outside and knock on the door, saying, 'Lord, open up to us!' then He will answer and say to you, 'I do not know where you are from.' "Then you will begin to say, 'We ate and drank in Your presence, and You taught in our streets'; and He will say, 'I tell you, I do not know where you are from; DEPART FROM ME, ALL YOU EVILDOERS.'"
—LUKE 13:24-27

Jesus told His disciples of the terrible events of 70 AD at the same time He warned them about the end of the age. Speaking about these times He said: *"At that time many will fall away and will betray one another and hate one another."* Paul made the same point: *"But the Spirit explicitly says that in later times some will fall away from the faith, paying attention to deceitful spirits and doctrines of demons, by means of the hypocrisy of liars seared in their own conscience as with a branding iron."*
—TIMOTHY 4:1,2

"that you not be quickly shaken from your composure or be disturbed either by a spirit or a message or a letter as if from us, to the effect that the day of the Lord has come. 3 Let no one in any way deceive you, for it will not come unless the apostasy comes first, and the man of lawlessness is revealed, the son of destruction, 4 who opposes and exalts himself above every so-called god or object of worship, so that he takes his seat in the temple of God, displaying himself as being God. 5 Do you not remember that while I was still with you, I was telling you these things? 6 And you know what restrains him now, so that in his time he will be revealed. 7 For the mystery of lawlessness is already at work; only he who now restrains will do so until he is taken out of the way. 8 Then that lawless one will be revealed whom the Lord will slay with the breath of His mouth and bring to an end by the appearance of His coming; 9 that is, the one whose coming is in accord with the activity of Satan, with all power and signs and false wonders, 10 and with all the deception of wickedness for those who perish, because they did not receive the love of the truth so as to be saved. 11 For this reason God will send upon them a deluding influence so that they will believe what is false, 12 in order that they all may be judged who did not believe the truth, but took pleasure in wickedness."
—2 Thessalonians 2:2-12

I realize that many believe these things have already happened or will not happen until the Church is raptured out of the world. In any event I repeat, we must be concerned for our loved ones and friends, if we feel comfortable, safe and are not concerned for our own condition.

SPIRITUAL HOMOSEXUALITY

This term is not in the Scripture, however, the concept is certainly there. I use it here to help define the process resulting in an individual or a whole society being given over to vain speculations, darkened foolish hearts, unthankfulness to God, and ultimately reprobate minds. A simple explanation of homosexuality is a man using another man instead of a woman or a woman using another woman instead of a man in sexual intimacy. This is sexual role reversal in a physical way. This same sex attraction and activity is against nature as explained in Romans 1:24-31. When this role reversal happens in the spiritual realm it is spiritual homosexuality.

Why is our sexual identity of such high importance to God? It is because He created us in His image and our union between man and woman are a sacred mystery showing whom God is and how He relates to Himself and to us. Philosophers and theologians have argued for thousands of years about the nature of reality. Some have said all is "one." Others have said the individual particular things have meaning in and of themselves. The Judeo-Christian view taught in the Bible gives a view, which is not intellectually understandable. This is why man in his arrogance fights against accepting this view of reality. It says that God is both one and many. A good discussion of this is in the book THE ONE AND THE MANY by Rousas John Rushdoony. God is both Divine and Human. He is both singular and plural. He is One and He is also many: Father, Son, and Holy Ghost. This can be seen by looking at the pronouns in the Genesis account of creation. He made man and woman to express His image. They are image bearers. Part of our understanding of who God is, comes from the picture He created in marriage of the two becoming one flesh. This whole theme of the one and the many is also expressive of Christ's relationship to His Church. Paul says this mystery is great. It is a sacred mystery about which marriage and family teach us. Satan has much at stake in destroying marriage and family – this picture of who God is – and pushing the lie that there is no distinction between God and His creation. Not only can he destroy the lives of children by having them grow up fatherless and motherless and the lives of adults living in rejection and emotional and economic pain, but he wants to destroy the truth of a Creator God to whom we owe allegiance. Satan starts with man who is created a little lower than the angels but is at the top of the visible created order by saying there is no distinction between male and female. Then he says there is no distinction between parents and children, employers and employees, mankind and animal kind and so on. The goal is to say that the creation is God and we therefore can worship ourselves. Our sexual identity and the acceptance of our sexual roles are at the very heart of our imageship. Satan's attempt is to destroy the idea of distinctions because he wants to deceive man into believing there is no distinction between God and His creation.

Of course men and women are of equal value and are coequal heirs of Jesus Christ. We are not saying that a woman should not be allowed to drive a bulldozer or that a man should be mocked for doing embroidery. Women should be paid equally with men for the same work. God anoints women in ministry and they should be released to utilize spiritual gifts. Nevertheless, women and men are not the same and God has given them distinctive roles and appearance to reflect the distinction they represent. Our culture has demeaned the traditional value of homemaking and child rearing in favor of being in authority and making money.

When men abdicate their role as spiritual leader in the family and women through fear from the history of abuse and neglect they have suffered, take control, this is spiritual homosexuality. Isaiah, in his third chapter warns about judgment coming and notes that a rebellious people display their sin like Sodom. He warns about the proud and seductive walk and dress of the daughters. He then bemoans the fact that their oppressors are children and women rule over them. The description fits our time well. American society is so far down this road that children reared in this climate have already been trapped by the satanic energy, which pushes them to make choices toward a homosexual life style and orientation.

Let me hasten to say that there is a ditch on the other side of the road regarding the error of this issue. Archie Bunker on television a few decades ago depicted the reason feminism is this country has gained so much momentum. On the other hand, the bourgeois idea that a good Christian home is a woman not working outside of the home, but remains in an isolated suburban cocoon ferrying her children to ball games and dance classes, while her successful husband works thirty hours a week and comes home to play with the children on the living room floor while making well into six figures is nice, but presents unrealistic pressures and expectations on most families in the real world.

SODOM

According to II Peter 2:6 Sodom and Gomorrah were destroyed for examples to people who would live ungodly lives thereafter. It is important for us to know what the sin of Sodom was. Most people equate the sin of Sodom with homosexuality and unnatural sexual acts. This was certainly the case but this behavior was the result of other sin before God gave them over to the lusts of their hearts to dishonor their bodies. We will look at the sins Peter, Ezekiel, and Isaiah observed. We will follow the progression Ezekiel gives in chapter 16 beginning with verse 46. We will add to Ezekiel's list from Isaiah chapter 3 and II Peter 2. Notice the spiritual progression in the sin before the city was given over to their sexual perversion. Notice also how the flood of evil in a culture overwhelms the individual. It is as we have learned in our culture: the abused abuse—the molested molest.

Ezekiel begins with the generational sin of mothers hating their husbands and children. This was no doubt, with good reason. Many of the husbands were probably abusive and the children were unruly. The children were oppressors and the women ruled. The women's walk and countenance was seductive and proud. They wore perfume and jewelry and dressed elaborately. There was arrogance, abundant food, and careless ease. The poor and needy were ignored and they did not help them. Rebellion and self-will were the routine and authority was despised. They indulged the flesh with sensual conduct and finally engaged in abominations. Sound familiar?

BABYLON

A little over a hundred years after God destroyed the inhabitants of the earth with the great flood, the descendants of Noah and his sons gathered together on the plain of Shinar in Mesopotamia by the Euphrates River. They decided to build a tower up to reach up to the heavens. God said that since they all spoke on language nothing would be impossible for them, so He dispersed them by confusing their tongues. About 1600 years later the first worldwide empire was established by Babylon. The Jewish people were taken in exile to that great metropolis which became known in later Biblical literature as all that is evil in fleshly, human effort empowered by demonic energy. The Greeks in their written observations of the great city were in awe of its majesty. The writers of Scripture were unimpressed, except to warn of the terrible evil of the culture.

In the book of Revelation there is a description of a re-established city of Babylon. The Great Harlot and Babylon of Revelation 17 and 18 are one and the same. She is a religious personage being dressed in religious vestments and carrying a gold cup with which she makes all the nations of the earth drunk with her immorality. She gets drunk on the blood of the saints. She sits on many waters, which are peoples and multitudes and nations and tongues. Apparently they are a melting pot and like the original Babel speak one language and nothing is impossible for them. Wealth obtained through a great worldwide commercial network causes all the merchants of the world to become rich by her consumption. She glorifies herself exports her immorality and over all the earth. She wallows in opulent luxury with much music and unexcelled consumption. Apparently she has a religious history, which becomes sorcery with a message of commerce, wealth, consumption and sensual gratification, along with human accomplishment perverting the whole earth. She has traded slaves and persecuted the saints who oppose her.

Many Bible scholars have thought that it was speaking of Rome and the Roman Catholic Church. Others, especially more recently have said it is the United States. I agree with those who say the United States fits the Biblical description. There is still a possibility that there is another explanation for this system of wealth, commerce, inordinate consumption, sensuality, immorality and sorcery. In any case the United States is the seductive 'Babylon the Great' to me and I must heed the warning:

> *"I heard another voice from heaven, saying, 'Come out of her, my people, so that you will not participate in her sins and receive of her plagues; for her sins have piled up as high as heaven, and God has remembered her iniquities."*
> —REVELATION 18:4-5 10

What we have said so far begins to set the stage for description of the conditions in which we live. When we ask God to bring revival, we are asking Him to crash though the carefully constructed stronghold in our churches protecting us from Him who is truth. We let the stronghold protect our comfort and ease, our riches, pleasures, and cares. Lie by lie the stronghold has been reinforced. A stronghold is a lie we have accepted and are unwilling or unaware needs to change. Ed Silvoso says, " a spiritual stronghold is a mind-set impregnated with hopelessness that causes us to accept as unchangeable, situations that we know are contrary to the will of God (Revelation 2:20-23).

The conditions we have discussed create a fertile ground for the sins of the four churches in Revelation which I believe make the lukewarm church of Laodecia a candidate to be spit out of the mouth of God. We live in a Laodecian Church age. When God removes His candlestick from a church it may be economically prosperous and have large numbers attending, but He is no more present than He is at General Motors, or Bell Telephone, who both have much success and which He holds together since He holds all things together. You will notice that much of Satan's lies have to do with our sexuality and sexual identity, so we will begin with the Spirit of Jezebel who is certainly the same spirit, which promotes the last days Babylon and The Great Whore of Revelation.

THE CHURCH OF THYATIRA

"But I have this against you, that you tolerate the woman Jezebel, who calls herself a prophetess, and she teaches and leads My bond-servants astray so that they commit acts of immorality and eat things sacrificed to idols. 'I gave her time to repent, and she does not want to repent of her immorality. 'Behold, I will throw her on a bed of sickness, and those who commit adultery with her into great tribulation, unless they repent of her deeds. 'And I will kill her children with pestilence, and all the churches will know that I am He who searches the minds and hearts; and I will give to each one of you according to your deeds."
—Rev. 2:20-23

The Spirit of Jezebel does have to do with control, but in light of what has already been said it certainly has to do with gender. Queen Jezebel had a passive husband who was King over Israel. He spent time pouting and being depressed. She was strong, took action, and was aggressive, religious, and seductive. She was controlling, quick to anger, and I believe would rather die, divorce, or commit murder rather than give up that control. I believe her motivation was fear of incompetent, emotionally unpredictable, irresponsible, possibly abusive male leadership. She did not have an intimate relationship with the God of Israel and so could not trust Him to care for her. She represents a form of witchcraft and harlotry (II Kings 9: 22). Where feminine rebellion and selfish ambition are used to gain power and control which are valued above love and family the Jezebel Spirit is at work. It is the denial of the distinction between male and female resulting in the reversal of sexual roles, which is spiritual homosexuality. Rebellion is expressed by not acknowledging male leadership as different, (I Timothy 2:7-15) or having respectful fear of husbands (Eph. 5:33). Harlotry (unfaithfulness to God) is expressed by resisting prophetic truth to the point of killing the prophets. False prophecy is embraced accepting and living out the lies we are discussing.

THE CHURCH OF EPHESUS

"But I have this against you, that you have left your first love."
—REVELATION 2:4

"At that time many will fall away and will betray one another and hate one another. Many false prophets will arise and will mislead. Because lawlessness is increased, most people's love will grow cold."
—MATTHEW 24:10-12

The Church of Ephesus is representative of Phariseeism, which after Jezebel is the second fruit of the flesh, which resists the presence of God. If Jezebel kills the prophetic, the Pharisee tries to kill Christ Himself. The essence of the spirit of phariseeism is replacing love relationships with doctrinal purity, legalism, and religious tradition.

In every human heart there is an empty place of the soul infinite in depth. It can only be filled with an infinite source. Communion with God brings the intimacy, which fills that hunger with Living Water, The Bread of Life and the Wine of the Holy Spirit. This vertical intimate relationship with God is worked out horizontally with other people. This is the law of God summarized by Jesus. Addiction is simply the substitution of anything in place of these two relationships. The Pharisee is an addict. He uses religion as his drug of choice, substituting it for love fulfilling relationships. As far as I can determine the only addiction for which the Lord did not express overwhelming mercy was phariseeism.

His view of truth is not in terms of a relationship with Him who is Truth, but in terms of black and white or right and wrong. He thinks he can grasp truth intellectually with his fleshly mind. He does not understand what Benjamin Franklin said, "Truth to finely sifted is error." He does not understand that truth often is in tension on a continuum balancing two seemingly opposing ideas. He therefore gets his doctrine well defined and in a box and cuts himself off from spiritual growth as defined in the context of relationships in Ephesians chapter four.

Here are a few more traits of the Pharisee gleaned from Scripture: He wants to be right and believes he is right. He is an evangelist trying to get people to accept his religion. He is proud and selfish. He bases his fellowship upon his doctrinal position, never questioning his views and rejecting others who differ with him and yet worship the same Lord as he does. He is provincial and traditional. His way, food, dress, and community are right and he rejects others who are different from him. He is easily threatened and equates his and others salvation to the acceptance of his culture and tradition rather than acknowledging God is above these concerns that are petty compared to Him who sits on the throne over all. Since a Pharisee has not been open to receiving God's love and mercy he knows nothing about compassion. He puts religious ministry over caring for his parents, using selfish lies to justify himself and so disqualifies himself from the blessings of the first commandment with promise and Isaiah 58;7-8. His ministry is his mistress displacing family. He has dealt with his emotional pain with his addiction and so he is past feeling and has a lot of energy in finding his feelings in things like sex and anger. He is able to hate easily justifying it with doctrinal or racial purity. He is filled with prejudice. He is rigid, not flexible, not broken, and not correctable. Ungodly people hate God because of his religion. He is spiritually in bed with the Jezebel or the Great Whore of Babylon.

Today many in modern churches are able to switch churches like choosing a fast food restaurant. "Where shall we go today?" "I don't really have a church home, I just go where the Spirit leads me." I wonder if I should capitalize Spirit in the last sentence. There is a consumer mentality about church. Long-term meaningful, community-building relationships are displaced by considerations about comfort and architectural ambiance. Buildings, programs, events, padded pews, the youth program, style and excellence of music, good preaching, fast and easy access to what I want is all more important than lasting relationships with the lowly or others. When it does not hurt to break relationships so I can get more of what I want outside of relationships, something is wrong. Switching churches easily is a symptom of trouble in the heart.

THE CHURCH OF PERGAMUM

Balaam's sin was using his prophetic gifting for his own personal gain. This was common in the early church as well. Paul remarked to the Philippians that there were no ministers except Timothy who were available to minister to them because they were all concerned with their own interests rather than those of Christ's. Balaam also thought that he could advance his own interests by pleasing an ungodly leader through the use of human means. He also believed he could disqualify God's anointed by getting them to sin and then finding fault. Christ gave his life to make the

Gospel available. We are challenged to do the same thing. When the Gospel is made into merchandise for selfish purposes, it is the exact opposite of the Lord's example of selflessness to the point of giving up His life. Paul said he did not peddle the Gospel. Peter and Jude both said this sin of Balaam's was the sin of evil men of their day for whom the black darkness is reserved forever.

Today in America commerce has reached a quintessential level of preeminence in our society and the Gospel has become a major product to market. Books, music, "Christian" performance and churches are all marketed like soft drinks or automobiles. How can a Holy Spirit given song or sermon become the exclusive property of the messenger and then hawked like pigs at an auction and no one think it strange? America has taken the idea of a corporation and built a mighty commercial culture around it. The science of corporate leadership has become a powerful influence all over the world. We have taken that model and superimposed it on the Church and now almost all churches are corporations, and are run like corporations. Where is this in the New Testament? Decisions are made like we have learned from the world of commerce. Finances are controlled in the same way. Staff members are hired and fired after the corporate model. For most of us shifting our paradigm to a New Testament model would be more difficult than for a hog to learn geometry.

I was a sophomore in college and came home at Christmas time and told my father that I believed I was called to the ministry. He had been a minister all his life. Men in those days did not cry—at least in public and I had never seen him shed a tear. He certainly had never given me any indication that he thought I would become a minister or that he wanted me to be. His eyes filled with tears and he looked me in the eye with penetrating warmth and passion. He said, "David remember this! The ministry is not a profession! It is a calling!" The ramifications of that truth are still resounding in my life today.

Another fatal aspect of Balaam's error was that he thought he could disqualify God's anointed by finding fault with them. Finding fault or accusing is satan's business, however he has been able to infiltrate the ranks of the Church with this critical spirit. Disqualifying Christian leaders by finding fault is easy to do. God chose the foolish to confound the wise and he chooses not many wise, or mighty. In weakness is His strength made perfect. Often this faultfinding is part of the motive of greed. It is used to advance one self to replace a person in a position or to gain power.

THE CHURCH OF SARDIS

"you have a name that you are alive, but you are dead. 'Wake up, and strengthen the things that remain, which were about to die; for I have not found your deeds completed in the sight of My God.' So remember what you have received and heard; and keep it, and repent. Therefore if you do not wake up, I will come like a thief, and you will not know at what hour I will come to you."
—REVELATION 3:1-3

Absalom, King David's son, killed his half brother, rebelled against his father, and tried to usurp the throne from David. Absalom is a good example of someone who has a name, is alive but dead and needs to wake up. He needed to remember what he had heard and repent. His father was a man after God's own heart, the king upon whom Christ established His throne forever, a tender passionate poet, a great warrior, and a loving father. He was also a repentant sinner and headed a dysfunctional family. Solomon was able to take this heritage and become a great king in his father's footsteps, but Absalom's life ended in a tragic ignominious death. He had the greatest educational and cultural advantages of his day. He certainly had an ideal role model. Even in David's failure and sin he became honest, transparent and repentant.

The last day themes we have identified do not work to bring about Satan's last day desperate attack on the Church individually or independent of each other. Rather, these concepts are so entwined; it is impossible to think about them apart from one another. They gain momentum from one another. They work synergistically. The focus we want to concentrate on here is fatherhood. Absalom effectively disqualified David from being a father to him. He prevented David from the love relationship David desired with Absalom, and so kept him from waking him from his deadness by pouring a father's life into him. This is the norm for our culture. We have disqualified the very idea of fatherhood and have cut ourselves off from life in the process. We do not respect age. Because of the rapid advancement of technology our mentors have become our children rather than our fathers. Mothers alone are raising children of broken homes and there is little acknowledgment of the tragedy. Men are now depicted in the media as sometimes comical incompetents, and more often now, as the unreasoning perpetrators of violence. It is true our society has robbed them of their role of protector, provider for the family, self-image builder, and identity giver for the children. So their frustration and anger has risen. The cycle continues its destruction of society by the progressing absence of fatherhood and male frustration in every succeeding generation.

It is probable that Absalom like Noah's son, Ham, saw his father's sin and refused to cover it by forgiving him. As Jesus clearly taught in the

Lord's prayer, this doomed Absalom to being unforgiven. Since sin is passed from generation to generation unless there is repentance and forgiveness breaking the chain of bondage, Absalom was compelled to commit murder and be alienated from his earthly and heavenly Fathers. We have many fathers: genetic, Heavenly, spiritual, and those who are willing to be role models and mentors. For the last day Church to wake up, we must repent of our attitude toward fathers and break with the mentality our culture has dictated regarding men and fatherhood.

THE CHURCHES OF SMYRNA AND PHILADELPHIA

These were the two churches with which Christ had nothing against. This is not an exegetical study and so we are not pretending to have gleaned everything we are saying from the specific passages regarding the churches of Revelation. What we are saying is, however, Biblical and these churches are examples of situations, conflicts, and challenges saints have confronted down through the ages and specifically today. On the eve of her execution during the Reformation Anneken Jans of Rotterdam spoke these words to her infant son. "Where you hear of a poor, simple cast-off flock which is despised and rejected by the world, join them, for where you hear of the cross there is Christ." The Lord said to the Church of Smyrna,

> *"And to the angel of the church in Smyrna write: The first and the last, who was dead, and has come to life, says this: 'I know your tribulation and your poverty (but you are rich), and the blasphemy by those who say they are Jews and are not, but are a synagogue of Satan. 'Do not fear what you are about to suffer. Behold, the devil is about to cast some of you into prison, so that you will be tested, and you will have tribulation for ten days. Be faithful until death, and I will give you the crown of life. 'He who has an ear, let him hear what the Spirit says to the churches. He who overcomes will not be hurt by the second death"*
> —REVELATION 2:8-11

It is interesting that He said to the Church of Laodecia that they were rich but they were poor and to Smyrna they were poor but they were rich. This kind of church is the type, which will not be spewed out of the mouth of God but will birth the John the Baptist Generation. Four things, which reflect the heart of God, are worship, community, the poor and the Jewish people. These things will be on the heart of that fervent generation which prepares the way of the Lord. When God's people become convicted about living in the city of Babylon and flirting with, if not sleeping with the Great Whore and going to the church of Laodecia, they can come out by getting a heart for the issues of God's heart.

We can worship the Lord by presenting our bodies, as living sacrifices which is our spiritual service of worship. Sacrificial giving of our tithes and offerings is worship. Making the sacrifice of praise is worship. All worship has to do with sacrifice. That which has to do with entertainment is not worship. We can find great joy in sacrifice; it is actually the Lord's joy into which we enter. We can even enter into The Lord's glory in these sacrifices of worship. Worship is on the heart of God and is a way out of Babylon.

Three great words in the bible are: love, grace, and community. *"The grace of the Lord Jesus Christ, and the love of God, and the communion of the Holy Ghost, be with you all"* (II Cor. 13:14). The word communion is translated in other versions as fellowship. It is actually our word for community. We can say God has a heart for His temple. His temple is built of the lively stones of the saints fitted together to make a spiritual habitation for Himself. The Psalmist comments on how lovely are His dwelling places.

One of the great tragedies of our society is the loss of community. With industrialization and now technology, mobility has increased and meaningful, long-term, supportive relationships have suffered. In the agrarian cultures of almost all of history, the extended family and community were usually constants in the lives of people. Part of the problem resulting in the recent school shootings and the general breakdown of our society is related to the isolation and independence individuals experience in our society. According to the New Testament plan local churches are to be small communities giving salt and light to a needy, lost people nearby. Many churches have almost lost the stability of the kind of community represented in 2000 years of history since Jesus set the pattern for Christian love and communion. Today corporations dictate to people where they live rather than family commitments or local church commitments. Vulnerability is always a component of love and so it is always difficult. Building meaningful long-term committed relationships is a second way out of Babylon.

A third priority on the heart of God is a concern for the poor. *"Be of the same mind toward one another; do not be haughty in mind, but associate with the lowly. Do not be wise in your own estimation. (Romans 12:16) Listen, my beloved brethren: did not God choose the poor of this world to be rich in faith and heirs of the kingdom which He promised to those who love Him?"* (James 2:5). In Isaiah 58, and in many other Scriptures, God makes his heart for the poor abundantly clear. He even tells us that when we give to the poor we are lending to God. He puts Himself in debt to us, when we choose to give to the poor.

A final way out of Babylon is to have God's heart for the Jewish people and Israel. In the past and in the future this may be a very costly love. Many have given their lives in their willingness to pray for and protect God's chosen people. According to prophecy there will be a great time of anti-Semitism yet to come. God has promised to bless those who bless Israel and to curse those who lightly esteem the Jewish people.

For the remnant of the called who bear His name every day gone by is one step closer to a "Godzone," but for Laodicean's one step closer to the "Dangerzone." In these last days we must put off the former things concerning the flesh, and delve ever so deeply into God's Grace He so freely offers at such a great price. We must untie the heavy yokes and unite locking arm in arm as we concentrate our prayer efforts in this arena of time. May we find ourselves at long last united in the tabernacle of God prevailing in unison as, "A City on its Knees."

All Scripture References, The New American Standard Bible, 1995 Update, (La Habra, California: The Lockman Foundation) 1996 unless otherwise noted.

About the Author

Pastor David E. Long is the founder of Grace Community Church in Whites Creek, TN. He and his flock were called from the country to Woodcock Church downtown in the East Nashville projects. He has the cry for the city and a message to free yourself from Babylon! He and his wife Sandra, have four incredibly gifted daughters and reflect the glory of what happens when children are brought up by God-fearing parents.

PART 3

REVIVAL AND
RESTORATION

*"The enquiry of our Lord, may, with great appropriateness,
be ours, 'When the Son of man comes shall He find faith on earth?'
We believe He will, and it is ours this day to see that the lamp of faith
is trimmed and burning, lest He come Who shall come, and that right early."*
—E.M. Bounds

THE NEW CITY

by Jeffrey M. Richfield

JUST AS JESUS Christ will bring down from heaven the new City of Jerusalem in Revelation 21:10, He will also be the Master builder of our city when we take confidence in Him. The Lord will build all its houses, and He will be the guard of this city. And its people shall not be ashamed (Psalm 127). The Master builder will lay a foundation of holiness in His City (Rev.21). From the mountaintop will flow a river of righteousness making straight paths that make glad the city of God. And the God of Jacob will be its refuge (Psalm 46). Wisdom will cry out and understanding lift her voice by the gates at the entry of this city taking her stand on top of its hills (Proverbs 8). The city that is called by His name that makes mention of Him, will lean on the God of Israel; the Lord of hosts is His name (Is.48). Finally, Jesus will declare His city to be the City not hidden but be the light of the world (Matt.5:14).

God has prepared for us a City in the state of heaven (Heb.11:16). There will be our living God, with an innumerable company of angels. See to it that you do not refuse Him who speaks now. For it is in a state of listening to the heavenly voice that is your roadmap to find this City of Grace.

Jesus promised that once more everything that can be shaken would be shaken. Therefore, for an unshaken kingdom, *"...let us have grace, by which we may serve God acceptably with reverence and Godly fear"* (Heb.12:28). Let us receive through grace the empowerment to do what truth demands. We must use the whole potential of grace. In carrying our faith, we must act in true commitment to our core beliefs about who God is in shaping our lives, our city, our nation, and this world into an unshaken kingdom.

In the New City, the foundation will be set with *precious stones;* the *pearly gates* will never close; the streets will be *pure gold,* and the face of Jesus will always *shine.* The city of our Lord's presence will be the Church on its knees in search for His presence. Finally, in Rev. 22:3 and 4 lies one of the many desires of my heart: that *we will see His face* in this New City!

"Once more I will shake heaven and earth...and they shall come to the Desire of All Nations, and I will fill this temple with glory...And in this place I will give peace, says the Lord of hosts."

—HAGGAI 2:6-9

The Spirit of Revival = Liberty

WHAT IS the Spirit of revival? How do we start to evaluate what God's desire is in bringing about a great spiritual awakening across our city? The apostle Paul gives us piercing clarity in this issue:

"Now the Lord is the Spirit, and where the Spirit of the lord is there is liberty. And all of us, with unveiled faces, seeing the glory of the Lord as though reflected in a mirror, are being transformed into the same image from one degree of glory to another; for this comes from the lord, the Spirit."
—2 Corinthians 3:17-18

With the Spirit of revival comes the *Spirit of the Lord, and with it Liberty.* For the individual, this liberty is the transformation of spiritual death into spiritual life. Ezekiel 36:25-28 graphically describes this change. *"Then I will sprinkle clean water on you, and you shall be clean; I will give you a new heart and put a new spirit within you; I will put My Spirit in you"* (Ezek.36:25-28). The Lord is giving His people *Understanding* as He did in past awakenings. They see the ruin of our city and the desolate condition it lies in and recognize the need to *repent.* They know the Lord's promise stands today as it always has for those who return to Him and become doers of the Word through Christ.

The Spirit of revival is directly related to the evidence of our faith in God. It is the carrying out of our faith that is *seen by others* that produces the evidence of our beliefs (the weightiness) to change lives. Active faith working through the Holy Spirit is the bridge to our Promised Land of revival. God's work of restoration is a work of the Holy Spirit in and through the lives of those who have been born from above (John 3:3). This is His Spirit of *Wisdom* and *Counsel,* which is being poured out not only upon those with ears to hear but also on those that are doers of the Word.

It is in the power of God's *Might* that this Spirit of revival is born. The same mighty spirit that established the firmament and breathed life out of dust will come again that we may have it more abundantly. This might is the release of God's power without measure to the Church. That release will come through His people as the gifts of the Spirit operate without restraint under the direction of the Holy Spirit in God's love.

Through the full operation of the gifts and ministries that God appoints the revival will bring *Knowledge* of God. Unity will be established as we trust Him for *understanding* and *wisdom* and *guidance* in following His divine appointments. This knowledge and unity will be needed as the church becomes a spiritual lighthouse inhabited by a royal priesthood, offering up spiritual sacrifices acceptable to God through Jesus Christ (Eph.2:20).

This Spirit of revival will also produce a newfound reverence or the *Fear of the Lord.* It will draw the lost, bringing conviction and obedience to the most fragmented of souls; it will bring with it an acute awareness of who God is: a holy God of divine order. It will be a transforming Spirit surging like electricity through the air. When the Fear of the Lord is in the air, there will be no questions such as, "Can this be God?" No, there will be no jesting or folly on that day. Obedience will be paramount. When the sound of that wind comes our only exclamations will be, "Jesus, revive my soul!" "Have mercy on me, O Lord!" And with that, an *afterglow* of joy will follow. For the Fear of the Lord is *pure;* reviving the soul (Psalm 19:9).

The Spirit of revival is seeking the Jesus of yesterday *and* the Jesus of today. The same Jesus who said, "Man shall live by every word that *proceeds* out of the mouth of God," beckons us to know what He is saying to us *for today* (Matt.4:4). It was Jesus who washed the feet of sinners and led the life of a servant; it was Jesus who said, *"If I then, Your Lord and teacher, have washed your feet, you also ought to wash one another's feet"*(John.13:14).

When God sends this mighty outpouring of the Holy Spirit, we will be a true reflection of Jesus. And as the Body of Christ reflects the glory of God with an unveiled face, we are responsible for clothing the naked, rescuing the poor and the widow in their affliction, healing the sick, setting the captives free, giving beauty for ashes, visiting those in prison, dividing our bread with the hungry, and comforting all who mourn (Is.58,62).

I am not saying we should make more dedicated efforts to please God by performing rituals and better works. My plea is for us to turn to God to allow Him to cleanse, restore, and work in us. The Holy Spirit is our agent of restoration. God's work of restoration is a work of the person of the Holy Spirit through love. Demonstratively, the Spirit of the Lord is Jesus Christ in active expression through His Body—His people. It is through a revival such as this that we will find true liberty and be called the holy people, the redeemed of the Lord; *"and you shall be called, sought out, a city not forsaken"* (Isa.62:12). God, grant this to be our testimony!

"The Spirit of the Lord is upon me, because the Lord has anointed me; He has sent me to bring good news to the oppressed, to bind up the brokenhearted, to proclaim liberty to the captives, and release to the prisoners; to proclaim the year of the Lord's favor..."
—ISAIAH 61:1,2

In Preparing for Revival

We must resolve that revival is something God desires in our city, for our generation, and that He has laid it on our hearts to pray for such a time as this. Second, we must come to grip with the fact that the Bible calls us to live a holy lifestyle—humble and contrite. For it is among the humble the Lord dwells. This is where our revival quest begins:

"I dwell in the high and lofty place, with him who has a contrite and humble spirit. To revive the spirit of the humble, and to revive the heart of the contrite ones."
—ISAIAH 57:15

We must seek holiness as our driving force. This is our "forgotten key" toward revival. Pure holiness comes through sanctifying ourselves by making a clear choice to walk with the indwelling of the Holy Spirit with His grace. It comes from taking every thought captive in accordance to the obedience of His will. It comes from *making* Jesus Lord of our lives not just *calling* Him Lord.

Third, we must become a city of prayer. I'm not talking about a trivial pursuit of prayer on your way to work or just before retiring for the night. I'm talking about time spent on our knees until we break through the heavenlies. Have you heard this call? Will you be one of those who push past the mountain peaks into God's eternal presence? When the people of God storm the gates for God with our whole hearts, then revival is imminent. Revival follows extraordinary prayer! History reveals this from past revivals. This type of prayer creates urgency from within us for lost souls, and enables God's manifest presence to spring forth from deep wells.

The fourth action we must take is to read, take inventory, and become familiar with the subject of revival, taking into account what God did in the book of Acts and later revivals of the 1700s and 1800s.

Finally, and most important, we must make a covenant of commitment today with God. *Prayerfully consider signing the Constitutional Revival Covenant and taking the personal revival quiz at the back of this book.* Let's tear it out and tape it to our bathroom mirror. This will bring honor and glory to God as we pray for revival in our lives, for our city, for our nation, and for the world.

In thinking on preparation, do you feel your church would be equipped to handle two hundred or one thousand new converts immediately? If we are convinced revival is just a short season away, we need to train ourselves for God's mighty move to be a rightly fit stone. Let us not fail in recognizing the Spirit of Revival in our midst. Let's become messengers and encouragers of revival. Let's proclaim it! God's word does not return void. Our words and proclamation are powerful also. According to scripture, the spoken word has the power life or death. Proclaim revival in Nashville's city streets! Prayerfully shout out the news of Jesus' imminent return. Let your friends know Jesus stands right at the door.

I plead with you—dedicate yourself to prayer for our city and devote yourself to become a prayer champion. Lead by example. Take relentless prayer time and seek a lasting encounter with God. Jesus will not beg you to spend time with Him. He has already done so much for us. It's up to you to say, "This is the time I'm setting aside for You, Lord." Have you set aside a specific time alone with God today?

It has been said that LOVE equals TIME. "Time spent" with God is "Father earned"—it's the most important aspect of our walk with God. I am a broken record on this issue! We are at a critical turning point on God's timeline. We are on one of two ships on the issues of intimacy and prayer. We are either looking towards heaven on "Glory bound" with our eyes fixed on Jesus, or we're on the Titanic headed for an iceberg. The Lord is so serious about a coming revival that He would do a "reversal of fortune" bringing judgment—if His people, who are called by His name, do not hear his voice for His purposes. The God who saves is the same God who judges! Lord, we need devotion and discipline in our prayer life with You! We are in desperate need of prevailing prayer! May we embrace prayer, oh Lord!

FOLLOW JESUS!

JESUS' disciples had to be with Him and follow Him to experience God at work. Where was Jesus? Spiritually speaking, He was abiding in the Father. He did nothing without hearing from Him! When Jesus wasn't in contemplative prayer, He was in streets—amongst the poor, the sick, and the needy. Where are the poor, sick, and needy of today? Can you hear the cry of the city?

In considering the land where God is at work we must call upon Him, hear His voice, and join Him. That is where His promises await us. That is where God will shape us for His next great outpouring. Just imagine God's people rebuilding God's house upon a foundation of prayer, *takin' it to the streets!*

"Let love be genuine; hate what is evil, hold fast to what is good; love one another in showing honor. Do not lag in zeal, be ardent in spirit, serve the lord. Rejoice in hope, be patient in suffering, persevere in prayer. Contribute to the needs of the saints; extend hospitality to strangers."
—ROMANS 12:9-13

CATCHING THE NEXT WAVE

by Jim W. Goll
Ministry to the Nations

THE EBB AND flow of revival throughout church history has often been compared to that of the waves of the ocean. The tides come in and out with subsequent waves of activity in between. Such it is with God's manifested presence and this wonderful thing called "revival", "the move of God's Spirit" and even "City transformation."

The thing we don't want, is settle in and passively become the stewards of the best of the past. We must press into the heart of God and cry out for a fresh outpouring of His grace in our time! We must continue to cultivate that pioneering spirit that seeks to go where no man has gone before. The question then can be asked, "What does it take to catch the next wave?" To begin to answer that question, let's take a peek at some historic revivals of the past to learn of some of the common characteristics they contain.

FIVE CHARACTERISTICS OF REVIVAL

Let's start this journey by considering five over all characteristics of classic revival. To recognize and catch the next wave, perhaps it will help us to know what some of the characteristics of classic revival in the past have contained.

1. Passionate Denunciation of Sin

There must be recognition that sin is an enemy - not a friend! James 4:4 reminds us, "You adulteresses, do you not know that friendship with the world is hostility toward God? Therefore whoever wishes to be a friend of the world makes himself and enemy of God."

We need a generation of anointed proclaimers like George Whitfield who in the 1700's preached like a lion and people had to listen whether they wanted to or not! Holy violence was often a characteristic of historic moves of God's Presence.

2. Revelation of God's Holiness

I Peter 1:16 tells us, "You shall be holy, for I am holy." Jonathan Edwards preached under this conviction in the 1700's. Many other revivalists did as well. Consider the late Leonard Ravenhill, author of *While Revival Tarries*. It was said that Edwards was consumed with the extraordinary sense of the awful awareness of the Holiness of God.

We need a return of standards of holiness that are not based out of legalistic laws but issues of the heart. We need a fresh holiness movement that actually has the fire of sanctification in it - much like the fire that rested upon the life of John Wesley. People would ask him the question, "How do you gather a crowd?" He would respond by saying, "I set myself on fire and people come to watch me burn!" Oh, we need the fires of Wesley once again!

3. Deep Awareness of the Love and Mercy of God

Romans 8:35-39 encourages with these words, "What shall separate us from the love of Christ? Shall tribulation, or distress, or persecution, or famine, or nakedness, or peril, or sword? Just as it is written, *'For Thy sake we are being put to death all day long; we were considered as sheep to be slaughtered.'* But in all these things we overwhelmingly conquer through Him who loved us. For I am convinced that neither death, nor life, nor angels, nor principalities, nor things present, nor things to come, nor powers, nor height, nor depth, nor any other created thing, shall be able to separate us from the love of God, which is in Christ Jesus our Lord."

It was said that Francis of Assisi, as well as the evangelist D.L. Moody only preached about the love of God. David Brainerd, revivalist to the First Nations People of America, was moved upon by the revelation that the Lord Jesus Christ was a kind and compassionate master. Brainerd would be moved upon with deep distress pleading with his hearers to accept the everlasting mercy of God as tears would stream down his face.

4. Heightened Consciousness of Eternity

Consider with me some of the sermon titles of the fabled Jonathan Edwards:

1. Sinners in the Hands of and Angry God
2. Wrath Upon the Wicked for the Uttermost
3. Eternity of Hells Torments

Revelation 20:11-15 describes this reality as follows: *"And I saw the dead, the great and the small, standing before the throne, and books were opened; and another book was opened, which is the book of life; and the dead were judged from the things which were written in the books, according to their deeds. And the sea gave up the dead which were it, and death and Hades were thrown into the lake of fire. This is the second death, the lake of fire. And if anyone's name was not found written in the book of life, he was thrown into the lake of fire."*

Today, we need a return to the teaching and revelation of eternal judgments of God and the realities of heaven and hell. When was the last time you heard sermon on hell? It's not popular to preach this stuff today—but we better catch God's heart to *plunder* hell to *populate* heaven.

5.   Experiential Conviction of Sin

John 16: 7-8 states, *"But because I have said these things to you, sorrow has filled your heart; But I tell you the truth, it is to your advantage that I go away; for if I do not go away, the Helper shall not come to you; but if I go, I will send Him to you. And He, when He comes, will convict the world concerning sin, and righteousness, and judgment."*

This is God's job - it is part of the job description of the Holy Spirit. Once again, we need God to squeeze our hearts. Notice I used the term "experiential conviction." Perhaps the move of God we need could be termed, "When the Holy Spirit came with conviction!" It was quoted from a scoffer of Whitfield, "I came to hear you with a pocket full of stones to break your head—instead—your word broke my heart!"

Yes, once again, we need a pure move of God like in the United Kingdom in 1859 when men "staggered down" due to the wounds to their conscience! In 1790-1800 in the frontier of rough Kentucky, people would cry out for mercy, as conviction would fall upon them. All I can say is, "More Lord!" Right here, today, in Nashville, Tennessee, or whatever city or nation you reside in.

THREE PRELIMINARY STAGES

Often times we are overly idealistic in our approach to revival. Many times leaders and other sincere believers are so focused on the "big enchilada" (the big tidal wave of gigantic proportions) that they miss the preliminary stages that might just lead to catching the big one!

The Old Testament prophets warned us to "not despise the days of small beginnings." Let's not miss birth in the stable while looking for the King to come riding on His victorious white horse! With this in mind, chew with me on three simple preliminary stages of revival.

1.   An Intense Hunger For Change

As I travel across the nations and denominational lines, I hear one main sound arising from deep within the global body of Christ. I call it hunger pains! I can hear a rumble deep within for change! Here are three little sign posts that the rumbles of hunger are getting stirred up.

a. Recognition of the way things should be.
b. Awareness of how terrible things currently are (Matt. 5:3).
c. Touched personally in your heart concerning these realities with the desire for things to change (Matt. 5:6).

Note: The first sign of "death" is the loss of hunger - you simply do not want to eat - you lose your appetite! On the contrast, the first sign of recovery is the return to hunger or the desire to eat! How hungry are you for more of God, His ways and His presence?

2. Prayer to God to Change Things

The desire for things to change is not enough. It is but the beginning. If it is not turned back towards God through prayer it will eventually result in frustration and then in criticism. Instead, turn desire into *intercession* and move deeper into the stages of revival.

Become a history maker and realize that we have been given keys that open heavens doors by the agreeing desperate prayers echoed from the heart of men and women, boys and girls. Cry out to the Lord for change to come to your life, your family, your neighborhood, and your congregation, your city and nation. Prayer is God's equal opportunity employment card. It does not take a special gift to prayer! It takes a desperate heart!

3. Networking Towards Unity

A third step towards "revival" that puts feet to your hunger and prayer is the relational work of networking resulting in progressive actions in a city or region towards unity. We need each other. Labor for the bond of unity and peace in the body of Christ. Remember that it takes a citywide church to win a citywide war!

I challenge leaders around the world, wherever I go—to get God's view of their assignment. Pastor a city—not just your flock! Come shoulder to shoulder with others in your area and just see what the Lord will do! Come lock arms with other pastors, intercessors and marketplace leaders and do something together for Jesus sake!

Get God's heart for your region and walk with others. The whole context of the teaching of I Corinthians 12 on the body of Christ is not set in the context of one congregation in a city. Remember, it says something like, "Can the eye say to the hand, I have no need of you?" This teaching is set in the context of the "one church with many expressions in a city."

Can Charismatic hands of healing say to the Evangelical shoes of the gospel of peace, "I have no need of you?" Give me a break! We really do need one another. The Calvinist need the Armenians and the Pentecostals need the Liturgical! Heaven help us to identify the redemptive gift of God found in each of the tribes of the Lord's body and learn to cooperate with one another instead of competing!

DEFINING WHAT WE ARE LOOKING FOR

What is this thing called revival? Let's continue to lay a proper foundation by looking at some definitions.

Definitions of Revival from Webster's Dictionary

1. Return, recall or recovery to life from death or apparent death; as the revival of a drowned person. (Revival brings something back to life that is either now dead or seemingly dead. Revival is not something that has never lived at all.)

2. Return or recall to activity from a state of languor; as the revival of spirits. Revival brings a holy shock to apathy and carelessness (Read Isaiah 64:1-3).

3. Recall, return or recovery from a state of neglect, oblivion, obscurity or depression as the revival of letters or learning. Revival restores truth and recalls to obedience that which has been forgotten.

4. Renewed and more active attention to religion, an awakening of men to their spiritual concerns.

Some Foundational Truths

Are your salivary glands getting whetted yet? Are you thirsting for more of Him? Then muse on these following truths and I promise you will truly be aching on the insides like I do for, "More, Lord!"

Revival is the restoration to life, vigor and/or to strengthen something that appears to be dead or is dead. Revival takes that thing that appears to be dead, so that it will be operative or valid again. Revival is necessary to counteract spiritual decline and to create spiritual momentum once again.

Revival includes the conversion of a large number of people in a relatively short period of time. It has been called the wave that carries the faith from generation to generation. When revival reaches its fullness it stirs:

a. The individual which impacts
b. The family which revives
c. A congregation to spread unity, inspiration, and the fire of God to influence
d. The church in a city or region; which then in turn
e. Releases societal change where the Kingdom of God comes on earth

Yes, Revival is the hunger for change. It is an extraordinary move of the Holy Spirit producing extraordinary results. It is an out right invasion of heaven that brings the conscious awareness of God on earth.

Charles Finney stated that revival is nothing more than a new beginning to obedience to the Word of God. A.W. Tozer remarked that revival is that which changes the moral climate of a community. We could thus conclude that it is a work of the Holy Spirit among His own people... What we call revival is simply New Testament Christianity—the saints getting back to normal.

I heard a message by the church historian, J. Edwin Orr, before he graduated to his heavenly reward on The Role of Prayer in Spiritual Awakening. In his stirring straight talk message he stated that a spiritual awakening as a "movement" of the Holy Spirit bringing about a revival of New Testament Christianity in the church of Christ and it's related community. This activity accomplishes the reviving of the church, the awakening of the masses and the movement of uninstructed people towards the Christian faith; the revived church by many or few is moved to engage in evangelism and demonstrating social action.

All I can say, is a loud AMEN to that. Help us to be prepared to catch the next and perhaps the greatest of all the waves of church history combined before the second coming of our Messiah and Lord!

LITTLE KEYS OPEN BIG DOORS!

Those of you, who know me, know the following statement real well! Little keys open big doors! It really is not complicated - it is an issue of a hungry heart! But what are some of these little keys that have been used before, and will be used again to help open the heavens over our homes, neighborhoods, congregations and cities?

Prayer Opens The Way!

Let me share a testimony with you from the Hebrides Island Revival right off the shores of Scotland in 1952. Two desperate women – Peggy & Christina Smith – 84 and 82 years old – were desperate for a revival. They began praying daily from Isaiah 44:3, *"For I will pour out water on the thirsty land and streams on the dry ground; I will pour out My Spirit on your offspring, and My blessing on your descendants."*

They reminded God of His word. Then they began to claim Isaiah 64:1, *"O that Thou wouldst rend the heavens and come down, That the mountains might quake at Thy presence...* The oldest sister was blind, but even in this state she received a vision and proclaimed, *"He's coming! He's coming! He's already here!"* Christina wrote the word from the Lord down and they proceeded to get the word to their minister.

That same night, the Spirit of God fell in a barn where seven young men were praying from Isaiah 62:6,7 where it tells us, *"On your walls, O Jerusalem, I have appointed watchmen; All day and all night they will never keep silent. You who remind the Lord, take no rest for yourselves; and give Him no rest until He establishes and makes Jerusalem a praise in the earth."* Sure enough God came. But He first came in His manifested presence to a group of young teenage boys in a barn!

This began the great Hebrides Revival, which then came under the stewardship and preaching of an evangelist Duncan Campbell. A spiritual radiation zone of conviction of spirit was created five miles in diameter and many souls came to the Lord! But the doorkeepers of that "new beginning" were not professional clergy – they were two elderly ladies who reminded God of His word!

Prayer was the key that used to open heavens big doors in 1952. Perhaps there are some Peggy and Christine's out there today. I have a word for you, "Keep on knocking on heavens doors!" Put in those keys in Jesus name!

The Key of the Prophetic

Another key that has often been used, is the key of the word of the Lord. Today we often refer to this as "the prophetic." The prophetic becomes a powerful tool to open closed minds, closed doors and closed situations. Seek God, get His word, put the key in the door and turn it!

We need a return of "Thus saith the Lord." We need the voice of God that thunders from heaven to earth to break things open. When you hear His voice, it produces faith in the hearer. Then all things are made possible to them who believe. Read the following scriptures and get inspired to call forth the key of the prophetic in your life and city.

1. Deut. 8:3 - man lives by God's Word.
2. Matt. 4:4 - by every Word that keeps proceeding.
3. Eph. 6:17 - the sword of the Spirit which is the Word of God.
4. Luke. 11:52 - we must use the key and not hinder others.

The Key of His Presence

We need His presence more than anything in this life! The one outstanding distinguishing characteristic of God's people is to be His presence among us! It is not as much what denomination you are, what type of faddish clothing you wear. His outstanding characteristic is to be "Emanuel" - "God with us!"

In Exodus 33:12-23, God gave Moses and invitation to step closer into His view. Moses gave his request that God's presence would go with him; he and His people. Thus God revealed a measure of His glorious Presence to him. Do you not want the same? Is this not what it will take for a City to be on It's Knees?

Exodus 25:30 gives us another glimpse into this key of His presence. The fourth station in Moses Tabernacle is the place where the priest would lay out the bread of His Presence (or shewbread). We need our daily bread! We need to eat of this bread at this table in an on going manner. I ask you again, "How hungry are you? Do you hunger for His presence more than anything in this life does?"

WHEN WE CARE FOR HIS PRESENCE

In rounding out this chapter, I want to tell you a dream that has gripped my soul. In January 1999 the Lord visited me with a piercing dream that is helping to set my course of direction right now and I believe is a clear word to His people.

In this dream, I was holding long loaves of bread each wrapped in their own individual napkin. I was holding these loaves of bread close to my chest right over my heart. Then I got our youngest child's (Rachel's) blanket she has had since birth. I now wrapped these loaves of bread in her dear baby blanket. I held the bread close to my heart and just kind of rocked the bread as you would a newborn child.

Then I heard the words, "When My people will care for, cherish, nurture and love the "Bread of My Presence" like a parent does it's new born child - then revival will come." I then found my self awakened out of the dream only to find my arms were held out as though holding and rocking something. I then heard myself prophesying out loud in the bedroom the same words I had just heard in the dream as the sweet presence of the Holy Spirit was lingering over my body. The Lord was emphasizing these words by having them be repeated twice!

This I know - He wants us to cherish, care for and love His Presence. Pray for His presence. Nurture His presence - after all - isn't this what you have longed for all your life? Isn't this what you were made and created for - to be a carrier of most brilliant presence?! Isn't this the answer to the church's cry for help? Isn't this how we catch the next wave?

When will revival come? You got it! When we get up in the middle of the night - do the night feedings, hold the child close to our bosom, and wash the child of new beginnings with the love and compassion - then revival will come! Let His Presence comes forth!

Now I could give you a whole bunch of technical points. But what I want to do is point you to the Heart of God Himself. Remember, the depth of your hunger, is the length of your reach to God! Want to catch the next wave of revival, the move of God in the earth today? Then cherish His presence - then revival will have already come! MORE LORD!

"Brokeness, redemptively, is the precursor to his fragrance being released."
—JIM GOLL

About the Author

Jim Goll is happily married to Michal Ann Goll and originally hail from Kansas City, but now reside in Franklin, TN. (Their new field of dreams). Jim is gifted in the prophetic and intercession and has a passionate heart for God's manifest presence to rain over Nashville. Let it rain, Lord! For more information go to www.ministrytothenations.org

Revival Nashville

by Steven Fry

IT WAS A dark hour for England, during the early stages of World War II, when German forces trapped thousands of British soldiers at Dunkirk. With the enemy all around them, it was either surrender or be pushed into the sea. For Britain's new Prime Minister, Winston Churchill, the situation looked bleak. Precisely at the point of what seemed like utter defeat, the pluck of the people and the courage of their leader were aroused, and the memorable evacuation at Dunkirk became one of the greatest testaments to human valor ever witnessed.

And so began the resistance. One island nation against the phalanx of Nazi evil threatening to engulf the entire Western World.

Today in America, we too face a rising tide of godlessness and secularism. The moral and spiritual struggle in which we find ourselves engaged, has increased in intensity as we have crossed the threshold into a new millennium.

Yet there are bastions of hope scattered here and there in which God has concentrated key spiritual resources; enclaves of significant numbers of believers who've been given strategic assets and unparalleled opportunities to take their stand on the beach, as it were, and begin to re-take the land for Christ.

Nashville is such an enclave. Few cities in America have both the concentration of forces and the communications systems in place to decisively alter the course of the nation. Like the soldiers at Dunkirk, their backs against the sea, we may feel trapped between our own 'sea' of limitations and the forces of moral turpitude. Yet, we can rekindle a holy fire of devotion to Christ on this beachhead called Nashville. For, unlike the soldiers at Dunkirk who had to evacuate, we who have so much at our fingertips, can help to lead a concerted effort to awaken our nation to its desperate spiritual state.

Nashville has a unique destiny. And yet...

In some ways, we as a Church are like the Church at Sardis in the book of Revelation: a reputation for being spiritually alive, yet actually in need of immediate reviving. Such a comparison is not meant to belittle the serious efforts being made at promoting Christian values, question the sincerity of thousands of well-meaning believers, or dishonor the many spiritual leaders in the City who labor intensively to see Christ glorified.

But it is to draw our attention to the subtle ways in which our zest for Jesus is being compromised.

OPTING FOR PROGRAM OVER PRESENCE

Because we are so adept at spinning out resources, we can find ourselves relying on the strength of our gifts and abilities, and not on God's invasive presence. We need to cultivate the kind of heart Moses had who earnestly sought God concerning the Israelites' trek to the Promised Land, *"Unless Your presence go with us, we will not go."* Moses would have rather died a failure in the wilderness, than attempt to do God's work his own way or in his own strength.

ALLOWING OUR SPIRITUAL PASSION TO WANE

We as the Church in Nashville can find ourselves lacking in holy desperation for God. The relative safety of our insular environment has not always produced a prophetic impulse to model kingdom life before the nation—rather, our cocoon has sometimes cushioned us, sedating our sense of spiritual passion. We allow ourselves to drift along with a 'business as usual' attitude; God wants to give us a heart that craves divine intervention.

SUCCUMBING TO THE SUBTLETY OF MIXTURE

One of the great dangers we face comes not from blatant sinfulness, but spiritual mixture. We can love the Scriptures on one hand, but compromise our standards on the other. We can worship sincerely, then pursue innocuous pleasures that rob us of time with our Supreme Pleasure, the Lord Jesus. Relatively speaking, an environment like Nashville is the kind in which the enemy seeks to distract us rather than destroy us; dull our discernment with good things rather than assaulting us with bad things—which over time causes us to miss the best things.

Spiritual mixture in one's life is deceptive. Just enough Christianity to avoid feeling guilty; just enough compromise here and there to neutralize our passion for Jesus. The result? We possess little power in our lives to be like Christ, but never quite awaken to our urgent spiritual need.

We can find ourselves like the Israelites of old, expressing a 'sound' that, as Moses said, is neither the sound of victory or of defeat but the sound of play. Would that it were one or the other. For the sound of victory reveals a people overcoming in God; the sound of defeat a people aware of their need who thus press into God. But the sound of play - there is the danger. For in that place we are neither attuned to God nor aware of our need. We simply drift.

It is an attitude of heart that I attempted to capture in a song called:

Rekindled Flames

It seems so right to buy and sell
Do all the normal things that gently lead to hell
As the song continues, the lyrics point to one solution for such a condition:
The drink that fills I find is still
Doing Father's will with joy and godly zeal.

The Church in Nashville has a destiny in God. There is yet enough critical mass in this city to spark a national explosion of genuine revival. Will we seize such a holy purpose?

God has always been at work preparing a people; a people who, by His grace and power, would arise to their destiny and fulfill His desires; *a people who would allow His kingdom to be expressed through them on earth as it is in heaven.* Yet so many times, through flagrant unfaithfulness or by simply allowing the humdrum of life to numb our spiritual sensitivity, we have fallen short of this high calling. The present yearning for revival is fueled in part by the need to recover this sense of destiny. For too long, we have preached a message to which few listen; too long we have heard the cynic tell us that while he respects Christ, he has little patience with a Church he sees as increasingly irrelevant and divided. Could it be that such dismissals reflect the sad reality that what the world *hears us say* and then *watches us do* don't add up? It is because a great chasm exists between our *message* and our *model* that many realize that it is not just *seasons of refreshing* that we need, but *strategies for reformation.* And it is that longing that must define our pursuit of revival today.

Perhaps we can frame this longing in a different more emotionally charged way. What kind of Church is Christ returning for: a divided body or a spotless Bride? Are we destined to just struggle along as His Beloved, settling for the status quo—a people shadowboxing the same fears and anxieties that so riddle the world, a Church fragmented and disunified?

There are many who love Christ, who desire that He be glorified through His church, who want to express His kingdom rule, and who long for the Body to realize her unity. There are many who fervently pray for the glory of the Lord to be demonstrated through the church until *"all flesh shall see it together"* (Is. 40:5). Yet, we staunchly support such propositions, there is a nagging doubt that it can ever become reality. Year after year comes and goes and though we see marvelous moves of God's Spirit we honestly see nothing that comes close to the awesome revival we talk about. It's still business as usual in the lives of many congregations.

For what kind of church is Christ returning? What will the Church look like at the end of the age? *Like heaven on earth.* It will be a place where the Church in a city worships with one voice; where pastors in a city are of one heart with each other; where each Christian home in a city becomes a haven of rest for unbelievers. In my song, *As In Heaven, So On Earth,* I tried to paint such a picture of the Church as it is in heaven:

> *"Consider a place where a holy race delights to please the Father*
> *As In heaven, so on earth*
> *Where everyone lives to spend himself on the needs of every other*
> *As in heaven, so on earth*
> *Imagine the time when men shall rush to behold His love through each of us*
> *As in heaven, so on earth*
> *Imagine believers flowing as one river to their city*
> *As in heaven, so on earth*
> *Binding the strong man, tending the weak and learning to be His Body*
> *As in heaven, so on earth"*

If this is what the Church will look like at the end of the age, then why not look like this now? For what are we waiting? Now is the time to lay aside every weight that would hinder us from seeing this fulfilled in our generation.

If Jesus taught us to pray, "Your Kingdom come, Your will be done; on earth *as it is in heaven"* He must mean that prayer to be answered. If Jesus is returning for a Bride without spot or wrinkle then that condition must be possible, by His grace, to apprehend. If we can refocus on this destiny, we will know better how to live our lives in the now. If we can rightly see our future, we can correctly prioritize our present. If we can once again grasp his overall purpose and align ourselves to it, then that will in and of itself provide the combustible material which, when ignited by the Holy Spirit, will explode into the flames of revival – a revival that does not necessarily take its cue from the past, but rather is the fresh application of kingdom precepts in the present; a revival that will, in turn, provide the momentum for the Church to confidently confront the emerging world order with the Divine Alternative; a revival that will catalyze the final thrust of world evangelization.

About the Author

Steven Fry is a conference speaker and worship artist who brings a call to revival and a passion for God to the forefront of his ministry. He is the author of the acclaimed musicals *We Are Called* and *Thy Kingdom Come,* as well as such well known songs as *"Oh, The Glory of His Presence"* and *"Jesus, You Are My Life."* To add to his list of anointed CD's, Steve has given the world *Higher Call* and *Fire In the Dark.* More recently, he has released a devotional entitled *I Am: the Unveiling of God*; an inspiring glimpse into the character of God which Moody Broadcasting called one of the best books written about God in fifty years. Steven has just recently released a new recording, *Rekindled Flame,* which calls the church to passionate pursuit of Christ. Steve has also produced *The Storyteller Project,* an evangelism tool combining a dynamic street musical with a literature distribution campaign, designed to get the teachings of Jesus into the hands of millions of people.

A HOUSE OF PRAYER

by Onnie Kirk
When Men Pray

IN 1994, AT the request of Roland Smith, the founder of Mission Omega Ministries, I was invited to attend the Mississippi Valley Prayer Conference in St Louis Missouri. Roland asked if I would be one of the representatives from Tennessee and share what God was doing in our region.

Some of the leaders at this conference were Francis Frangipane, author of *"The Three Battlegrounds,"* David Bryant, the founder of Concerts of Prayer, and Joseph Garlington of Promise Keepers. The first night of the conference there were approximately sixty leaders from around the nation. As each representative spoke there seemed to be one continual theme. *Reconciliation.* Throughout the nation there seemed to be a mandate from the heavenly throne room.

Our heavenly father was calling for the church to be reconciled.

While listening to the representatives speak about what God was doing in their cities, I pondered why the Lord had commissioned me to be at this conference, I asked myself, "who was I to speak on behalf of the capitol city of Tennessee."

Then the time came for me to speak; I spoke about the twenty-four hour prayer chamber that had been established on the twenty-seventh floor of the Stouffer Hotel. The prayer room was a gift to the body of Christ from a group of local Christian businessmen. The room had been established for the purpose of continual intercession over our city. I shared about Nashville's call to the Jewish people and the nation, Israel. (This year our mayor Bill Purcell, along with several other U.S. mayors will be visiting with mayors in the nation, Israel).

It had also been prophesied that Nashville was to be a city of refuge. Today Nashville is home to thousands of Vietnamese, Koreans, Kurds, Ethiopians, Sudanese, Laotians, Hispanics, and a host of Middle Easterners.

The conference in St Louis ended and I began the drive back home to Nashville. My heart was full of the testimonies I heard from around the nation. Somewhere between St. Louis and Nashville the Holy Spirit spoke to me and said, "Call the men of the city together for prayer." I immediately dismissed the Holy Spirit's assignment deciding it was not the Lord I had heard …it couldn't be. It would take time, energy, and money. I had none of these three requirements. Certainly the Lord was not calling me to call the men of Nashville together to pray.

Approximately two weeks later the Lord woke me at around five in the morning. There seemed to be a sense of urgency in his beckoning. I went into my study area and began to pray. I grabbed my bible realizing there was a reason for this summons. As I opened my bible the pages fell open to Exodus 23:17... *"Three times in the year all thy males shall appear before the Lord God."* As I read this scripture I began to weep uncontrollably. I realized it was the Lord who had spoken to me on the way from St. Louis.

I began to repent for ignoring him and asked him what I should do. He gave me his plans for calling the men of Nashville together for prayer. I called for a council of pastors to meet with me to share with them what the Lord had spoken concerning the men of Nashville. The pastors represented the diversity in the body racially and denominationally. I explained to them what the Lord had spoken to me. After they had heard the testimony they were all in agreement, and "When Men Pray" was born.

When Men Pray hosted it first prayer gathering on May 14, 1994, at Pilgrim Emmanuel Baptist Church, in south Nashville. Approximately three hundred men gathered at 6:00 a.m. to pray. Denominational and racial strongholds crumbled in the presence of the Lord. These men represented the Baptist, United Methodist, Catholic, Presbyterians, Pentecostal, Charismatic, Episcopalians, Apostolic and Nazarene denominations. As the Lord's presence filled the sanctuary men cried out to the Lord in humility, asking forgiveness, and repenting of personal and corporate sins. The men of the city interceded on behalf of fathers, families, business, government, and the Jewish people. At the end of our prayer time men embraced and wept. We all rejoiced to see the sprouts of reconciliation begin to break through the crusty religious topsoil of Nashville, Tennessee.

When these tri-annual prayer vigils began we were not aware of the erosion in the spiritual landscape of our region. We were not aware that Tennessee, and it's capitol city, had been birth from the blasphemous loins of Masonic fatherhood. Many of its founding fathers had been members of the Masonic order. During the first hundred years of Tennessee's statehood it was almost impossible to hold a governmental office if you were not a member of the Masonic order.

We are given instructions in Matthew 5: 33-37 that we should not make an oath or make a vow unto anything. The Masonic order defies the word of God by having its converts declare blasphemous oaths.

"Again, ye have heard that it hath been said by them of old time, Thou shalt not forswear thyself, but shalt perform unto the Lord thine oaths: But I say unto you, Swear not at all; neither by heaven; for it is God's throne: Nor by the earth; for it is his footstool; neither by Jerusalem; for it is the city of the great King. Neither shalt thou swear by thy head, because thou canst not make one hair white or black. But let your communication be, Yea, yea; Nay, nay: for whatsoever is more than these cometh of evil."

—MAT.5:33-37

William Strickland who was the architect of our state capitol and a Mason are buried in the foundation of the Capitol building. The burial of his body in the foundation of our state capitol building opened the door to a floodgate of evil. God, forgive us!

The bible tells us we are not to learn the ways of the heathens. The Egyptians and many other pagan cultures worshipped their dead. The burial mounds and pyramids around the world are evidence of this abominable practice. In the Old Testament books of Numbers and Leviticus scripture gives us witness of the dead being defiled.

"And there were certain men who were defiled by the dead body of a man, that they could not keep the Passover on that day and they came before Moses and before Aaron on that day: And those men said unto him, We are defiled by the dead body of a man."
—Numbers 9:6-7,

During the earthly ministry of Jesus all that were dead when Jesus came near were brought back to life. Jesus is our high priest. If he had been in the presence of the dead and they had not come back to life, Jesus would have been defiled.

"If the foundations be destroyed what can the righteous do?"
—Psalm 11:3,

The foundations of Tennessee were defiled through Masonic fatherhood. As a result of this defilement Tennessee became the birthplace of organized racism and prejudice. The Ku Klux Klan was born in Pulaski Tennessee and held its meetings in Nashville. It was Tennessee that gave evolution its entrance into the educational system of our nation through the Scope's Monkey trial in Dayton Tennessee. It was a Masonic Andrew Jackson that established Memphis, Tennessee. In ancient times Memphis was the capitol of Egypt. Throughout biblical history Egypt is generally synonymous with sin. Ironically, Martin Luther King, the drum major of justice and racial equality was killed in Memphis, Tennessee. The city fathers of Nashville have proclaimed her, "the Athens of the south." The Parthenon was built in honor of Nashville's one hundredth birthday and a forty-foot idol of Athena is erected in the Parthenon's main hall. Police reports indicate that Centennial Park is a prime location for heterosexual and homosexual prostitution. These were the same practices of the ancient Athenians.

On April 16, 1998, the Lord allowed tornados to attack the Capitol City of Nashville. Two of the hardest hit areas were the Andrew Jackson Hermitage and Centennial Park. The day after the storm the newspaper printed a picture of the flag flying over the state capitol building. The three stars in our state flag representing West, Middle, and East Tennessee had been cut out by the storm.

I firmly believed the men of this region praying in agreement over our families, churches, businesses, and government provided a prayer shield for our city. The storm hit during rush hour traffic around 4:30 p.m., however, there were no fatalities during the storm. One young man died three weeks later who had been struck by a tree in Centennial Park.

In Ezekiel 22:6, the Lord tells us he is looking for a man who will stand in the gap. In Isaiah 28:6, the Lord decrees strength to them that turn the battle to the gate. When the men of the region gather on one accord to fast, pray, and worship the Lord. The unity and oneness among these praying men send a resounding message to the forces of evil, "You will not prevail in our city!

The Lord has always held men accountable. When Satan tempted Eve in the garden, the question God asked was, *"Adam where art thou?"* (Genesis 3:9). He has ordained men to cover their families. I Corinthian 11:3 reads, *"But I would have you know, that the head of every man is Christ; and the head of the woman is the man; and the head of Christ is God."* Ephesians 6:4: *"Fathers, provoke not your children to wrath: but bring them up in the nurture and admonition of the Lord."*

When the Lord began the world he created one man—Adam. When the Lord destroyed the earth he saved one man and his family—Noah: When man failed again the Lord chose a family—Abraham, Isaac, and Jacob. When that family sinned and went in to bondage in Egypt he brought them a deliverer—a man called Moses. In the book of Isaiah, the ninth chapter, we read about the man-child:

"For unto us a child is born unto us a son is given: and the government shall be upon his shoulder: and his name shall be called Wonderful, Counselor, The mighty God, The Everlasting Father, The Prince of Peace."
—Is.9:6

The men of Middle Tennessee are responsible for being at the forefront of this spiritual battle. As men humble themselves and commit to pray collectively the Lord will strengthen and direct us in the battle.

When the men have gathered three times each year there has been an increase in the Lord's presence. Many have received emotional and physical healing. Some have been delivered from demonic oppression. Others have been filled with the Holy Ghost. We have laid aside our religious garments and asked the Lord to wash us and cleanse us from all of our iniquities. As we have humbled ourselves and prayed, and turned from our wicked ways, he has heard from heaven and is healing our land.

For eight years the spiritual fathers and elders have gathered at When Men Pray to stand in the prophetic gates of our city. At these gatherings proclamations of righteousness, truth, and the fear of the Lord are decreed. As our offerings of praise and thanksgiving ascend into the heavens our heavenly father meets us with his glorious power. He has begun to transform us into 'One New Man.'

This 'One New Man' is consumed with the passion and fire of the Lord. The Joy of the Lord in him is electrifying. He is a living epistle of God's word. The Light of the Lord radiates through him just as it did through Moses and Stephen. He speaks the word of God with power and authority. The presence of the Lord is his only desire. This 'One New Man' is the blood washed progeny of Noah.

Noah and his sons Shem, Ham, and Japheth labored one hundred and twenty years to build an Ark that would carry mankind through the flood. Shem is the father of the Jews and Shemites, Ham is the father of the people of color, and Japheth is the father of the Caucasians. The flood was God's judgment upon mankind because man's heart was continually evil. In the biblical record we read that the last days shall be just as it was in the days of Noah. It must be the reconciled Noahatic Family that builds the Prophetical Ark. This Ark will carry us through the perilous times ahead.

Nashville's economy is flourishing. We rejoice over this visible evidence of reconciliation. However, there is much work to be done in Nashville. Our city ranks in the top ten nationally for sexually transmitted diseases. There is a strong spirit of lust over the city resulting in an increase in sexual perversion. The increase in homosexuality, rape, incest, adultery, and prostitution are evidence of its power. Police reports indicate an increase in domestic disputes and violent crime. The plague of divorce is running rampant in our city. There is a strong spirit of religion that has a form of Godliness but denies his power. This spirit continues to weaken the church.

The Lord is raising up men from every walk of life to stand in the gates of our city. The common bond is a love for Jesus and a willingness to forsake our personal agendas in pursuit of Holiness. The scriptures confirm that the fear of the Lord is the beginning of wisdom. This 'One New Man' the Lord is raising up will have no spiritual superstar. The nurturing of the five-fold ministry, Apostle, Prophet, Evangelist, Pastor, and Teacher will mature him:

"And he gave some, apostles; and some, prophets; and some evangelists; and some, pastors and teachers; for the perfecting of the saints for the work of the ministry for the edifying of the body of Christ: Till we all come in the unity of the faith, and of the knowledge of the Son of God, unto a perfect man, unto the measure of the stature of the fullness of Christ."
—EPHESIANS 4:11-13

Father we pray that Ephesians 4:11-13 will be fulfilled in Nashville. In Jesus' name. AMEN!

In becoming this perfect One New Man we are coming closer to the stature of Christ and are forerunner's in our plight to bring Nashville the Unity, the Peace, the Joy, the Love, and the blessings it so richly must bear as a spiritual beacon in the world.

Just as When Men Pray came into existence for the glory of God, it is in this same way, Nashville will be a light of the world—by first becoming, a city on bent on its knees in prayer.

About The Author

Onnie and Margienell Kirk reside in Bordeaux and currently have eight healthy God-fearing children. Onnie is gifted as a Prayer Champion of the city and leads a ministry for the fatherless called Family Foundation Fund. Anyone who knows Onnie knows his passion for God and integrity to the Lord. He is blessed with "the voice of Moses" as his prayers are heard on high! More information on the ministry can be seen at www.WhenMenPray.com or call 615-876-7170.

Shut in With God

by Becki Fortner

AS A NASHVILLE intercessor of 30 years, my heart both rejoices GREATLY as I see the hand of God stirring a new "prayer movement" in our city! And, at the same time my heart aches with MUCH sorrow and pain as I see the great gaps of prayerlessness throughout the Nashville area. Throughout the many years, I have been used of God to organize, lead, and/or participate in many different types of Nashville prayer gatherings for various purposes of Our Father's heart: Prayer Director at a large local church for 10 years; led midnight Prayer Watches every Friday night for years; organized and facilitated "Churches Uniting in Prayer", a monthly prayer gathering of pastors/ministers/worshippers of all denominations and races from the Nashville area meeting monthly at various churches throughout the city area; organized and facilitated city-wide Prayer Conferences; organized and facilitated city-area Nat'l. Day of Prayer gatherings; Prayer Director for Promise Keepers Regional Clergy Conference and various other conferences and gatherings such as the Sons of Thunder Roundtable; State Coordinator for TN-KY Prophetic Intercessors under the leadership of Bobbie Jean Merck, Founder and Pres. of A Great Love, Inc.; Administrator/Prayer Coordinator for Shirley Stockton's Feed My Sheep Ministries out of Jacksonville, FL; etc.

I was born into a humble Pentecostal home in Memphis, Tennessee, where every night before retiring our family knelt to pray and read The Holy Word together! These memories are the VERY BEST memories of my childhood! Yes, FAMILIES WHO PRAY TOGETHER STAY TOGETHER! However, I am moved to say the most important times of my prayer journey are kneeling in my private closet! The more I have prayed privately, the more I have been drawn by the Holy Spirit to pray privately; THUS the more I desired TO GET SHUT IN WITH GOD IN A SECRET PLACE...as the old Pentecostal hymn goes. (Why would we not RUN to have the HIGH HONOR of being "alone" with Our Best Friend, who is the Great Creator of all the universes and who willingly diminishes himself to our level, the mere dust of lowly man...to merely fellowship and enjoy each other!?) Here is where Our Lord desires for EVERYONE to go every morning 1st thing: to minister unto Him, to be renewed by His love and power, to gain new wisdom, to know Him, and to grow in Him!

As my adult life progressed, I became aware of the vast majority of Christians who never took the time to get alone with Our Lord Jesus, nevertheless join in an announced prayer gathering! I am saddened to say that prayer gatherings would always have the least number of participants present, whereas an announced Covered-dish dinner or some type of a party would easily draw hundreds. Trying to appeal to the masses for prayer gatherings, would take MUCH PRAYER AND FASTING to obtain a "catchy" slogan with a "catchy" purpose...to my dismay! However, at those times I felt I was hearing from the Lord that at least "some of His lambs" would follow after His call, as I would bitterly CRY ALOUD for God to reveal Himself to His precious people: every age, race, profession, economic and social status!

As I led prayer groups, I noticed the Holy Spirit starting every gathering with hymns of praise and worship, and then moving in and out with songs of love and adoration unto The King of Kings! As a matter of fact, many a day in this city from 8am until 3pm, an entire day given unto leading scores of men and women in intercession would go no other direction but the high praises sung unto Our Loving Father!! As I moved into higher levels of intercession, simply praying for others as the Holy Spirit directs, I was led to incorporate MUCH "WORSHIP"! And, as I followed 'hard after My Master," I was soon incorporating in the city prayer gatherings the MUSICIANS, the WORSHIPPERS, the INTERCESSORS IN SONG!! Our God was bringing us together as "ONE" in His heart!

Our Wonderful Lord is SO AWESOME! When he pours out His heart upon His people, He leaves NO ONE out who will receive!! And, I soon discovered Our God was drawing His minstrels EVERYWHERE in this city, Worship City USA! And, His hand began networking me with these dear SINGING WORSHIPPERS! Then, I noticed I was being encircled with these musicians as I was learning we had "one" heart: Our Father's! Our Great Teacher was instructing us that HIS HEART desired to receive our praise and worship together; however, I noticed an EXTRAORDINARY ANOINTING in this city for the worshippers and intercessors to join together!

As the Holy Spirit led me into the importance of "prophetic" intercession, which is hearing the heart of God and then praying His heart "through" in the Spirit and/or declaring it in the Spirit and/or prophetically acting upon it! ("Praying through in the Spirit" means that one prays fervently in the Spirit until there is a release in the Spirit that our work as intercessors, along with The Great Intercessor, is completed, ...or the peace of God overtakes us revealing to us our prayer assignment is completed, or at least the particular part at hand is completed).

ALL MUSIC WORSHIPS SOMETHING OR SOMEONE! And, what one listens to is what he/she becomes! With trembling and a TRUE "Fear of God" upon me, I have witnessed in this city false shepherds stopping the true move of the Holy Spirit...to move in REAL power and TRUE conviction. Not only has prayer been removed from our schools but gradually true prayer has been removed from many churches, until now the churches are TOTALLY unaware of their prayerlessness! (Allowing only a written short prayer that is so "perfectly" worded from pulpits to not offend anyone, whether in large churches or small groups!)...

While sins continue to be covered and hidden to protect "reputations"...to the point that deception has set in SO VERY deeply, these congregations are TOTALLY unaware!! In this religious arena, carnality, which leads to death, has gradually taken over until the Spirit of Death (instead of THE HOLY SPIRIT, the Spirit of Life) even resonates through the notes and tones of the hymns and songs, choirs, and musical groups, even to the point that no one is even aware that this Spirit of Death is ALL AROUND THEM...AND "IN"THEM! These groups have become so accustomed to this carnality until they do not realize they are deceived! Some churches have been bewitched...having been led into hypocritical self-righteousness, full of outward form but devoid of inner spiritual truth and reality! Yes, even the church music "sounds" wonderful to the ear, seducing the listeners, as the lyrics and "sounds" draw the hearers in the soulish realm (because this is the realm in which these worshippers/leaders live.)...but NOT Holy Spirit to spirit! If the Holy Spirit doesn't anoint the music, it is producing death. (One may have 'goose-bumps' by a seducing spirit in the soulish realm, which is NOT produced by the Holy Spirit!) Our Father is 'shouting' forth to HIS PEOPLE to humble themselves and pray with a sincere, Godly sorrow and true repentance, which includes turning from all wicked ways! T H E N, He has promised to hear from Heaven, forgive the sins and HEAL OUR LAND, OUR CITY of NASHVILLE (II Chron. 7:14)!

Even though in our land there is an unprecedented acceleration in lawlessness and wickedness, this has not taken Our God by surprise! There is ALSO an UNPRECEDENTED ACCELERATION in a EXCEEDINGLY GREATER MEASURE of the Spirit of The Living God!!! Something MAJOR is about to happen! We are at the very brink of it! We don't know "what" exactly, how it looks or feels; BUT we know it is GOD!!! And, I see the MUSICIANS WHO ARE FOLLOWING HARD AFTER GOD leading this "MAJOR" move! God is beginning to release a new HEAVENLY SOUND that will be heard around the world .. to bring unto Him His due PURE, TRUE praise and worship!!! EVERYWHERE!!!

In mass large gatherings as well as in small gatherings ...in the inner-city and neighborhoods...as well as on the streets, in businesses and schools, and in taverns and whore houses!! And, as this NEW SOUND is heard, thousands of lost humanity in this city and around the world will fall to their knees that will totally surrender to Jesus Christ, Our Lord and Savior! The PURE, TRUE, HEAVENLY SOUNDS that satan stole are being restored in this Third Day...with the anointing for salvation and healing in HIS GREAT LOVE, like we have never known!!!

I am sensing the hour is LATE! God STRONGLY DESIRES to use every one of His sons and daughters as "prophetic intercessors"!! God wants to use EVERYONE, whether you have a history of prayer and intercession and worship, or NOT!! God delights in using all of His sons and daughters, whether you have been highly successful or have been highly unsuccessful! Our God takes GREAT PLEASURE in using the "most unlikely" to confound the wise of this world! All of Heaven is responding and erupting to the purposes of God in this 3rd Day!! Our Loving Father is EXTRAVAGANTLY pouring forth the culmination of HIS BLESSINGS AND ANOINTINGS of the generations past and present upon whosoever will decide to join in His Army of Worshipping Prophetic-intercessors...for the Great Harvest of S O U L S!!! Rightly blessing Our Commander and Chief with the obedience to the first and greatest commandment: Deut. 6:5 *"...to love the Lord Our God with all our heart, soul, mind and strength!"* And, then in obedience to the second: *"...to love your neighbor as yourself!"* Then, *"...on these 2 commandments hang all the Law and the Prophets!"* Thus, we prove to Him that we truly love Him, when we obey His commandments (John 14:15)!

I praise God and sincerely support the scores of His newly appointed Nashville PRAYER leaders and warriors joining with the older persevering, faithful ones...in every zip code of this city and all the surrounding areas...a GIANT move of prayer that is sweeping our city!! The devil will not render this city helpless! Our Jehovah God is Faithful and True!! He is establishing A 'JESUS' revolution! YOU can elect to join, asking the Holy Spirit to ignite His fire in your heart! And, if you are already a loyal worshipping intercessor, you can elect to ask the Holy Spirit to stir the flame within to a BLAZING TORCH, with an ever increasing anointing and empowerment combined with true humility, wisdom and purity!! OUR LORD JESUS IS CALLING YOU BY NAME!!! Get in the harness...begin on your knees!

The old Pentecostal hymn, "Shut in With God," still rings true:

"Shut in with God, in a Secret Place!
There, in His beauty, beholding His grace!
Gaining NEW power to run in this race!
OH! I love to be shut in with God!"

GOD SEES THROUGH COLOR

How a White Guy Became a Black Preacher by Crossing Racial and Denominational Lines
by Pastor Steve Simms

ONE DAY IN November 1999, my wife, Ernie, and I came into our office to check our messages. We pushed the play button and heard the voice of a new friend of ours, Dr. Larry Britton, who is the editor of The Whole Truth, which is the national magazine of the Church of God in Christ (COGIC), America's second largest black denomination. He said: "Steve, I want you to write an article for the March 2000 issue of The Whole Truth on 'racial reconciliation in the new millennium'." Ernie and I both began to weep. It was a "God" moment and we were overwhelmed and in awe. We didn't know anyone in COGIC except Pastor Britton and a few of his members. Yet here was an open door. Ernie prayed fervently for me and God allowed me to write the following article.

The Article—"Racial Reconciliation: A Possibility in the New Millennium"

The Creator made His pots, various shades of pots, and filled those that were willing with the gold and treasures of salvation and set them in His shop. Pots with eyes, and ears, and mouths. The pots saw each other and saw themselves and realized that some pots were similar shades to themselves while other pots were darker or lighter than they were. So the pots moved about and got together with similar pots. The group of lighter shaded pots began to laugh at the darker pots and the darker pots made fun of the lighter pots. There was much cruelty among the groups of pots, much hatred. The Creator wondered why His pots treated each other so badly, based only on their color. "Look at the gold and treasures inside each other," He said. But the pots wouldn't take their eyes off the colors.

So the Creator began to crack the pots. And the treasures and gold were exposed sparkling and dazzling! The pots were amazed that they carried within themselves such precious gifts and that the pots of the other color did as well. In every person is a treasure. In every true Christian lives Christ, the hope of glory. God wants us to look beyond the color and find the glory.

Genuine, heartfelt, racial reconciliation is based on seeing the treasures in people of a different color—looking beyond skin color to the riches the Creator has placed within. I love to see the glory of God on a saint's face when the anointing falls. In moments like that, I can't see his color or gender—I just see the treasure and fall in love with Jesus in my brother or sister. Racial awareness flees before the glory of God.

A few months ago a friend of mine who pastors a racially mixed church in Las Vegas, invited me out to hold a series of meetings. The anointing fell and no one seemed to notice what color anyone was. We just saw brothers and sisters in Christ. Racial awareness fled before the glory of God.

In 1906 at Azusa Street, Bishop Seymour embraced all people. And God sent the great Holy Ghost revival in a racially mixed group. One of the early Azusa members said, "The color line was washed away in the blood." I was asked to preach recently at a COGIC congregation in Nashville. The glory of God fell and I loved everyone in that congregation and I felt like they loved and accepted me as well. My wife, Ernie, and friends, Dale and Melanie, and I laid hands on and prayed for many members of that congregation. We hugged them, cried with them, told them we loved them--simply because God cracked us and blessed us with His love for them. And they let their treasures and love flow to us. Racial awareness fled before the glory of God.

God gave us color to beautify us, not to divide us. Our race is not black or white or yellow or red. If you are reading these words, you are a member of the human race! And if you are saved, you are a member of the greatest race on earth--God's amazing grace race! Heaven bound. Part of the body of Christ along with every believer on the planet. We are family. Sure someone of another color has hurt you. Most of us have been. But we have also been hurt by people of the same color as well. God wants us to love and forgive those who hurt us. When we are hurt, our pot cracks a little, and God's treasure, Jesus, will shine through us, if we allow Him to.

It has been 2000 years since our Savior was born. May He give us eyes to see and a heart to embrace the treasures He has placed in our Christian brothers and sisters. May we reach out in love to those of a different color in this new millennium. And may racial awareness fade before the glory of God!

BACKGROUND

I was saved in 1970 and baptized in the Holy Spirit in 1971. I went to a Charismatic Seminary, Melodyland School of Theology in Anaheim, California for a year and then transferred to Memphis Theological Seminary and finished in 1977. I became a Cumberland Presbyterian pastor for a few years and have been non-denominational every since. I have pastored about 10 years of my adult life. The past ten years I have been a professional motivational speaker. I moved to the Nashville area 11 years ago and married my wife, Ernie.

About 3 years ago we both began to be stirred up by God. Financial struggles began to plague us. We began to long to know Him better. Ernie began praying regularly with several prayer partners. I began reading everything I could find about the Azusa Street Revival and about early Pentecostalism.

We began to feel led to conduct a weekly "miracle meeting" in Murfeesboro and God confirmed it with an amazing series of confirmations. I called a friend who lived in Murfreesboro and he gave me Pastor Adam Swanson's number. Adam (a white brother), who pastors in Murfreesboro, offered his church to us and we began the meetings. Adam became a great prayer partner for us. Although we never had large crowds in the Murfreesboro meetings, we began to see the power of God and learned how to flow in the Holy Spirit. We held the weekly meetings for about a year.

One night Adam and I were the only ones there. We began to pray for each other to have a healing anointing. We embraced and were so moved by God that we held each other weeping. When we finally opened our eyes a dear sister had walked in. She went to the kitchen, got a bucket and washed the feet of both of us.

About the summer of 1999, Ernie received several prophetic words. Once at Abounding Grace Church in Williamson County, Sherrie Turner, a black sister from St. Louis, spoke over her, "God is about to show up and show out in the lives of you and your husband." The presence of God was so strong; Ernie and several ladies who were also praying with her began to weep. Around the same time, a sister told Ernie that she and I were going to go to a 'spiritual Disneyland' and never come back." Another sister heard that God was taking us to a lavishly overflowing banqueting table.

THE DREAM

One morning, (late summer or early fall of 1999), Ernie began to tell me about a dream. She had dreamed that I was passionately preaching in a black church and that I was surrounded by fire. As I was thinking about the dream I remembered that when I was in seminary in Memphis, I had felt a leading to approach the Church of God in Christ and see if I could be a pastor in their denomination. Suddenly the Holy Spirit spoke to me and said, "You never acted on that leading." I felt so convicted that I picked up the Nashville Yellow Pages called every Church of God in Christ in town. But except for some answering machines, no one answered.

To the answering machines I said something like, "Hello, I am a white minister and feel like God wants me to become part of the Church of God in Christ. Can you help me?" No one returned my call.

Finally, I called the COGIC headquarters in Memphis and someone gave me the home phone number of Pastor Larry Britton. I called him and he invited me to come to a prayer meeting at his church and to talk with him afterwards. As I walked into King Temple, people were prostrate on the floor and crying out to God with their whole hearts. I was very moved. Afterwards I began to tell Pastor Britton what God was doing in my heart. He encouraged me and invited to visit his church on a Sunday morning.

PROPHESY AT KING TEMPLE

As my wife, daughter Amelia, and I, entered King Temple on Sunday morning, we were a little self-conscious so we sat toward the back. We may have been the only white people there. The service was powerful-- anointed worship, great preaching. In the middle of his sermon Dr. Larry Britton left the pulpit and began to lay hands on people. Everybody stood up. I closed my eyes to savor the presence of God.

Suddenly I felt a hand on my head and heard Dr. Britton praying for me. As he walked away a sister, Eucretia Johnson, came up from be hind me and said, "The Lord would say to you. Great doors are opening for you. I am sending you to a great and mighty people. You will see again the great things you have seen in the past." (When I was in college in the 70's I was privileged to witness dozens of people getting saved, delivered from additions, and baptized in the Holy Spirit.) As she walked away I unintentionally fell back in the pew and sobbed for ten minutes.

CONFIRMATIONS

During this time I was praying regularly with Steve Allen, pastor of Oak Hill Assembly of God. He helped counsel me and pray through. Once after praying with him about direction for my life, I picked up the magazine, Pentecostal Evangel, at his church. When I opened it up there was a picture of COGIC Elder Larry Chrisman along with his Assembly of God counterpart in Shelbyville, Tennessee. Elder Chrisman is now my "District Superintendent" in COGIC.

Ernie is a consultant and trainer and has a client in Shelbyville. As she was meeting with a lady with this client, the lady told her she had to leave to go to revival. Ernie asked her which church. She told her Bright's Temple Church of God in Christ with Pastor Larry Chrisman. Ernie asked her if she knew Pastor Larry Britton and she said he grew up next door to her. For several months after meeting Pastor Britton, Ernie and/or I kept meeting people who knew him!

Once Adam Swanson and I were in his father's business in Murfreesboro. As we walked pass a trash bin Adam saw an art easel had been thrown away and asked me to fish it out. As I got it out I saw an upside down license plate. I picked it up and turned it over. It read "Church of God in Christ." I keep it in my office. Before the dream Ernie began to feel a desire to feed the poor in Murfreesboro. She called a friend who lives there and asked her if she knew someplace to help feed the poor. The lady told her to call a friend of hers named, "Sara Armstrong." Ernie called Sara and she and I went to Murfreesboro to pray with Sara. After we prayed awhile, Sara mentioned she belongs to a Church of God in Christ. Ernie asked her if she knew Pastor Britton. Sara said she had been with his wife the night before. Sara has driven from Murfreesboro to help us with our new COGIC church in Franklin many times. She and her husband, Odell, are some of our best friends.

PREACHING AT THE TEMPLE

After I had known Pastor Britton a couple of months, he called me and Ernie answered. He told Ernie he wanted to ask me to preach at his church the coming Wednesday night. When I picked up the phone he said the Lord told him to ask me to preach on Sunday instead. That Sunday I was so excited. It was my first time to preach in a black church. I sat up front and felt great freedom to worship God. I clapped, danced, and shouted. Once I opened my eyes and saw my own hand raised. I did a double take because at first it looked like my hand was black.

After the service I told Ernie, "It's a miracle. For the first time in my life I had rhythm." Ernie replied, "The miracle is that you thought you had rhythm. She said I was clapping off beat, dancing out of step, and swaying the wrong direction. God blessed the service powerfully. Dale and Melanie Jackson, Ernie, and I got to pray with dozens of people. We were blessed and surprised by people wanting to hug us and by them telling us how glad they were to have us.

BECOMING OFFICIALLY COGIC

Ernie and I continued to talk with Dr. Britton about how we could officially become COGIC. He called Bishop James Scott, his Bishop and introduced me to him over the phone. Bishop Scott asked me to come and preach for him in Chattanooga on a Saturday night, which I did. It was a great service and Dale, Melanie, Ernie, Amelia, Spike Blake, and I were all very well received. Bishop Scott asked me to come back in a couple of weeks and meet with his official board, which I did. He had me tell the board what God was doing in my life.

I told them about Ernie's dream and about my desire in seminary to become COGIC. I told them I wanted to start a multi-racial COGIC church in Franklin, near my home. After I finished, one brother said, "If God sent him, we want him. I move we receive him." Someone said, "Second." The Bishop took a vote and it was unanimous. Before I knew it they were all hugging me and welcoming me to the Church of God in Christ.

After we all sat down, one brother looked at me and said, "You do, by the way, believe our doctrine." I was happy to say "yes" to that. A little later that day, they brought me before the pastors and other leaders of the "jurisdiction" (which includes about 40 churches). After the Bishop told them how God and how led me to them and how they had commissioned to start a multi-racial COGIC congregation in Franklin, they gave me a standing ovation and I believe everyone in that room hugged me and welcomed me. These weren't cool; polite hugs, but warm and enthusiastic. The COGIC has given me the warmest reception I have ever had from any group of people in my life!

GOD'S GLORY AND GRACE AT COGIC

We started God's Glory and Grace COGIC the first Sunday of May in 2000, with Ernie, Amelia, and I, Dale and Melanie Jackson, and Spike Blake. And we have been richly blessed with the presence of God in our midst. Almost every service someone is deeply touched. We've seen God work in many ways. Our welcome and support form our COGIC family has been awesome. Two Churches of God in Christ have come to Franklin to hold services for us. Two COGIC churches have given us money to help us get started. The Bishop and the Jurisdiction have given us money. Two COGIC churches have released a member to be a part of our church. Several COGIC pastors have invited me to preach for them. Most of them are praying for us.

We have made some wonderful and lifelong friends in our new denomination. Ernie recently said to me, "Steve, I think we now have more black friends that we do white." And I think that is correct. Our church has been blessed with people who want to serve and minister to hurting people. After every service we have time for prayer when anyone can get prayed for by our members. Often during this time words of knowledge or prophecy comes forth and like the Scripture says the secrets of people's hearts are laid open and they are able to receive comfort and healing.

Last summer we were allowed to regularly visit the Boy's & Girls Club after school program. We brought the kids hot-dogs, played games, sang worship songs, prayed with them, and just hung out with them. We have also been going door-to-door in inner-city Franklin and asking people if we can pray for them. Most people say sure. As we hold their hands and pray, in their living room or on their front porch, people are often moved to tears.

OUR VISION

We believe God's desire is for all of His people to be one (see John 17). Our desire is to have people from various races and denominational backgrounds passionately loving one another. We want to see God use us in Franklin, TN, as a model of racial reconciliation and in the COGIC denomination as well.

Our vision is not for a huge church. Once our church gets to 150 or so members, we envision sending out a racially mixed group to start another COGIC church. We would like to plant dozens of multi-racial churches.

A CHALLENGE

I believe God's special blessing is on people whom cross racial and denominational lines. For years as a white pastor, I used to try to get black people to come to church. Some would visit, but no black brother or sister ever stayed. God showed me that I was wrong to wait for other people to cross the racial line and come to me. He has shown me that I must be the one to cross barriers and be a part of my black brothers' and sisters' church.

Black and white preachers often preach in other's pulpits. What I believe God wants is for black and white preachers to exchange members. I encourage you to go visit a church of another race and see what God will do. Praise His holy Name!

About The Author

God has called Steve and his wife to a ministry of racial reconciliation. He is now teaching in a COGIC Bible School. He has been on several TV broadcasts. "God is amazing me with open doors. We have started a COGIC congregation in Franklin (May of 2000). We meet at the Senior Citizens Center. Me and a few other people have been going door to door in inner city Franklin neighborhoods and asking people if we can pray for them. Ninety percent of people will let us pray with them on the spot. We've been able to minister to many people right in their living rooms or on their front porch. God is good all the time."

REDISCOVERING COMMUNITY

by Pastor Jerry Bryant

AS A YOUNG believer I experienced living in the radical Last Days Christian community in Woodland Hills, Ca. One of the things that I learned there was that community requires openness, transparency, confrontation and disclosure. In other words, one couldn't carry an agenda and live in isolation. It was hard to hide and harbor an offense. The nature of community required everything remain in the light. There was no separation because of title or financial status. We had found relationship free from leverage. Unity was the basis for harmony.

In a culture filled with diversity of gifting, religious expression and individuality, it is hard to capture the passion of community, even though it was a meaningful New Testament lifestyle. The truth of Christian relationship is best displayed through commitment. Winston Churchill said, "Men occasionally stumble over the truth, but most of them pick themselves up and hurry off as if nothing happened."

Amidst the business of the pursuit for success where does one take time or interest in cultivating that which was modeled by the early church? As one man said, "It is easy to spend too much time doing church, and not enough being the church."

In the 70's, I was a "JESUS PEOPLE." As I recall, the mark of the Jesus movement was that our personal time was God's time. After the necessary work and time in cultivating relationship and caring in families our time was His to use as He saw fit. Believe it or not, we really believed that!

We had a sense of DESTINY and PURPOSE for our generation and discovered that what you belong to shapes your character, and character shapes your destiny. There was no price to high to pay.

In a city on its knees, we are re-discovering Christian community. There is an openness to share a common cup again, to spend time connecting with divine purpose. The result of walking in light is expressed in humility before God and each other. We are re-discovering our need for intimacy. As we find God approachable and accessible, we also find each other in that light.

The destiny of our city is indeed unfolding. There is much hidden treasure in this city to be revealed in committed relationships disclosed through unbridled worship—worship with out limit and unified prayer. Let's allow God to mold our character through truthfulness and belonging.

About the Author

Jerry Bryant is Senior Pastor at Vineyard, Nashville. He and his wife, Cindy, have two grown children. Pastor Jerry was pastor of Last Days Community with Keith and Melody Green. He was a pioneer in the '70's as a host of Jesus Solid Rocks nationwide radio broadcast.

THE NORTH GATE

by Tony Woodall

A WELL OF LIVING WATER

IN 1784, PIONEERS from North Carolina and Virginia settled in what is known today as Hendersonville, Tennessee. Two families, the Daniel Smiths and 20 year old James Sanders (who would later marry and have 4 children) were sent as military surveyors to scout out the land. However, after arriving their industrious hearts were soon captured by the fertile soil along the banks of Drakes Creek and the opportunity for their children to live in a community that would be dependent upon the divine providence of God. During these years Sumner County was governed by a group of leaders known as the Quarterly Court who governed the people based on moral values as expressed by the Bible. Only fifteen years after God founded this community, a move of God's Spirit was welcomed and received into our city. This period of time was later called the Great Revival of the West. In late October of 1799 a meeting took place at what is now known as Beech Cumberland Presbyterian Church in Hendersonville next to Beech High School. William McGee, an unusually fervent man, led the meetings. This Sumner County meeting initiated an upswing of spiritual enthusiasm and awareness. In the summer of 1800 a fiery Methodist, John Page, successfully stoked the smoldering spiritual zeal in the area. In Sumner County the coals burst into flames. A month later, William McGee began to plan a five-day meeting at Drakes Creek Meeting House. This building was located at the end of Hendersonville's first road, Sanders Ferry Road, in an area we now call Sanders Ferry Park (land that was given by James Sanders). He was assisted by four other local ministers and over one thousand people were in attendance. By late summer the Baptists, Presbyterians, Methodists and the Reforms had joined together to hold one successive revival after another. The crowds swelled to over five-thousand (an L&N Railroad Production in 1866 showed our city with only 36 inhabitants). Meetings that customarily lasted for days went on for weeks. Worshippers exceeded the capacity of any and every building, so services were moved outdoors. Young Methodists circuit riders on horses set this region on fire with their bold sermons and willingness to die for their God (many of them did while on the road). Their revival sparked the spread of spiritual life into Tennessee, Kentucky and surrounding areas.

MUDDY WATERS AND THE WELL IS CAPPED

At the same time that God was transforming the lives of the city's population however, there were three practices being participated in by many people in the Church that were not repented of nor abandoned. One was the practice of slavery, second was Freemasonry and the third was the expulsion of the Indian (Native American) nations. At one point in our city's history, there was one slave to every two free persons. The geographical center of the slave trading industry in our city was located at the intersection of Long Hollow Pike and Shackle Island Road (named after the locations major activity, the "shackle-ing" of slaves). Many in the church today are not comfortable identifying Freemasonry as an evil force. However, research into it's foundational rites and practices show it's origination from ancient Egyptian and Babylonian occultism do involve the activity of demonic forces. The expulsion and murder of the Indian peoples was an atrocity that was done under the religious imagery of the "chosen people" being led by God into the "promised land" and defeating the "enemy" that is in the land.

The good fruit of the Great Revival of the West was experienced into the early 1820's. Morality was at an all-time high and our Sumner County communities were known for their fervent zeal and commitment to God. However, the (1) humility, the (2) fervent faith, the (3) cooperation of church leaders, the (4) unity of God's people and a (5) hunger for God's presence in time gave way to (1) religious pride, (2) trust in man's ways, (3) competition for converts and credit, a (4) divisive spirit among God's people and (5) self-pleasure. The well of Living Water that flowed so freely from our city to the surrounding communities had been capped. The move of God's Spirit had been quenched.

HENDERSONVILLE TODAY

History through man's eyes would tell us that Daniel Smith and James Sanders founded Hendersonville. However, God says that, *"For by Him (Jesus) all things (Hendersonville) were created: things in heaven and on earth, visible and invisible, whether thrones or powers or rulers or authorities; all things were created by Him and for Him."* Colossians 1:16. Since Hendersonville belongs to Jesus and was created for His purposes, we must then receive revelation from God about His purposes for our city. So what are those purposes and where are we today as a city in relationship to God and His redemptive purposes for us. God is continually releasing revelation to His people about the many purposes that belong to Hendersonville. However, I believe that two of them have eternal significance for us as a city today.

God has called Hendersonville to be a city that produces and trains strong, courageous, industrious and pioneering young men and women (like James Sanders who founded Hendersonville at age 20 and the young Methodist circuit riders that set this city ablaze with their zeal and commitment) for the purpose of advancing God's Kingdom through the specific ministries of worship, healing and the proclamation of the Gospel throughout the world but specifically in Greater Nashville.

God has called Hendersonville to be a well of Living Water, a River of God's Presence, that people from all over the Greater Nashville region come to for refreshing and reigniting.

God's call on our lives as the Church of Jesus Christ in our city is to cooperate with the Holy Spirit as He removes all sinful hindrances that stand in the way of His purposes being fulfilled and the re-establishment of our City Father's original intent for our city. Again, I realize that there are many sins that we as a city have committed. However, after years of prayer and seeking God for revelation about those hindrances, I believe the following "city sins" have crippled our city from fulfilling its destiny.

City Sins (Principalities)	What we see…(Strongholds)
Self Pleasure	greed, lust, addictions, rebellion, complacency, racial prejudice, laziness, divorce, abandoned children, sexual perversion, drunkenness, ungratefulness
Social Pride	competition, intimidation, discouragement, vengeance, gossip, vanity, extravagance, self-exaltation, woundedness, elitism
Religious Pride	judgementalism, criticism, cynicism, closed mindedness, stubbornness, division, envy, strife, arrogance, gossip, spiritual blindness, elitism, decrease, weak leadership, haughty spirit, bitterness, unbelief, fear
Power & Control	elitism, racism, shame, guilt, discrimination, condemnation, fear, manipulation, violence, corruption, hatred, unforegiveness, self-idolatry
False Religion	lying, unbelief, cults, New Age, satanism, white-magic, fear denial, ancient spirituality, false teaching, entertainment, legalism, conformity

It has now been approximately 175 years since Hendersonville has experienced a city-wide move of God's presence that has widely effected the unchurched as well as the churched. God speaks of geographical locations having the opportunity to accept His truth or reject it. Cities that accept His Truth are blessed, but cities that reject His Truth speak curses on themselves.

"If anyone will not welcome you or listen to your words, shake the dust off your feet when you leave that home or town. I tell you the truth, it will be more bearable for Sodom and Gomorrah on the day of judgement than for that town."
—MATTHEW 10:14-15

I know that many of you have been living in and praying for this city much longer than I. I and many other newer residents are truly grateful for your love for the city and willingness to labor on its behalf. I submit this to you only because I, like many of you, believe that our city is at a crucial time in it's history. We now have an opportunity to cooperate with the Holy Spirit as He heals our city or to reject God's hand and leave our children and grandchildren to pay the price. May God give us power and humility to repent and say yes to God.

Laboring with you for Nashville...Tony Woodall
—II CHRONICLES 7:14

FROM THE REVIVAL JOURNAL

If (all the things Jesus did) were written down, I suppose that even the whole world would not have room for the books that would be written.
—JOHN 21:25 NIV

Blessed are you, Oh Lord our God, King of the Universe, Who has preserved us, Who has sustained us, Who has enabled us to reach this season.
—TRADITIONAL JEWISH PRAYER

In every crowd, there are people, each with their individual stories, desires, dreams and hurts. Jesus, omnipresent, omnipotent, is ministering to each person, taking care of as many things as they are able to turn over to His care.

In every great event, there are many ministers on earth, and in the atmosphere, accomplishing bookworthy tasks, praying earth-moving prayers, seeing results worth of print.

Our attempts to relate what happens in even a moment in time are encumbered by our physical restraints. We do not have enough paper, enough time; we cannot see, comprehend, know all that has gone into even one moment.

The August 6 Belmont Rivers youth group did not exactly have a stellar beginning.

It was a pretty evening, and the group decided to meet outside. As they stood in the parking lot, deciding where to go, a white van drove up and stopped. The passenger door flew open, a teenage girl jumped out, bent her head back into the van, yelled, "Shut up!" to her mother, slammed the door and turned to us. Shannon had arrived at youth group.

Shannon and her brother were rebellious. Their single-parent family was the product of a difficult divorce.

"Flood" that night was perhaps not boring, but definitely "low-key," "laid back." They decided to meet in the meadow next to Drake's Creek. Worship consisted of three songs hardly anybody sang. None of the older kids had shown up (the oldest present was 14). Tony's teaching was described later as "good but not exciting."

In the midst of it all sat Shannon, her face like cement. "It was obvious," Tony recalled later, "that she did not want to be there."

It was in a closing activity in which Shannon was supposed to "bless Tony in the name of Jesus" that the Spirit fell. Shannon had just screwed up her face and protested, "I don't know what to say!" when, perhaps in answer to her dilemma, the Spirit baptized her. It hit her so heavily, she could barely stand. She began crying and smiling, gasping, gulping, clawing the air. She reached over and grabbed Tony, trying to keep from falling. When she touched him the surge of power almost knocked him off his feet. "Can you feel that, Shannon?" he asked her.

"Yes!" she said, excited. "What is it?"

"It's the Holy Spirit!"

At Tony's direction, other kids lined up for Shannon's prayers. Each time Shannon extended her hand towards one, they would immediately fall to the ground. One boy lay on his back prophesying. Bonny Jobe was out for 2 1/2 hours, had to be physically carried to her car and dressed for bed.

Two years before, Kathryn Royster, then 16, had given Tony a scripture after the Holy Spirit had fallen on the Community Church youth:

"I will pour out my Spirit on your offspring...They will spring up like grass in a meadow, like poplar trees by flowing streams."
—ISAIAH 44:3,4 NIV

"You're seeing some of this tonight," Kathryn said. "But you will see a lot more in a couple of years."

The parents, wandering over to see what was taking so long, found a little group in the meadow, next to the stream, plastered by the Holy Spirit.

Since that time, the youth, baptized in the Holy Spirit, minister to each other. One lays hands on another asking for prayer, and another quickly takes position behind "to catch." They are overwhelmed by intercession for their schools, receive visions, words and scriptures. Parents report changed lives. God has used the youth as "fire starters." Other churches visit the meeting, coming away drunk with the Spirit. The Spirit graciously fell when they ministered at Belmont Central's youth group, even before any hands were "laid on." Central reports lives are already being changed.

Some adults have gotten hit too—if not at church, then at cell group watching a video, at Pensacola, at the Brown's house, during a visit from a minister brought from Florida, from England or Ohio.

A group of prophetic intercessors have begun to pray. After they met the first time, a barrier seemed to splinter at the weekly Saturday night meeting; visitors came, worship was heavenly, the Spirit fell.

When some of the youth began fretting because they were not feeling the Spirit as strongly as they had at first, Tony spoke to them of loving Jesus just for Himself, not for the charismatic fireworks. That night, Shannon wrote on the blackboard, "God is good all the time."

On November 12, Tony told the youth, Bring your friends next week. Aaron's going to give his testimony, and kids are going to be saved in this very room."

The next Tuesday in obedience, the kids showed up with friends in tow. After Aaron's talk, visitors stood for prayer. The Holy Spirit fell. By the end of the night, one girl lay in a back room, eyes closed, having a vision of Heaven.

"Everyone's loved! Everyone's happy!" she was saying.

"Is that your friend?" I asked Shannon.

"She's my best friend. We used to do drugs together. She went to church once and said she'd never go again. I really felt like she was supposed to come tonight."

That same night, Emily Smith, one of the original youth group, related the following—every day, without warning, seemingly out of context, a still, small voice speaks unmistakably to her heart. It's message never changes: "I am coming soon."

The following was compiled by the hungry church youth and staff in Hendersonville, and is listed as a valuable resource to recognize the prayer strategies laid which prepared the road to Revival.

DEMOGRAPHICS OF HENDERSONVILLE

Hendersonville Total Population

1990	Census	36,841
1993	Estimate	39,135
1998	Projection	43,500

Hendersonville Population by Age

0–18 years	27%
18–24 years	9%
25–44 years	35%
45–64 years	21%
65 years & up	8%

Hendersonville Population by Race

White (96.8%)	35,652
Black (2.3%)	863
American Indian (0.2%)	86
Asian (0.5%)	190
Other (0.1%)	51

Religious Community

16 Denominations

40 Congregations

Total Membership Less than 15,000 Members

IDENTIFICATION OF PRINCIPALITIES AND STRONGHOLDS

Principalities	Strongholds
Religious Pride	Judgementalism, criticism, cynicism, close mindedness, stubbornness, division, envy, strife, arrogance, gossip, complacency, woundedness, blindness, elitism, decrease, bitterness/unforgiveness, intellectualism, Ahab & Jezebel

Strategy

A youth representative from all sixteen denominations in the city of Hendersonville must come together in the name of Jesus and:

1. Repent
2. Forgive
3. New covenant

False Religion | Lying (no truth), unbelief, control (self god), masonry, Bahai, satanic/white magic, Indian Spirituality, New Age, Jehovah's witness, false teaching, entertainment, deception, distraction, legalism, fear, denial, conformity

Strategy

God's intention for Hendersonville was that it should be led by divine providence. For this spirit to be recaptured we must pray in the name of Jesus against the spirit of false religion.

Pride | Competition, intimidation, discouragement, vengeance, extravagance, gossip, vanity, self exaltation, woundedness, elitism

Strategy

The youth representatives from each denomination should go "as one" to the mayor, school officials and city council in the name of Jesus and:

1. Repent
2. Forgive
3. New covenant

Self Pleasure Greed, lust, narcotic, rebellion, complacency
(bored), deception (lack of identify),
purpose/destiny, slavery, enmity (divided families),
poverty, drunkenness, laziness, sexual perversion

Strategy

God's intention for Hendersonville was that its people would have
a strong work ethic and would be people who gave into the city. For this
spirit to be recaptured two things should occur:

1. pray against the spirit of self pleasure in the name
of Jesus
2. As a believer in Jesus search your heart to be sure
you are walking in God's original intention for
the people of Hendersonville.

Power & Control Elitism, racism, shame, guilty, discrimination,
condemnation, manipulation, violence, hatred,
unforgiveness, deception (God-complex), self-pity, fear

Strategy

God's intention for the city of Hendersonville was that it be a city
controlled by and empowered by the Spirit of God. If this spirit is to be
recaptured we must pray against the spirits of power and control in the
name of Jesus.

A City on its Knees

HENDERSONVILLE AND THE WILDERNESS

One of our team members, Josh Deaton, was reading scriptures pertaining to spiritual mapping when the Lord told him to review the Biblical areas in relationship to Nashville. Geographically, the Hendersonville Peninsula, before the manmade creation of Drake's Creek, was the same shape as the Sinai Peninsula. Hendersonville, like the Sinai Desert, was to be a place used as a training ground for the prophets (proclamation: music industry, Trinity Broadcasting Network, Great Revival of the West, etc.). However, the people of our city, like the children of Israel, have spent generations wandering in the desert of no spiritual direction or purpose.

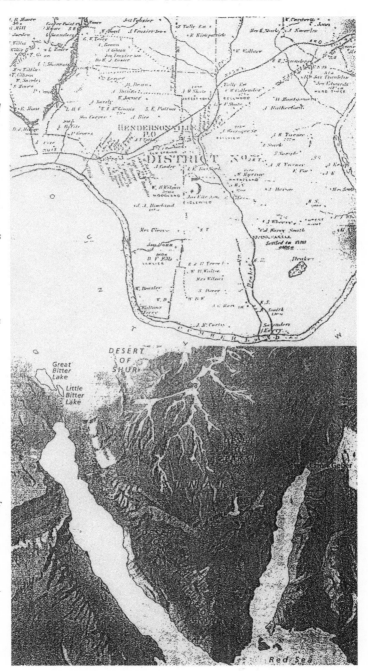

The Kingdom of God on Earth

by Tod Bell

*"The kingdom of God is not coming with signs to be observed; nor will they say, '
Look, here it is!' or, 'There it is!' For behold, the kingdom of God is in your midst."*
—Luke 17:20-21, NASB

*"...for the kingdom of God is not eating and drinking, but righteousness and peace
and joy in the Holy Spirit."*
—Romans 14:17, NASB

IT BEGINS AS a seed. A seed of desire. A sense of
disjointedness, of things terribly out of order.

A question rises, "Surely, this is not the way things ought to be?"
A sense of frustration takes hold of your mind as you look around you, in
your life, in your city. A cry forms, a longing, a prayer, if you will, "God,
if you are there, set things right. Fix me! Fix my world!"

This is the longing for the way things were, when the world was
first made and God pronounced it, "Good, very good!" (see Gen. 1:31)
God breathed His life into that first man, Adam, and told him that he was
a co-regent over the place where God had placed him and that he was to
rule it and tend it and cultivate it.

This world became horribly corrupted, wasted and infiltrated by
death the moment Adam turned from dependence on God. An alternate
power came in, saturated mankind and the whole atmosphere with sorrow,
hatred and pain.

Even then, however, man had a memory, a shadow of a picture in
his mind and heart of the way things were and the way things ought to be.
There was and continues to be a sense of loss and lack due to the breaking
of fellowship that occurred between our loving Creator and us.

THE KINGDOM OF GOD- WHAT IS IT?

When Jesus spoke of the kingdom of God, He spoke in clear
terms of *rule, relationship* and *righteousness*. He did not speak in esoteric,
obscure terms like the mystery religions. He spoke of earthy practical truth
in life and the way we treat each other. He spoke of men and women,
rightly related to the Father and ordering all their earthly relations in
response to learning His way of doing things.

1. *The kingdom of God is about rule.* Rule deals with geography. God is interested in land! He wants area! He reigns first in our hearts. Then, as we come into loving submission to Him, we begin to rule our personal geography along with Him, in His power and in His love.

    This has to do with every area we as Christians ("little christs") touch in our lives. Can you imagine a people who, in all their dealings with others, truly lived according to the Word of God? What power that would give to our words!

    No longer would the church have such a black eye when we try to tell others about Jesus Christ. When we tell of a heavenly kingdom, our lives would have told the story first. Our motives and way of spending our money and raising our families would bring the conviction of God into our words so they would not seem so empty.

    I was preaching once in a Shoney's parking lot down on Woodland Street in Nashville. I was telling anyone who would listen about the salvation that Jesus offers. One young guy walked up to me and got right in my face and said, "If I believed that, like you claim to, I would sell everything I own and leave home to tell as many people as I could how to be saved!"

    I told him, "I've done that." His mouth was shut and he had nothing to say (see Romans 3:19). I was able to lead him to Jesus right then.

    When our lives back up our gospel, we will see the kingdom of God manifest in our city.

    The kingdom of God is "righteousness, peace and joy in the Holy Spirit."

    When God rules in our lives and in our city, rival powers are displaced. Where once selfishness was the rule of the day, love has the upper hand. Real love that puts the needs of others first, not the kind that manipulates to get what you want.

    Where judgment and condemnation once ruled, peace and blessing now characterize the way we treat others. When we have God's heart, we learn His way of treating those who are out of fellowship with Him. Remember, He is the one who died for us while we were still sinners (Rom. 5:8). He did not wait for us to repent or clean up, He acted first in the power of blessing and love. This breaks down the hardness of our hearts and opens the way for His grace to win us back to Him. For too long our witness has had too much self-righteousness in it and that wins no one to God. The gospel of peace is the welcome mat into the kingdom of God.

2. *The kingdom of God is about relationships.* Jesus made it abundantly clear that the kingdom of God is manifest most powerfully in the way we treat each other (see Mat. 5:21-48).

   This is where the rubber meets the road in our entire walk with God. There is not room for theory or fantasy in this arena. Either we are honest to God and others, or we are merely religious. Jesus could stand in front of His most vehement opposers and ask, *"Who among you can find me guilty of sin?"* (John 8:46). In my home, my children must see me following as hard after God in loving my wife and loving them as they see me on Sunday morning leading worship.

   My dealings with my boss or my clients must be able to withstand the white-hot scrutiny of the words, *"Be perfect even as your Father in Heaven is perfect."* (Mt. 5:48). This is a tall order under any circumstances, but understood correctly it is within the reach of all of us as we live in the grace of God. Simply put, it means living according to the light we have in the way we deal with others. Without mistakes? That's not what Jesus means in the context of when He said this. He is talking of living without offense to our conscience and the mercy of God in relating with others. And when we do offend because of ignorance or sin, we quickly make things right in order to see that the witness of God's love and glory is maintained in that relationship.

3. *The kingdom of God is about righteousness.* Jesus is preeminently interested in fruit, not anointing or ability. The fruit of our lives will be the measuring stick when standing before the Lord in judgment. Jesus said the way to know a false prophet from a true one will be the fruit of his or her life (see Mt. 7:20). Not accuracy, not anointing, not miracles, not prosperity, not speaking skills, but *fruit!*

   There will be anointed, gifted ministers cast out of God's presence because they did not walk in righteousness (Mt. 7:21-23). It is God's kingdom we represent, not our own. It is His character that we are to be most interested in promoting, not our own ministries or doctrines, styles or projects, churches or missions.

   Imagine our city where the one consideration among Christians would be "What will promote the interests of Christ? What will please Him most?" Then imagine congregations, ministers and ministries working in step with each other, blessing each other, not competing but *completing* each other to see that Jesus Christ and His desires are served. Imagine a city where no one has too little and no one has too much, but all things are shared freely among the people of God (2 Cor. 8:13-15). This is a true representation of the blessing of God, not wealth and prosperity to a few who can whip up the crowd and receive large offerings as others struggle. The whole example and precept of the word of God demonstrates something altogether different than that. Another word for "righteousness" is "justice". They are interchangeable in the Bible. When justice rules our way of life and behavior among believers, the lost world will stand in line to see what we have. It has happened before and it will happen again. Let me tell you why...

THE UNSEEN ALLY

When we go back to the beginning of the kingdom of God on earth, what do we see? We see God and man (man being male and female), together:

- Man under God, submitting and loving,
- Man with God, ruling and tending,
- God over man, covering and providing.

That longing is still within us *and we know it.* It is the source of all strife and depression, frustration and madness, restlessness and longing, this shadow of a memory of the way things should be.

This longing explains all of our restless attempts to create a perfect world, to actually form something we cannot form on our own. It explains the reason our heart responds to words like "family" and "home" and "gift" and "love."

The prophets spoke to this when they called Israel to see what God would do when He comes in His power and glory and makes things right. This longing is the heartbeat of hope in every human heart. *It is our unseen ally in the heart of the lost!* When they see this openly lived out among a body of people, that heart within them that knows things can and should be different will be drawn to Christ and His kingdom.

There are actually people in our cities that have given up this dream. These are the areas that have been taken over by hopelessness, violence and darkness. Those who can afford to avoid them bypass these areas. But for those who live there, they have stopped trying to create a "heaven on earth" and have simply given themselves up to the apathy. That is why Jesus went into these very places with light, because it stood out in stark contrast (Mt. 4:15-16).

When the kingdom of God is bursting into our lives, individually and corporately, the values and priorities we live by go under a major overhaul. The carefully crafted church life which avoids all sharing in the suffering of the Lord (Phil. 1:29, 3:10) will be replaced with a people who live for what God's heart beats for, the restoration of a city horribly out of step with Him.

A Cry...

That's how it begins. It is a cry in our hearts, "Lord! Your kingdom come into full swing in our lives and in our homes and into your church in this city. Then, Lord, let your kingdom take over in every arena, in the marketplace, in our schools, in the government, in the courtrooms, in the law offices and police stations, LET YOUR KINGDOM COME! LET YOUR WILL BE DONE!"

We do not have revival, we do not have an in-breaking of the power and glory of God in our city, because we are content to live without it! Yes, that's right, we have been content to go about our feeble church lives, our normal, business as usual work and family routines without taking stock of the fact that everything we are doing we can do without God's supernatural power breaking in to our lives.

We must look upon our city and say, "It must change because it can change!" We must pray as if we cannot be denied, because God's word is unchanging. He desires to send forth His power more than we could ever want His power to come!

There is a harvest to be reaped, and dry and dead religion will not answer the call. Many thousands of souls will perish if we do not cry to God to send forth His Spirit to bring conviction of sin and the need for the Lordship of His Son, Jesus.

A Correction...

When this cry reaches critical mass, then we see God making things right, we see supernatural evidence of the kingdom of God breaking into our city. The Holy Spirit moves in power and those who have opposed God's ways turn back to Him or at least begin to fear Him! That is the beginning of wisdom.

Empty religion gives way to "truth in the inward parts." God moves in individuals and in the community to set things in His order, under His command. We refuse to bow to the spiritual chill around us and to the common, low conception of what Christianity is thought to be. We do not fear abuse or ridicule, we see them as badges of honor.

Ray Comfort, a New Zealand evangelist, says a lamb can look very white standing in a green field, but standing in a snowdrift, he looks almost brown! When the kingdom of God is openly demonstrated by Christians repenting of all known sin and compromise, the ugly stain of sin will be more visible. Sinners will awaken to their need, to their fearful condition, and will either rise up in open opposition or melt down in humble repentance to God.

When the cry of our hearts reaches a corporate pitch, pastors and marketplace leaders laying down their personal agendas to pursue this one thing, then He will hear from Heaven and send His correction, His making-things-right outpouring of His Spirit.

Right now, the current level of righteousness in the church generally is no higher than the world's. We worry the same as those without God. We spend the same way, cheat the same way, have sex the same way, divorce and are entertained the same way. *And the lost know it because they do business with us, they live next to us, they hear our conversations and see the jostling and jealousy in the church.* The pornography houses, strip clubs, and other sex-related businesses are a testimony to the fact that these problems have not been solved in the church. Every line of iniquity in the city can be traced back to the strongholds in the church.

We could focus on these things with a lot of information and statistics. We could concentrate on the evil and wickedness around us. We could cast our eyes on the corporate sin of our city, those things in our city that actively oppose God's righteousness and kingdom.

But God says, *"COME UP HERE and I will show you..."* (Rev. 4:1). When we seek Him and His pleasure, we will see where He wants to take us and this will help to break the yoke of unbelief and sin.

When we turn and team up to cry out to God, we begin to focus on something different. We see God, high and exalted, overruling all things, and we see our own desires change. We begin to see what God intends to do and we begin to come in line with what He wants. We receive His correction. We see we have not loved our city, we have not loved the lost, we have loved our own lives and our own ministries and works. God turns our focus onto Himself and His heart for this city.

A Community...

We are living and spreading community not concepts. This is the missing link in most Western Christian living. We are have concentrated on the message, forgetting that the church *is the message.* How we live is the key to the hearts of the lost.

Martin Luther recovered the crux of the message of the Gospel: salvation is by the grace of God through our simple trust in the finished work of Christ on the cross. Praise the Lord for this recovery that helped to bring the world out of the darkness she had sat in for so long!

However, this message was poured into old wineskins that had been around since the time Constantine had made Christianity the state religion of Rome (312 AD). The church had become a place to go with special buildings, special priests, special clothing, special music and special rituals, removed from daily life and normal believers and placed in the hands of professionals. The message was recovered but the structure was untouched.

If you will look into the word of God at what Jesus Christ demonstrated and taught, at what His followers then demonstrated and taught, you will find nothing remotely resembling what we have called Church for so long.

Jesus is the Life. He came to bring Life. He taught us the God-way of Life. He lived with, walked among, and shared His life with men. He then sent them out to do the same. When He trained them for spreading the Kingdom of God, he taught them to go two-by-two and live among the people (Luke 10:5-7). They were to stay in their houses, speak peace, live among them, serve them, bring the power of the Living God to bear in their situation, then and only then to tell them that what they had seen and experienced was the Kingdom of God!

He taught us to spread the *community* of the Gospel, not just the *concept* of the Gospel. In 1998, I and a faithful team of believers knocked on every door within about a two-mile radius of the central part of Nashville. We loved praying with the people we met, sharing God's love with them and how to be saved. This particular area had a lot of foreigners who had moved from many different countries. It struck us when so many of these people, particularly those from the Middle Eastern nations, would open the door wide and invite us in to come in and sit with them, share a little food and drink with them, and share time with their family. This is life for them, and what they believe is central to their life as well.

Imagine we come and tell them Jesus is the only way, and they come to check out how we live our faith. What would they find? When we invite them to join our community of faith, what would they see? So often, they would experience meetings in large buildings, sitting on benches looking at the back of someone's head, listening to someone talk for an hour, and then shuffling out again. Where is the life? Where is the community? To ask someone to leave their family groupings to believe as we believe and then do as we do, I am afraid what we have would not be very attractive to them.

What we see pictured in the Bible as the life shared by the body of Christ is central to the family, not filled with a lot of fluff, but made of the stuff that daily life is made of, with GOD IN THE MIDST. The church is then a *relational,* not *informational,* way of living out the life of God in the midst of where the people are. The church becomes the living picture show of God within walking distance of where people live and work. Church is in our homes, in our neighborhoods, in our offices, in our schools, it is *who we are,* not *where we go or what we say.*

I have seen most remarkable miracles done in the power and name of Jesus. I have seen blind eyes have sight restored; torn knee ligaments repaired instantly; speech given to someone who had never spoken in her sixteen years of life. I have also seen where, even with all of these things, if people are not adopted into the family of God and given truth in the context of life rather than classrooms, that the power of the miracle to keep them walking with Jesus is limited. We see this in the ministry of Jesus as well as experience all over the world.

The Kingdom of God on earth is a shared life! Jesus taught us to pray, "On earth as in Heaven". This prayer takes into account that there is perfect unity and love in the relationships between the Father, the Son, the Holy Spirit and all other Heavenly beings. If we would see the Kingdom manifest in our city, let us *become* what we say we *believe!* Let us share the Life that Jesus has shared with us. What a privilege to walk with the Living God and be the aroma of Christ among those who are saved and those who are perishing (2 Cor. 2:15-16)!

A COMMANDMENT...

Then we can hear God. We can hear His command to share what He has given us. This soul-cleansing power of the Blood of Jesus is available to everyone. God desires that none perish. He desires that all come to know that there is one God and one mediator between God and men, the man Christ Jesus. (I Peter 3:9; I Timothy 2:1-8).

The Lord releases His strategy to us as we come to Him in His Name, waiting, uniting, praying. He sees that we are dying to ourselves each day, living under His ownership, yielding ourselves to His leadership. That is His kingdom made visible in our hearts.

Then He sees us living real church. He sees we have traded our "pristine" religious lives in for the real stuff of cleaning out our closets of hidden sin, ripping off the Christian veneer to go for the real variety, all in response to His cleansing and wooing us by His wonderful Spirit.

We share in His commandment to *"believe in the Name of His Son Jesus Christ, and love one another, just as He commanded us."* (I John 3:23)

We begin to take seriously the call to reach the whole city with the gospel, to pray for everyone, to take every person before the throne of God and plead for his or her salvation (I Timothy 2:1-2). Then it is no longer a matter of protecting our turf, controlling those whom we lead, or being jealous over the success of other ministries or businesses. It is a shared joy of seeing Christ exalted, whether by me or someone else (Phil. 1:18). Let's just get His name preached and miracles done in His name! Let's see the Kingdom of God break into our city! Let's see Nashville become a "praise in the earth" because God reigns here!

About the Author

Tod and Emily Bell have lived in Nashville since 1992, and are raising their six children to follow Jesus Christ. Since 1995, they have served at Abounding Grace Church in Franklin as Associate pastors, worship leaders, children's ministry coordinators, and outreach leaders. In December 2000, Tod and Emily went full time with their call to the city of Nashville. Their mission is to reach the city of Nashville by helping to change the mindset of "church" from a place to go to a people who are what Christ has called them to be.

They started their ministry, New Vision, as an expression of faith in Jesus to supply all their needs and to spread the gospel of the Kingdom of God. New Vision is called to serve the body of Christ in the city, to "go public with the gospel" in every arena, to see every home, every street, every business, every school, have a living example of God within sight so that He can draw people to Himself.

For more info about New Vision, or to contact us for ministry, either leading prophetic and declarative worship, or speaking and training in "prayer and Presence evangelism", call 615-365-4457 or write New Vision, 741 Greymont Dr., Nashville TN, 37217

PART 4

LORD, SEND ME!

"Revival is a community saturated with God."
—Duncan Campbell

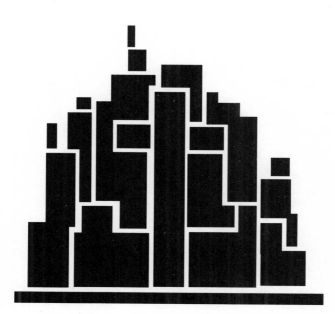

GO VOLUNTEERS!

by Jeffrey M. Richfield

TENNESSEE PRIDES ITSELF on being the Volunteer State. Throughout its history Tennesseans have volunteered for combat in American wars. During these times, there were a number of soldiers who held rank as volunteers. Part of their agreement was to serve for a time as 'volunteers' in combat. These Tennessee volunteer's were stationed in regiments, many on the front lines, who gave their lives in honor for some of the freedoms we still enjoy today.

What was it about these volunteers that made them unique? *Willing service.* The words "Here am I! Send me" (Is. 6:8) are the volunteer's motto. The book of Nehemiah may be considered the volunteer's handbook. From rebuilding the walls of Jerusalem to offering his heartfelt intercessory prayers for God's people Nehemiah applied divinely inspired principles and highly effective volunteerism. He not only rebuilt the wall, but also led a spiritual reformation and restoration of God's chosen people. We can apply much of Nehemiah's reforms to our day. Nehemiah helped to preserve Jewish identity; we must preserve the royal priesthood identity. Nehemiah protected Israel from compromise from a pagan community until the promised seed of Abraham, Jesus the Messiah. We must stand for truth and protect what has been entrusted to us in spite of all adversity until the return of our King, Jesus.

Nehemiah was a man of prayer. Ten recorded prayers range from the quick "arrow prayer" (Neh. 2:4) to the Bible's longest recorded prayer (Neh. 9). There are prayers of confession and repentance, delivered in mourning in sackcloth and ashes, and prayers of praise and adoration, delivered with jubilant singing and musical instruments. There are prayers of supplication and weakness (Neh. 6:9) and prayers for God's judgment on Nehemiah's enemies (Neh. 4:4,5). Above all Nehemiah desired the approval of God more than the approval of people.

Nehemiah prayed and then put his request before the king (Neh. 4:9). He exhorted the people to *"remember the Lord and fight"* (Neh. 4:14).

The opposition of enemies and spiritual warfare are inevitable when people are doing the work of God. Satan's purpose is to destroy God's people and God's work. His tactics as seen in Nehemiah include ridicule, slander, opposition from within and without, oppression and unrighteousness, discouragement, demoralization, distraction, and physical threat. Nehemiah combated these tactics with continual prayer, single-mindedness, wisdom, and righteous living. God's people in every age must employ these same weapons and use the heavy artillery given to us by our Captain!

Leaders are called to faithfulness more than success. Becoming entrapped by sin through compromises weakens our authority and position in the army of God. Escaping these things can be difficult, but all things are possible through God. Through faithfulness, Nehemiah succeeded in escaping the wiles of the enemies of his day.

As Nehemiah carried the message of rebuilding; we are to carry the message of the power of the cross to all people, races, and nations. Nehemiah saw the deprivation and derision of his people, and was resolved to act upon his beliefs of a Holy God. Nehemiah also had a vision to rebuild the walls of God's chosen people, and was fervent in accomplishing this task. We are called to produce good works for Jesus to read about when He opens the Book of Merit on judgment day (Matt.25:23 and Matt.5:16). Happy are those who are called to enter the joy of the Lord!

VOLUNTEERS AND THE CROSS

As Nehemiah did in his day, we must plug into the power source of God and make a commitment to rebuild our city on the spiritual building blocks of prayer and active faith. As committed volunteers in God's army, we must enlist our services through the power of Jesus. We must become the true embodiment of His message of the cross. The cross is the center and power of everything we are called to live by. From there the living waters flow in the streets of our city in a spiritual bathing.

Truly, as we lay *our* personal agenda and *our* goals at the foot of the cross, God will then give us -a starting place- in our quest for our city's revival. Test Him in this. Call upon God, praying for the welfare of the city as Jeremiah urged long ago:

"But seek the welfare of the city where I have sent you into exile, and pray to the Lord on its behalf, for in its welfare you will find your welfare...Do not let the prophets and diviners who are among you deceive you, and do not listen to the dreams they dream..."
—JER. 29:8

The trump is sounding! We must call upon God in behalf of our city. We must search for Him with all our hearts and pray He will let us find Him on our watch. We must enter into the gates of prevailing prayer! Only then will He fulfill His promises in bringing Nashville to its appointed hour of visitation.

"Then, when you call upon Me and come and pray to Me, I will hear you. When you search for Me you will find me; if you seek Me with all your heart, I will let you find Me, says the Lord, and I will restore your fortunes and gather you from all the Nations..."
—JER. 29: 12-14

TIME TO TAKE INVENTORY

CONSIDER carefully what your part is in preparing for the coming wave of spiritual awakening in Nashville. What eternal rewards and imperishable crowns will you inherit at your appointed time? The Bible says we (the redeemed) will be wearing crowns symbolic of our eternal rewards that reflect the glory of God. They will be crowns of righteousness, crowns of glory, crowns of life (James 1:12). The crowns will be given based on what we *did* with this guy we call Jesus, and what we *did* with the irrevocable gifts he allotted to us. What will your crown be? The apostle Paul pursued righteousness faithfully and ran a great race. We are in a race too, and time is fleeting by and by. Now is the time for us to live lives worthy of your calling. It is time to produce *good works* worthy of repentance that will last through the fire. Paul said in 1 Corinthians 3:14-15:

"If what has been built on the foundation survives, the builder will receive a reward. If the work is burned up, the builder will be saved, but only as through fire."
—1 COR.3:14-15

And in Ephesians 2:10,

"For we are what He has made us, created in Christ Jesus for good works, which God prepared beforehand to be our way of life."
—EPHESIANS 2:10

Look deep within and ask yourself, "Are you building on hay, wood, and stubble or the eternal works of bronze, silver, and gold?"(1Cor.3:12-14). When was the last time you gave tithes of time to the needy? You may claim that your works have been financial gifts. If so, great! I learned through much suffering that the rewards are greater for gifts of time than for a quick "hand out." Our culture is in "fast-food/take-out" mode, but there is a greater giving that develops relationships: TIME. No, in the end our gold will not save us. Paul exhorted Timothy, *"Be rich in good works, ready to share, storing up for yourselves the treasure of a good foundation for the future"* (1Tim.6:18,19). Real faith manifests itself in good works. Our claims of faith without works is dead (James 2:14-26). It is time we took inventory of the costly oil and perfume (good works) we have stored up in our lamp to pour on the feet of Jesus upon His grand return!

DECEPTION BY DISTRACTION

In these latter days, we know that Satan is deceiving some by distracting them. He would actually have us think our circumstances *must* be dealt with *before* we can move on with God. As he did in the Garden of Eden, Satan might even use Jesus' own words against us. He may say something such as, "Be still, and know He is God." He might actually have us believe we are to wait on God to give us a ministry *before* acting upon what God has already commissioned us all to do(Matt.28:18-20)!

I'll be the first to point out that while there are seasons for being still before God, there is a time that we leave the mountain because we have circled it long enough (See Deut.1:6-8). Some of us wait, and wait, and wait, procrastinating at the expense of God being able to use us in a mighty way today. Please do not be deceived. Our faith is not fixed on circumstances but upon God alone! We are to use our present adversity to further the cause of Christ, bringing men and women into the kingdom of God, possessing the land for Christ. The real tragedy is living life roaming endlessly, drowning in the affairs of men, instead of trimming our lamps for God's eternal purposes (Matt.25).

Do you have a true perspective on Jesus' imminent return? The truth is we are all but one heartbeat away from eternity. No one is promised tomorrow. Our life-span is but a mere vapor in God's eternal eyes. Looking back, we must consider the enormous consequences of wasted time and lost potential in our joint sonship with Christ. Looking ahead, we, like the apostle Paul, are to press on toward the mark of our high calling in Jesus. Now is the time we consider Jesus crucified and Jesus resurrected. He is reigning on high! He has conquered death for us, and we are His chosen royal ambassadors who carry the Ark of God inside us!

The Lord is calling out, "Where are you?" What is stopping you from stepping out from behind the "fig leaves" (coverings) of fear, intimidation, and shame to get real with Jesus today? Or have you forgotten: there is no hiding from an all-seeing God. Choose this day to present yourself a living sacrifice, and say, "Here am I!" "SEND ME!"

On the following page my Lord gave me these words that I pray will spark a fire unrestrained in you...

Go Volunteers!

CHOOSE THIS DAY

Salvation is free, but at such a great cost,
For each moment that passes is forever lost;
Why then, Oh wanderer, why must you fight?
Remember His words, "As a thief in the night."

For He will soon come with a trump and a shout,
Parting sheep from the goats without question or doubt;
That the only difference between the two,
Will be what they did and they did not do.

Make no mistake: the appointed hour
No one knows but the Heavenly Father;
All we need to do is press on toward the mark,
Of the high call of Jesus, and each play our part.

So not my will, Oh God, but Yours be done,
Here am I, Lord, your servant, a son;
Father, forgive, I choose Jesus this day,
Make me bold, for the debt I could never repay!

PART 4
LORD, SEND ME!

AFTER GOD'S OWN HEART

by Jim Freedman
Executive Director
Nashville Baptist Association

THE YEAR WAS 1991; the month was May; and what I was soon to discover was the first whisper of God's still voice coming to me in the form of a telephone call from a friend in North Texas. I was serving the Lord through Union Baptist Association in Houston, Texas, and had been in this position for ten and one-half years at this time. Union Baptist Association is the organization of the Southern Baptist Churches in Harris County, Texas, where there is a population of four and one-quarter million people and nearly five hundred Southern Baptist Churches. My ministry with the Association was as the religious education director for these churches.

I had been doing this ministry with Southern Baptist churches for the first seventeen years of my vocational life on a volunteer basis and for these ten plus years as a fulltime denominational worker. However, just three years prior to this moment, in whatever way it is that God "speaks" to His own, I had heard His voice whisper that one day I would be called to be the Executive Director of a Baptist association. So when my friend called in May, 1991, to tell me that the Executive Director of the Nashville Baptist Association in Nashville, Tennessee, had retired and that he wanted to recommend me for that position, I was not totally taken by surprise! In the back of my mind I was thinking, "but an association as large as Nashville Baptist Association will certainly want to call a man who has been serving as pastor of a large church somewhere in the Southern Baptist Convention." But I found myself saying "Yes, that will be fine." We talked for another minute or two, and when we said goodbye, I turned back to my work at hand and more or less put the phone call out of my mind.

Two weeks later another phone call brought me to "alert status!" It came from a member of the Search Committee in Nashville. He was calling to ask me if I would send a resume to the Committee! God now had my full attention, to say the least, and again, I found myself saying, "Yes, I'll send one right away!" I'm sure that many of you reading these words know how slowly committees work. They are certainly seeking the mind and the will of God as they consider every candidate recommended to them. And so they move with great deliberation. Hence, I did not hear from them until August. I had spent the Summer with training sessions, planning meetings, travel, budget projection, and on and on and had not given a great deal of

187

thought to the Nashville position. But when the call came in August to inform me that I was one of three candidates the committee had determined to interview in September, my prayer life took a dramatic turn to the specific prayer, "Lord, if this is where you want me to serve, make it clear to me and to the Search Committee!" And He did just that!

In mid-September I experienced the most relaxed job interview in my life, and a week later the Committee Chair called to say, "You are the man we will nominate to serve as Executive Director of Nashville Baptist Association." Three weeks later the Executive Board voted to call me to this position.

On January 1, 1992, I arrived in Nashville, Tennessee to begin the greatest years of ministry in my life! When people ask me how my work is going, I often respond, "God saved the best for last in my life!" I knew I was coming to work with, minister to, and serve alongside the more than one hundred and fifty Southern Baptist Churches of the Greater Nashville area, but again, God had more in store for me and for this great metropolitan area!

During the first twenty-one months of this ministry God gave II Chronicles 7:14 to me and to Nashville Baptist Association as the scriptural basis for all that He was to do in our midst during the last decade of the century. He led the Association to start several new churches, to enlarge and build upon a fledgling prayer ministry, to replace two retiring staff persons, and to carry out the five year strategy plan that had been approved in 1991. Personally, He began laying on my heart the need for revival and spiritual awakening, not only in Nashville, but across our nation. I began reading about the three Great Awakenings that had touched the United States in the previous two centuries and my mind and heart were continually being opened, challenged, and stretched. During this period of my ministry in Nashville Baptist Association we expanded the Prayer Committee of three persons to become a Prayer Team of twelve persons touching every facet of Association life and organization.

The more I read about the Great Awakenings, the more I realized that each of them began with diligent, heart-searching, God-beseeching prayer. The prayers of an individual or of a faithful few soon became the prayers of hundreds and then of thousands of believers. And to praying believers God sent the Pentecostal fires of revival to burn in their hearts, setting afire lives that aforehand had been but warm coals at best on the fire of God's holy altar! I was reminded that when the fires of Revival came to believers, their lives were transformed into living testimonies to the mighty work and power of God. Then, as unbelievers saw this living, breathing testimony to the One true and living God, they began to be drawn to Him themselves. Soon, believers were sharing the Good News and unbelievers were crying out for salvation. By the hundreds of thousands men, women, and children were saved! This is called a "Great Awakening!" First come the prayers leading to the revival in the hearts of believers. Secondly, comes the salvation of hundreds of thousands of lost persons — the Great Awakening. Thirdly, comes the by-product of all of this God Thing — believers, new and old, joining together in great choruses of praise to God the Redeemer! In other words, believers new and old become worshippers in spirit and in truth.

In my own life, the more I read about the three Great Awakenings in our country, the more I was led to pray more and more fervently for a fourth Great Awakening to sweep our country, and I even began praying with boldness that God would let it begin in Nashville, Tennessee! In Nashville Baptist Association the concept of a Prayer Team was enlarged to become the Spiritual Awakening Council with the three components of the Great Awakenings: Prayer, Evangelism, and Worship.

Now it was time for God to begin a work in my life, which I have only been able to describe as a "stretching" process. Again, it all began with a simple phone call from a friend. It was mid-September, 1993. This time the friend was a staff person with the Baptist Sunday School Board in Nashville. He called to tell me that an ad hoc Prayer Committee had been formed in the city to discuss the need for a prayer conference of some kind to be conducted in Nashville. This Committee consisted of ministers representing several different denominations. The prayer conference was envisioned to be a citywide conference to which persons from all evangelical denominations and cultural backgrounds would be invited to attend. He told me he had heard about the work of the Prayer Team in Nashville Baptist Association and of my leadership for it. The committee had just begun to meet, he said, and he just wanted to invite me to join them for lunch and sit in on this meeting. I agreed, and the date was set.

When I arrived for the luncheon my friend introduced me to several ministers from other denominations whom I had not previously met in the city. Then he told the group that he had accepted a position in another city, would be moving there in November, and Jim Freedman was taking his place on the Committee! No one was as surprised as I, since he had not given even one hint that he would make this announcement. Quickly my mind assessed the situation and concluded that if this man who had been a close friend for many years thought that I should serve with this group, then it more than likely was God's hand leading me in this new direction. So, without the rest of the group knowing that any of this was racing through my mind, I was accepted as a committee member, and the meeting continued unabated.

During the weeks and months that followed, the Prayer Committee met regularly, and the plan for the Prayer Conference began to evolve. It was scheduled to take place Monday through Friday the last week of June, 1994, just prior to the Third Annual March For Jesus in

Nashville. As we sought God's leadership for the week we were drawn to several Scripture passages. Among them were these two:

"If my people, who are called by my name, will humble themselves and pray and seek my face and turn from their wicked ways, then will I hear from heaven and will forgive their sin and will heal their land."
—2 CHRONICLES 7:14 (NIV)

"How good and pleasant it is when brothers live together in unity!...For there the Lord bestows (commands) His blessing, even life forevermore."
—PSALM 133:1, 3B (NIV)

Focusing on 2 Chronicles 7:14 led us to provide opportunities for God's people to pray together during the week. Downtown First Baptist Church opened her Worship Center every weekday morning for people to gather for prayer before going to work. Focusing on Psalm 133 led us to provide a Reconciliation Gathering on Thursday evening featuring the inspired preaching of Bishop Wellington Boone. David Bryant was invited to conduct a Concert of Prayer on Friday evening. These events were not attended by vast numbers of people, but in the words of David Bryant, "A beachhead has been established in Nashville, and from there we would move inland taking the city for Jesus!"

The six months just prior to the Prayer Conference saw two additional movements take place in Nashville - one in Nashville Baptist Association and the other a citywide prayer initiative. During the fall of 1993 word had come to the Committee planning the Prayer Conference that a dedicated Christian businessman in the city had begun a prayer ministry called "Nashville On Its Knees." A room on the twenty-seventh floor of the downtown Stouffer Hotel had been leased and designated as a prayer room. Twenty-three prayer group leaders had been enlisted — one for each workday during the month. Each leader was assigned a prayer concern and a meeting day. The leader had the responsibility for enlisting a number of prayer warriors and setting the time of the prayer meeting. They gathered once each month in Room 2712 and prayed specifically for their assigned area. The prayer assignments included: City, State, and National Government Leaders, Education, Entertainment Industry, Reconciliation, Pastors and Churches, Evangelism, and other topics of concern in the city. This prayer ministry continued for nearly three years from Room 2712.

The ad hoc prayer committee received word from Nashville On Its Knees that the prayer room was available for other prayer meetings as well as the twenty-three established groups. Don Finto, Senior Pastor of Belmont Church and member of the ad hoc committee, and I determined to invite ministers from across all denominations and races to join us for a Citywide Ministers Prayer Meeting in Room 2712 at 3:30 p.m. each Tuesday afternoon. The first of these prayer meetings was held on the first Tuesday of January, 1993. It was a blustery, cold day, and few prayer warriors turned out, but it was the beginning of what has been one of the most consistent and powerful prayer meetings in the city. The prayer time was enhanced by the view from Room 2712! The room had windows from floor to ceiling and wall to wall. It looked out over downtown Nashville and directly across the way to the State Capitol building. We also had a spectacular 180 degree view of the surrounding hills and countryside. It made praying for revival and spiritual awakening in the city a challenging and richly rewarding task each week.

During the third year of Nashville on Its Knees, we "lost our lease" on Room 2712. The various prayer groups that had been praying in that room either found other places to meet for prayer or disbanded. The Ministers Prayer Group, though, decided that our decision was not whether or not to continue praying every Tuesday afternoon, but merely where would we find a place to meet? I invited the group to use my office at Nashville Baptist Association. Its location at 420 Main Street in East Nashville gives it a beautiful view of downtown Nashville. And although it is not as large as 2712, and it only is two floors tall, it does have windows floor to ceiling and wall to wall just like 2712! We began meeting there during the spring of 1996, and this prayer meeting continues to the present time. It has never been a large group — we have never had more than sixteen persons present. But, as stated earlier, it is a powerful prayer time. One of our most delightful prayer targets has been the Adelphia Coliseum. Since it is in sight of my office windows, we were able to pray over it from the groundbreaking until the last light pole was in place. We have thanked God for providing this magnificent stadium for God's people to gather in and celebrate His presence in our city! The first opportunity for that to take place was, of course, the Billy Graham Crusade, June 1-4, 2000! We had prayed that God would fill the stadium for the four nights of the Crusade. We saw crowds numbering from 40,000 persons to 54,000 persons on Thursday, Friday, and Sunday evenings, but on Saturday evening an audience numbering 72,000 filled the stadium to overflowing! We had prayed; God had heard; and His Spirit filled the stadium. It was an awesome night for Nashville as we worshipped, prayed, and heard his preacher, Dr. Billy Graham.

The second major initiative of the spring of 1994 was the formation of the Spiritual Awakening Council as a major part of Nashville Baptist Association. As I have already written, God had led me to read about the Great Awakenings in our country's past. He had impressed upon me that the components of these Awakenings had been prayer, evangelism, and worship, and so we organized our Council with these three component parts. The Spiritual Awakening Council sponsored three weeks of prayer gatherings across the Greater Nashville area each year: one in February, one in May, and one in October. We focused on praying for revival and spiritual awakening to begin in Nashville and spread through the country. We encouraged all of the churches in Nashville Baptist Association to enlist a Prayer Coordinator and begin a prayer ministry. We offered training for beginning or for maintaining a prayer ministry.

Meanwhile God was continuing to draw His Body in Nashville toward unity. Jesus' prayer in John 17 was being laid upon the hearts of many of His prayer warriors in the city.

"My prayer is not for them alone. I pray also for those who will believe in me through their message, that all of them may be one, Father, just as you are in me and I am in you. May they also be in us so that the world may believe that you have sent me. I have given them the glory that you gave me, that they may be one as we are one: I in them and you in me. May they be brought to complete unity to let the world know that you sent me and have loved them even as you have love me."
—JOHN 17:20-23 (NIV)

I mentioned earlier that the Prayer Conference planned by the Ad Hoc Prayer Committee was scheduled to be held the week prior to the March For Jesus in June, 1994. This was to be the third March For Jesus to be held in Nashville. It had begun in 1992 with several hundred people participating in the march and had swelled to include several thousand in 1993. From Room 2712 the ministers gathering there each week had looked out over the very streets where the march would be conducted and had prayed specifically that it might be used of God as a symbol of the building sense of unity among the Body of Christ in Nashville. We had prayed with great fervor that the unbelievers in Nashville would see such a great demonstration of celebration and joy by the believers, that they would only be able to see it as a great God Thing in the city! And God honored those prayers. In 1994 there were 30,000 marchers; in 1995, 35,000; in 1996, 40,000; and in 1997, the last year of the citywide march, more than 45,000 marchers. Indeed, the March For Jesus in Nashville was the largest march to be held in the United States. I believe it was due to the prayers of His children in our city, and especially the powerful prayers prayed from Room 2712!

By 1996 the stage had been set for yet another "act" in the great drama God was playing out on the Nashville stage. Again, this act opened as the preceding ones had—with a phone call from a pastor-friend. L. H. Hardwick, pastor of Christ Church, called to invite me to attend a breakfast meeting for the purpose of discussing the need for a citywide prayer meeting which would include laypersons as well as pastors. Twenty-five persons gathered for that breakfast time, and after prayer, determined to join him in calling believers to this once-a-month prayer time. We scheduled it to be held on the first Friday morning of each month and to be hosted by a different church each month. Again the prayer warriors responded! The attendance ranged from forty to fifty persons each time. And the prayers grew out of 2 Chronicles 7:14. I can still hear the fervent prayers for revival to wake up our city and for another Awakening to begin in Nashville and sweep across the country! In the fall of 1996 we were praying on a Friday morning at Alta Loma Baptist Church in Madison, Tennessee. The group was gathered around the altar as was our custom in each church. Our prayers on this particular morning had centered more around Psalm 133 and John 17 as we prayed for unity in the Body of Christ. Pastor George Adebanjo from Living Word Church of God in Christ broke into the praying with a fervent appeal for a Reconciliation Gathering of some kind to be conducted in the city. He felt it was time for the Body of Christ to demonstrate this unity about which we had prayed. I can still see Pastor Finto stepping up beside Pastor Adebanjo, placing his arm around his shoulders and saying, "George, if you will take leadership for this Rally, the rest of us will support you and work along side of you!"

Pastor Adebanjo took that challenge, and within a couple of weeks, he called together a group of interested persons from all denominations crossing all racial lines for the purpose of discussing a Reconciliation Gathering. The group was named the Racial Reconciliation Task Force. We prayed together about reconciliation, and under God's leadership, planned the first of several Annual Reconciliation Gatherings. It was conducted in the spring of 1997 in the Worship Center of The Temple Church. Nearly 2500 people gathered on a Sunday afternoon! We worshipped, prayed, and heard testimony from various leaders of reconciliation in the city. The number of persons attending and the intensity of their worship and prayers seemed to be God's stamp of approval on the work of this special group. The Task Force in its next monthly meeting determined to continue its work in the city and has sponsored a Reconciliation Gathering each year since that time.

One of the speakers in that first Reconciliation Gathering challenged us to make a commitment that would lead us deeper into the matter of reconciliation with a person of a different race than ourselves. His challenge was to find a person of a different racial background and make a commitment to meet together once each week for seven weeks. The meeting could be at breakfast, at lunch, or at any other time convenient to the two of us. The purpose of our meeting was to be friendship! We were simply to get to know one another — to find out about the each other's family — to pray every day for the partner. I took that challenge and became close friends with Pastor Warner Durnell of St. Andrews Presbyterian Church. These seven weeks of meeting and eating together led to a bond which continues to the present time. We have rejoiced with one another and prayed for one another. It became a picture of what reconciliation looks like when applied on an individual, personal basis.

In 1999 and 2000 the Reconciliation Gatherings were held on the National Day of Prayer the first Thursday of May. The Gatherings have continued as meaningful expressions of racial reconciliation while the Task Force has enlarged the scope of its work to include an evangelism initiative in the city. As of this writing the evangelism initiative has been assigned to a sub-team of the Racial Reconciliation Task Force and has produced a training manual and conducted the pilot project in February, 2001.

In February, 1996, yet another event took place which had a part in shaping my life. It was the Clergy Conference in Atlanta, Georgia, sponsored by the Promise Keepers organization. More than 32,000 ministers from around the world gathered in the Georgia Dome for three life-changing days. On the first evening as we worshipped and prayed together, tears of joy, repentance, and devotion filled my eyes and spilled over time and time again. As we left the Dome that evening I thought, I have done all the crying I can do ... there are just no more tears! But I along with everyone else discovered that there were more tears and more expressions of life-changing devotion to come on Wednesday and Thursday!

As Wellington Boone preached on servanthood on Wednesday morning and as he knelt on the platform to wash the feet of Tony Evans, God spoke to me. His words to me were about my role in what He was doing in Nashville and led to my commitment to indeed be His servant more than ever before in my life.

That decision in the Georgia Dome led me to seek out additional ways to serve my city and to express that servanthood to spiritual leaders in the city. One of those leaders was Pastor Michael Graves of The Temple Church, a predominantly African American church in North Nashville. In a discussion with him shortly after the Clergy Conference, we talked about reconciliation — the need for it to happen and how it actually does happen. He told me about the Interdenominational Ministers Fellowship, and that this group had been composed of both white and African American ministers until the Civil Rights Movement came to Nashville in the Sixties. At that time the white ministers ceased to attend, and the organization from that time until now has consisted mostly of African American Ministers. It meets every Wednesday at Noon at Jefferson Street Missionary Baptist Church. As Pastor Graves shared this information with me, God again spoke to me. His word was that I should attend the Interdenominational Ministers Fellowship. On the next Wednesday I walked into the meeting room shortly before noon and said to the three ministers who were already there, "I'm Jim Freedman, and just want to fellowship with you!"

I have been a regularly attender of IMF since that day, have served for two and one-half years as secretary of the group, and have been stretched by God in the arena of reconciliation through my participation with IMF more than in any other activities in the city! I believe the main thing He has taught me about reconciliation is that it is a personal, one-on-one relationship. It does not happen through Gatherings — although the Gatherings are important and play a significant role in reconciliation. It happens when one gets to personally know and work alongside of a person or persons of a different color or cultural background. It happens between friends!

For the past four years the Interdenominational Ministers Fellowship has joined with the Covenant Fellowship in addressing the problems of racism in the city. During the first year of this relationship the two groups met every other month and addressed the issue of racism — what is it? How does it affect life in the city? What can the faith community do to correct it? The second year we dealt with the issue of the school system coming out from under court-ordered desegregation. The third year we dealt with the issue of guns in schools, and the fourth year we dealt with ways the faith community can be a part of reducing violence related to racism in the city. This relationship between IMF and Covenant continues as we seek to lead members to form relationships that cross racial lines and become the strong basis for reconciliation.

During the fall of 1997 a beautiful packet of materials reached my desk under the caption, "Celebrate Jesus 2000." The materials came from a newly formed national organization called Mission America and outlined a vision for our country: "to pray for and share Jesus with every person in the United States by year end 2000!" As I read the materials, my heart burned with an excitement and a passion that this vision would happen in Nashville! I began to pray about the response of our city to this stirring challenge. I also began sharing the vision with the Spiritual Awakening Council of Nashville Baptist Association. In a March, 1998 meeting the Council asked me to bring together a number of the spiritual leaders in the city and form a local organization much like the national, Mission America organization for the purpose of challenging the more than eight hundred evangelical churches in Nashville *to pray for and share Jesus with every person in Metro Nashville by year end 2000.* My initial response was that this was not a goal for one denomination or for one group in the city...it was a challenge for the entire Body of Christ and the goal could only be achieved if we worked together.

In April twenty-one leaders met in the offices of Nashville Baptist Association and formed the Nashville Bridges Coalition. These leaders

represented a networking of many of the groups in the city that had been
filling a particular need and reaching a particular segment of the
population. Nashville Bridges Coalition was to be the "glue" that pulled all
of these groups together and set our minds and hearts on the common goal
of praying and sharing Jesus with the more than one million lost persons in
the Greater Nashville area. The leadership of the Coalition included:

George Adebanjo, Racial Reconciliation Task Force
Bob Cook, Saturday Search Chair
Don Finto, Tuesday Afternoon Ministers Prayer Group
Enoch Fuzz, West Nashville Ministers Group
Frank Gill, Member at Large
Michael Graves, Member at Large
L.H. Hardwick, Metro Pastors Fellowship
Forrest Harris, Kelly Miller Smith Institute
   & American Baptist College
Onnie Kirk, When Men Pray
John Ledford, Mapping Center Specialist
Fred Lodge, Nashville Baptist Association
   Spiritual Awakening Council
Scott MacLeod, Provision
Mark Puckett, Jesus Video Distribution Chair
Lew Reynolds, PrayerWalking Chair
Ed Sanders, Interdenominational Ministers Fellowship
Rubel Shelley, Project Goodwill
Brett Stewart, Canning Hunger Chair
Steve Tackett, Public Relations Chair
David Thompson, Evangelistic Block Parties Chair
Drew Wileczek, Antioch Churches Together
Kerry Woo, Promise Keepers
Yvonne Wood, U.S. Center for World Mission
John Yancey, Kindness Outreach Chair

At each monthly meeting, the first agenda item was prayer for
the city and for God's direction in implementing the great vision which
was our driving force. We soon saw the need to appoint a Task Force to
suggest some specific tasks or events that a church could use as their
members accepted a specific geographic area for which they would accept
responsibility. Their assignment would be to pray for and share Jesus with
every person living in their assigned area.

Nashville Bridges Coalition became a member of the Mapping
Center for Evangelism, a national organization providing data on every
household in the nation! We hired a part time mapping center consultant
and made his services available to every church that became a Celebrate Jesus

2000 participant. The data included a map of each block in the assigned area, demographic information about the persons living on that block, and the name, address, and phone number for each household on that block.

The Task Force suggested six events that a church could conduct anytime during the year to carry out the vision of praying for and sharing Jesus with every person in Metro Nashville by yearend 2000. They were: PrayerWalking, Evangelistic Block Parties, Saturday Search, Jesus Video Distribution, Kindness Outreach, and Canning Hunger. Chairpersons were enlisted for each of these events and three training sessions were planned to give instruction to local church chairpersons. By January 1, 2000, one hundred and five churches in the Metro Nashville area had officially accepted a geographic area and made the commitment to pray for and share Jesus with every person in that area by yearend 2000!

God has been at work in many areas and through many individuals in our city! It is my conviction that the Revival and Awakening for which we have prayed is tied directly to reconciliation. We are first to be reconciled to God through Jesus Christ. That reconciliation with Him leads to reconciliation with brothers and sisters in His Body. The extent to which we are reconciled in the Body of Christ across all of the lines we have drawn — race, denominations, gender, age, etc. — will measure the extent of the fires of revival and of the Awakening.

We continue to see powerful prayer meetings and powerful worship gatherings across the city. We continue to see God's servants serving Him, serving one another, and serving the lost and the poor of the city. But while we continue to hear the reports of revival and awakening sweeping entire cities in other parts of the world, we have not seen that kind of transformation in our area. So our continuing cry to God is: *Let it happen in Nashville! Let the fires of revival and of awakening sweep across our great metropolitan area and let it happen in our day! May we be a city on its knees!*

About the Author

Jim Freedman is a man after God's own heart. Above all we are to first be reconciled to God. And this is Jim's call to ministry as he pursues it with a great zeal. If you think the older generation has no grasp of worship let Jim prove you wrong! Originally from Texas, He and his wife Sandra now reside in Franklin, TN., and attend The Peoples Church. They are blessed with two boys, Kennie and Kyle.

Jim hosts "Bridges Network" which is a spiritual incubator which partners with other Nashville ministries to bring the body of Christ together in unity and reconciliation. Email jwfreed@aol.com for more information.

True Transformations

by Ray Elder
Teen Challenge

IT'S FRIDAY NIGHT in Nashville, Tennessee, and the streets of Music city are awaiting the big red London double-decker bus to roll down the streets heading for its Friday night rendezvous in the heart of the city. On board the bus tonight are a good selection of Tennessee *volunteers* from all walks of life, and different denominations that have been picked up from the bus's starting point, all chatting away excitedly on their way to yet another encounter with the inner-city and its inhabitants.

As the "big red" arrives and docks opposite the American truck stops of America parking lot and restaurant, the rest of the team who have motored there from other points of the city are there to greet its arrival.

The familiar noise of the trucks entering and leaving the truck stop lets us know we have arrived at the correct location. The team swings into action, as the bus and location must be prepared for the night's activities. The smell of diesel coming from the bus and the hundreds of trucks parked in the truck compound in front of us will be our constant companion for the next few hours. As we prepare to do the Lords work on the opposite side of the road we can see young girls getting into and out of trucks involved in prostitution.

The round tables and chairs are taken off the bus and set up on the street. The steps to get up onto the bus are put in place—the generator is started, the crock pots of soups are plugged in too stay warm along with the home-made cookies/biscuits and other goodies made by the volunteers, are all placed on the counters. Prayer having been given—we await what the Lord will send along tonight. Every week is different, though there are regulars of course. Last Friday for instance was a sober time, as one of the street people's number had come up, committing suicide rather than face a slow death with aids. That only went to underscore their desperate circumstances and broken lives.

This being the South, it is still warm enough to sit outside the bus at night. On the upstairs deck already two of our Lady volunteers are speaking to a woman in her forties. This is the first night that she had been on the bus. She is very lonely. She had reached out to a homeless man that soon got out of control and at times she had to call the police to intervene. She had met him when she phoned the Salvation Army's Nashville headquarters to have them take some furniture away. She realized tonight as the ladies were talking with her that she had a Divine Appointment to be on this bus to night. She was only passing by, when a friendly voice offered some refreshment in His name. They talked; they laughed; they cried, and they prayed. Stay tuned as the Lord completes this story.

Cowboy arrives. You would not think of the word cowboy to describe this man. He is about five feet 5 inches tall. His face is hardened from living on the streets for so long, and he talked continuously from the time he got there, until his sudden dramatic departure one hour later with "Bear." He consumes cups of hot soup while complaining that the free giveaway supper at a local church was not up to scratch tonight. He gives himself a compliment that he is not as drunk tonight as he was last week at the bus. He is 47 years old—had been a truck driver, and lived on the streets since 1979. He was from Alabama, and served a number of prison terms here in the Volunteers State. He stated proudly that he was a tenant of "Bear" and they lived down by the river under the railway bridge in a tent—adding "a big tent". He thought he might retire to bed early tonight, because early this morning a girl had awoken him and Bear up looking for a man who owed her money.

Bear joins us. Bear, unlike Cowboy, was fully satisfied with the supper tonight at the church giveaway, and so refused our soup and cookies handed to him by one of the faithful volunteers who had spied him coming down the road. But not to worry, "yes" Cowboy, once again came to the rescue, and ate the whole thing. Bear did take the cup of coffee and in fact had three cups of coffee, and thought he would take one for the road. Bear and Cowboy discussed their program for the next day, Saturday. It was a string of free giveaway meals at various churches, soup kitchens, community services, clothes distributions, etc. They had all the times down. They obviously knew their way around this town. Suddenly in the midst of all this, Cowboy jumps up and runs across the street to ask a truck driver if he needed any help in unloading his truck into another man's truck. He called after Bear to join him, but the truck drivers turned down their willing offer. They came back to the bus, took their coffee, and off down to the river they went—to dream they were riding the overhead railway cars across America. I declined their invitation to visit their street house until a daytime hour, as it was dark.

News reached us at the bus tonight, that the 22 year-old boy, who we got out of the woods living in a car sniffing spirits off a rag, had left our crisis home. This is where we take the prostitutes, street people, alcoholics, and drug addicts off the street and put them into our crisis home when they accept Christ as their Answer. It is here where we prepare them to go into a Teen Challenge center, once we have dried them out from drugs. The good news here on Saturday is that David has phoned, and asked one of our staff members to meet and talk to him, and now I can report he has returned to the crisis house.

Many other cups of coffee, ice tea, and drinks were given out tonight. These are only but a few whose stories the Master knows, and sends us out each week to call them to Himself. At the end of the evening, everything is packed back onto the bus, and this mobile coffee house on wheels winds its way back through the streets of Music city—with the volunteers waving back to the street people—who are waving at them along the streets. Our bus driver and captain of the team, Tod, blows the bus horn which gives out such an alarm that you would think that men had heard the "trumpet sound" on That Day. Of course that is our hope and the reason that we are on this front line—so that many will hear the *Masters call* with us, on that glorious day!

Here I am Lord; Not my will, but Yours,
Ray Elder
TEEN CHALLENGE INT'L.

NATHAN'S TESTIMONY

My name is Nathan. When I arrived at Nashville Teen Challenge in September of 1999 I was 17 years old. I was a broken reed. I was confused, chaotic, fearful, dejected and introverted. I literally arrived in shackles. The chains that bound me were not only physical but spiritual as well. I had lived my seventeen years bound by the chains of darkness but under the nurturing of the Holy Spirit I have been set free!

This past year has been difficult, enlightening and humbling and I could not have completed this program without the merciful love of Our Father in heaven. How priceless is His unfailing love! In Teen Challenge I have experienced the magnificent hand of God upon my life and the lives around me.

I came to Teen Challenge because my parents pastor is a graduate of Teen Challenge. I was incarcerated for possession of LSD and was facing several years in prison. The pastor went to the judge on my behalf and I was brought to Nashville in shackles from Montana.

My life has been changed. I have had Jesus in the morning, lunch, supper, snack and at the going down of the sun. I have learned to do chores, to respect others rights and space and to submit to authority.

I have learned to walk a straight line. I have learned to ask, "Lord, what will thou have me to do: Speak Lord, thy servant heareth: Not my will but thy will be done." I have learned to focus on God, not on man.

I believe that God has called me to be a youth pastor. Job 14:5 says *"Man's days are determined; you have decreed the number of his months and set limits he cannot exceed."* I believe that I am to use these days to reach out to other young people to share my testimony and to help them fulfill the calling God has upon their life. I was recently watching a tape of the Brownsville revival and Steve Hill said the only thing we can take to heaven is other souls, so, I must win souls for the Kingdom of Heaven.

In order to fulfill the call that God had placed upon my life, I needed to continue my discipleship training when I graduated from Teen Challenge in August of this year. I chose to continue that training at the Master's Commission in Griffin, Georgia.

I had completed all the prerequisites to enter Master's Commission, which included obtaining a GED. The one obstacle was raising the $3,650.00 tuition. My mother in Montana held weekend yard sales and the family donated as much as they were able, but I was still short of the required amount. I had made pleas to area churches and pastors. I had learned to surrender all to God for He is my provider.

Four days before the time for me to leave for Georgia, I still did not have the required funds. God used that time to teach me to trust in Him and to reveal His awesome power. While sitting in the YMCA gym, my Director received a phone call from the last church I had made a plea too and they were turning down my request because they had four of their members going to the Master's Commission. We then prayed and the Director made a call to an individual who pledged one thousand dollars. A second call was made to a business. An individual from that business called back in fifteen minutes and said not to request the donation from the corporation, that he and his wife would make the donation of one-thousand-four-hundred-twenty dollars instead.

Within a matter of minutes, God turned a seemingly hopeless situation around to a reason to rejoice in Him and to stand in awe of His Mighty Power! I give God all the glory for what He has done in my life and I thank Him for the power of His love that enabled me to be called as one of His disciples.

I am now at Master's Commission continuing my discipleship training. I could not have made it here without the Masters intervention. I thank the Lord for Teen Challenge for that is where the training began. I pray that I continue to be the clay in the potter's hands and to be molded into the pastor He has called me to be.

CHERYL'S TESTIMONY

No, I didn't have a disease, I wasn't crazy nor did I just wake up one morning to set out to be on drugs and alcohol for the next 30 years. But at 45 years old I found myself in a desperate and hopeless situation.

My youngest daughter dragged me off to Freedom Chapel, which is a church that was born out of the Long Island Teen Challenge. My ex-husband who went through Teen Challenge in Brooklyn and is now a pastor there; along with a very close family friend who we grew up with and who also went through Teen Challenge in Brooklyn and is now the Director of Teen Challenge in Long Island and the Senior Pastor, urged her to bring me there. You see, we all grew up in the same neighborhood and had drugs, alcohol, pornography, prostitution and other life controlling problems.

As I sat there, feeling sick in tired of being sick in tired my daughter had her bible open to Proverb 3:5-6, "Trust in the Lord with all your heart, and lean not on your own understanding. In all your ways acknowledge him and he will direct your path."

At the age of 13, I ran away from home. My father, who was an abusive alcoholic and my mother who took the abuse were separated. That abandonment and rejection set me out on a search looking high and low to be loved, needed and accepted. By the time I was 19, I had two daughters and was divorced from my husband. Being a single mom was not an easy task, but I was determined to be the mother, father, provider, nurse, taxi driver, cheerleader and friend, to give all that I had. I worked from time to time, and had two and three jobs. I wanted my children to not want anything.

To get me through the day I started out having a few glasses of wine and would smoke a joint (marijuana). Not wanting to feel the pain that I stuffed, and stuffed, and stuffed, from the hurts of the abandonment, rejection, shame, guilt, anger, resentments and the abusive relationships that came upon me. I started using anything and everything to numb the pain. (acid, pills, sex, men & women, cocaine, and heroine). I was a functioning addict that was right at the door of suicide and death.

Whether you are functioning or not when you are living like that it not only affects you but everyone around you. So, when my oldest daughter went to college she too became a victim in an abusive relationship with a young man who transported drugs through out the United States. We became a gun toting, drug-dealing commodity from coast to coast and even came up against each other on the streets of New York in competition in selling the drugs. My daughter got shot in the leg in the midst of a stick up, and shortly after that she lost her 4-month-old son. She went into Teen Challenge first, and soon found out that what the Lord had done for her He could do for me. She and my youngest daughter, along with those Teen Challenge people began to pray.

After going to a couple of the Teen Challenge outreaches and visiting their chapel it wasn't long before the Lord gave me the willingness to seek Teen Challenge for help. With God ALL things are possible.

My ex-husband, a hard core heroine addict (now a pastor), and our close family friend (Long Island Teen Challenge Director and pastor), along with his 10 brothers and sisters who also were on drugs, many cousins, nieces, nephews and extended family members, a total of 44, have gone through the program, and are now serving the Lord. I am now the office administrator of the Teen Challenge in Nashville, my oldest daughter who has been married now for two years to a graduate of Teen Challenge now pastor and living in California. I had the opportunity to visit with them and my daughter and I was blessed to minister together to two of the California Women Teen Challenge's. When I think about Jesus and what He has done for me I SHOUT, SHOUT, SHOUT !!!!!!!

LORI'S TESTIMONY

Hello, my name is Lori. I was born and raised in Kentucky. My family knew the Lord, and they took me to church and Sunday school. I believed in God, but I didn't trust him. I was never able to distinguish between truth and feelings. I believed what I felt. As a child I didn't know what the Word said about who God really is. The only thoughts I had of God brought fear and damnation. I rebelled as a teenager against all authority, teachers, and especially my dad. I had decided I would do what I wanted to do. I also made an inner vow that I would never allow anyone close enough to hurt me. I experimented with sex, cigarettes, beer, and friends that weren't Christians, just to fit in and receive love and acceptance. Little did I know it was a trap. I spent eighteen years of my life trying to escape the hurt caused as a result of compromise and playing with sin. I never said I want to be a drug addict, or never said I want to be an alcoholic. I didn't ever say I want to be arrested. I didn't decide to spend time in a mental hospital.

By age 30, I was a heroine/cocaine drug addict, living in a lesbian relationship. I had no hope and I knew I would probably die. The sooner the better is how I looked at it. I had tried AA and NA programs, I had tried self-help groups, and I had tried psychiatrists. Nothing worked, I didn't realize I was soul-sick. I jumped out of a window in the building I was living in at the time. I couldn't keep living like I was living. I wouldn't even call it living; it was more like existing. I broke both my hips, my pelvis, my left foot, my left arm, and dislocated my left elbow and shoulder. The hospital staff knew me; they knew my story; they knew I would probably die. It was just a matter or time. They released me one week later with out treatment or plan for rehabilitation. I was staying with a friend I had been riding with to AA meetings.

Out of nowhere I heard my grandmother say I love you. She had been gone about 2 years. I just knew it was time to call my dad and go home. The Holy Spirit began to minister to me through my family. The Lord began a physical healing. He also breathed a new spirit of life into me. Out of obedience to my earthly father, I agreed to go to Teen Challenge. My dad said I needed a long-term treatment program. He wanted me to go to Teen Challenge. He said I needed to allow these Christian people to love me back to life. He said they had been where I was and they had the way out.

That way out was Jesus. I have graduated the program, and now I am working here. The Lord has given me a new life and a new hope in Jesus. Instead of suicide, drug addiction, and perversion, God has redeemed me by the blood of Jesus. He has called me to minister to others and share what I have seen and heard. The key was in the washing and renewal by the Holy Spirit and the Word of God. I praise the Lord for taking someone like me and loving me and giving His way of life to me.

THE STORY OF TEEN CHALLENGE

40 years ago, Life magazine carried the story of a crippled 15-year-old who was brutally beaten in New York City by a teenage gang. That story captured the attention and the heart of a young country preacher - in an unusual way God gave him a burden for the gang members! That young preacher was Rev. Dave Wilkerson.

Rev. Wilkerson saw those gang members as troubled youths whose lives were being snatched away from them. His burden became a vision - a desire to reach teenage gang members with the message of God's love and changing power. In 1958 Rev. Wilkerson established Teen Challenge in the slums of New York City. Forty years later, Teen Challenge has grown to be not only one of the most successful programs dealing with lifecontrolling issues, but also one of the largest.

Today, Teen Challenge has become Teen Challenge International, a nonprofit international ministry with more than 125 ministry centers in 43 states and Puerto Rico and established in more than 60 countries around the world. it has expanded to not only offering hope and healing through discipleship training to teens with lifecontrolling problems, but also to adults.

Teen Challenge International, Nashville Headquarters
PO Box 187, Madison, TN 37116
Phone (615) 868-7300   Fax: (615) 868-3301
Email: tenashville@juno.com

THE URBAN CRY

by Scott Macleod
Provision Ministries

THERE IS AN urban cry that ceaselessly goes out from the center of our city; it is a cry for mercy! The big question is ... Can you hear it?

I have a couple of other extremely important questions for you.

No. 1. Are you interested in seeing this city changed from the inside out? No. 2. Are you interested in serving the poor and the lost? If so, you need to know about Provision Inner City Ministries. First we'll let the Word of God speak for it's self...Jesus said:

"I tell you the truth, whatever you did for one of the least of these brothers of mine, you did for me."
—MATT. 25:40

Jesus said, *"They also will answer, 'Lord, when did we see you hungry or thirsty or a stranger or needing clothes or sick or in prison, and did not help you?' He will reply, 'I tell you the truth, whatever you did not do for one of the least of these, you did not do for me.' Then they will go away to eternal punishment..."*

"Religion that God our Father accepts as pure and faultless is this: to look after orphans and widows in their distress and to keep oneself from being polluted by the world."
—JAMES 1:27

"The righteous care about justice for the poor, but the wicked have no such concern."
—PROVERBS 29:7

The inner cities of America are some of the most ripe and crucial mission fields that we could ever work. Jesus is there, waiting for us to join Him!

The truth is—and I speak for most inner city ministries—we need all the help that we can get! The situation is no less than urgent!

As you read this note people are literally perishing because of brutal violence—drugs are ravaging and enslaving multitudes; the little that is left of the family unit is continuing to crumble; desperate crack addicted prostitutes are walking the streets; many elderly are sick and lonely and multitudes of precious children are being abused and neglected. If someone does not intervene there will be no hope for them.

If you are interested in being a light shining in the midst of great darkness then there is a phenomenal opportunity awaiting you; the good news I have to report to you is that the gospel of Jesus Christ really works—especially in the darkness! By God's grace, we are seeing the power of God's love when it is extended through His people bringing about miraculous change in people's lives. God's love in action brings an end to the perpetual misery, poverty, corruption and bondage that have plagued the inner city for decades!

I want to ask you to seek the Lord and see if He would lead you to help us. The harvest is awesome, but just as Jesus said, the workers are few. This is precisely the reason why most of the inner cities in America remain in the desperate condition that they are in.

We need more volunteers, more money and resources, more prayer and most of all...we need your heart! Come and see what God is doing in the inner city! You will be challenged and blessed!

I believe that God's desire is to open every believer's ears and heart to the urban cry. According to scripture it is imperative that we hear and respond. To those who are willing to respond out of love to this cry for mercy Jesus has extended these awesome promises...He has declared them his true *"sheep."* He called them *"righteous"* and He has pledged to give them *"eternal life!"* (See Matt. 25:46) May we all find a place to truly touch and minister to the King through serving the poor and the lost!

If you're interested getting involved in this kind of work please call: 615-327-1200 or for directions and schedules call 615-327-4003.

You can write us or send contributions to:
Provision Ministries, PO Box 330061, Nashville, TN 37203.

Our Web sites are:
www.provisionministries.org or www.zadokministries.org.

Our location is:
1419 Clinton Street in Marathon Village close to downtown Nashville, TN.

God bless you much!
Hold fast to the Lord!
Scott MacLeod
President of Provision Ministries & Pastor of the Fortress Fellowship

OPEN YOUR EYES

by Pastor Mark Goad

I WOULD LIKE to begin by acknowledging God for this opportunity to share a portion of the vision that he has given to me back in November of 1996. It was then that God began revealing His will for Nashville to me personally...

A few of us were meeting in a two-car garage that had been converted into a "little" church with four pews, a wood stove, and a homemade pulpit. There was an awesome presence of God that afternoon, the air was filled with an aroma, a fragrance that I had never smelled before, while I was prostrate on the cold garage floor. Praying, I started getting intoxicated in my spirit. The presence of Jesus was now filling the room, and in the most simple way the LORD began to open His will to me. He showed me a date, and a time, and a place in the future—April 7, 1997, 9:00 am. I saw the State Capital Building of Nashville, Tennessee. The picture of the Capital was clear, I knew exactly what it was and where it was. My response to God was "Yes LORD, I'll go and I'll pray". I was so filled with peace that it really did pass my understanding. This peace is still a part of His mission to Nashville to this day.

Being excited I went the very next day to downtown Nashville. I wanted to find the exact spot that I was to pray the next year, April 7, 1997. I went strait up to the Capital walking and searching for the exact place. I walked around the very porch of the Capital, laying my hands upon the walls praying for those in Legislative positions, for senators and congressmen, and for lawyers and judges. I was asking God to raise up Holy men of God to lead and make right and just decision for Nashville, Tennessee.

After awhile I began to realize that I was not in the "spot"—the very place that God had called me to pray. So I went walking around the streets praying and walking, looking toward the Capital so that I would see it the same way I saw it in my vision. After about two hours of walking around searching for the place of anointing, I couldn't feel the peace of where I should begin to pray.

ASK AND YOU SHALL RECEIVE

I remember asking God to anoint my eyes so that I could see the spot where He wanted me to pray. About ten minutes later, WHAM! Like running into a wall I saw it. God had opened my eyes to the future...April 7, 1997. Right where I was standing, the LORD showed me leaves on the trees that I wasn't seeing because of the fall of the year. In the natural there was no leaves. God enhanced my vision as I was standing in "the place," and by His Spirit I saw the Capital just as I had the day before in prayer.

I was standing on the concrete plaza that cuts over beside the Municipal Auditorium. Benches and tables were all around me. And I knew that place was the place of anointing. WOW! So I walked around in prayer thanking God for His Spirit, and for what He was going to do through prayer on April 7th. From this point on, April 7th was on my heart, mind, and spirit every day since.

Finally, April 7th, 1997 had come! I was so excited I got to Nashville an hour early. I parked by the War Memorial Building and waited until 9:00 am. Time passed quickly and I could feel a battle commencing in my spirit. Being determined, I knelt down on my knees over one of the benches about half way through the concrete plaza and began to pray. My face was in my hands and my "flesh" was warring against my spirit. My knees were feeling the weight of gravity against the concrete(a miserable place for my flesh, but I had already been assured months ago in November of 1996 that this was God's will for my Life in Christ. I knew my "flesh" had to begin to become subject to the authority of my assurance. I had prayed a good hour for everyone I could think of that might be up in that Capital Building that day. With open voice, I would pray for God to raise up a man of God that would stand for justice and morals in decision making, and votes that were to come—that every choice would be made in the fear of the LORD.

Then I guess it was right around the time of that first hour when the heart of the prayer was changed by the Spirit of Prayer. I had begun to cry out with groaning and deep breaths of elongated cries for revival and salvation for Nashville, the City, and its people. The more I would cry for God to deliver souls into His Kingdom, the more I became broken, weeping like one who has heard the news of a very close loved one being taken by unexpected death. It was overwhelming. It seemed as if Jesus was right there as I was interceding and travailing coming into the very throne room of God. I was being turned upside down—His will turning. For a time I felt absolute numbness as I was poured out before God.

The Spirit of Prayer had reached a pinnacle cry in my spirit and now everything was quiet in heaven and on earth. I don't recall a sound at all. After a time I had found myself prostrate on the concrete plaza, it was hot—sweltering hot. I was sunburned on my lower back, where my shirt had come up while in travail. I felt the burning. I began to come back to my knees and lean back across the bench, and asked the LORD if He would send a cool wind over me because I was utterly famished. I was dry. My back now blistered. No sooner than I had asked, a brisk breeze encompassed me, as if in a counter clockwise manner dropping the temperature to 65° air conditioning for a quick five minutes or so. You can't imagine how thankful I was for that moment for immediate relief! *Answered prayer!*

Then, while in thanksgiving and praise, I felt the Lords' presence intensify, and I put my face back into my hands in reverence before Him. I saw the most brilliant hues of color that were so clear, so bright, so pure. *Nothing* on earth compares. In my minds eye I saw the colors of a rainbow. A deep red hue went through, and all around me. Following that, an orange-gold hue went through, and all around me. Then green. Then blue. And finally, a deep purple, all passed through, and around me. I was so intent on capturing these elements in my memory, because of the brilliance of it. I knew the Covenant of God was upon me.

THE FIRE FELL

God then gave me a vision of fire poured out upon Nashville. Not just a flame of fire, but a pillar of fire—liquid fire. It was as if a five gallon bucket of water was poured out all at once on ones' feet. This liquid fire was poured down upon the center of the City of Nashville. As it fell, it splattered all around Nashville like water or liquid would splatter. The liquid fire had splattered everywhere causing fire to break out in the suburbs of Nashville. First it fell on the North Side. Then the East. Then the South, and finally, the West. All of the liquid fire began to burn its way back into the heart of the City (downtown area). God had assured me that He would pour out His Spirit upon Nashville.

From that time forward, *every time* I approach the city of Nashville, I can still see the pillar of fire vividly being poured out over downtown. The more I walk with God, the more I understand that the things of God, and timing of God, all have their place in the Master's plan. I just sigh, "Thy will be done on earth as it is so in heaven". The LORD has so encouraged me about this very personal vision for Nashville in my life, even though He didn't really need to...

THE MISSIONARY

In 1998 I met a missionary who had just gotten back from Pakistan. We had fellowshipped for about thirty minutes one night. I shared my vision with him and he got rather excited; you see he had made several trips over to Israel bringing Christians out of persecution through underground means to save their lives. This particular instance he had brought several Jewish people (Messianic Jews) from Israel to Nashville. That same week they went back to Israel informing their communities and neighbors that Gods presence was in Nashville. They were testifying among people that there was a strong Authority over the City of Nashville. The missionary went on to tell me that many more were leaving Israel and coming to Nashville because they believed that God was doing something in Nashville, Tennessee. AS DO I BELIEVE!

AN ARMY OF THESE

June 6, 1999, I was compelled to begin reaching out into the city of Nashville. Earlier in the month of March, I was down at the Nashville Rescue Mission, near the front steps witnessing to a man, and a *bright light* had caught my eye down the sidewalk. It was around midday, so curiously I peered at it while talking to this man. It was a bright sunny day outside. I saw a purer light than I can describe coming from around that corner. It captivated me. Then two homeless men walked around the corner as if they were coming to the front door of Rescue Mission. The LORD spoke to me and said, "I will raise up an army of these!" And I said, "Yes, LORD."

At times I wonder if God would not prevail more through the efforts of reaching a city one soul at a time. One on one. Won by one. I just wonder at times.

THE CARE OF SHEEP

My pastor and I began to take bologna sandwiches and ice water down to the streets, and hand them out with tracks, doing 'one on one' witnessing for Christ. In the beginning, it was peanut butter and jelly, and ice water with bologna three times a week. The LORD blessed us with a great sale on bologna, but before long the people were "full of bologna." We were tired of bologna too, so we began seeing a greater need for hot food. Through prevailing prayer, we were serving hot soups for crowds up to 30 by that September, and we have served HOT meals ever since.

The first winter it got down to 13° one night, and we still served about 12 people who were staying out in the cold. I recall one guy who had a camp about five miles from the River Front Park who said he was going to sleep on the "hot rock" (a warm concrete pad that has steam coming up under it). I convinced him I would give him a ride to his camp so he would not have to walk. When we had gotten to his campsite, we found his brother passed out in a chair. He was drunk. We carried him inside a "little" shack that kept the wind off, and laid him across a very dirty mattress. We covered him up with several dirty blankets, and thanked God that we came back to his camp that night because he probably would have froze to death. I think the wind chill that night was something like 10° below zero.

There are so many other glorious things that have happened to people down on the streets of Nashville that it would take another book to write about it.

BUT TRAGEDY STILL OCCURS

The violence among the street people and the homeless, yet alone amongst the thugs, is very depraved at times. I remember one guy who waited until a man he had a conflict with earlier that day went to sleep, and after drinking a lot of alcohol, he poured gasoline on the other man's covers which caught him on fire. *LORD, save your people and deliver them from that old spirit of hate and murder!*

During the summer, the crowds get up to around 120-150 people. Some just passing through Nashville, were brutally mugged; some are simply stranded. The crowds are made up of many different types of people. Quite a few Mexican people migrate for work in Nashville. Some have had nervous breakdowns; some are on the run; some are murderers; some are sowing wild oats; some are veterans; some are schizophrenic, and some are possessed. But the majority are alcoholics and crack heads. Shockingly, the majority say they are Christians!?

Who discipled this majority who will not repent for their pride and rebellion, to obey Gods calling, to be separate and Holy?? Who discipled these "Christians" who run to the bottle or run to the one who has a 'rock to smoke' to be a part of the family on the streets?? Who taught them through the steps of faith that when you fall you don't get up, and obey God's Word after you truly repent, with a brokeness and a shamefulness over that sin? Who discipled those who have no reverence for the Word of God, and are convinced that everything is all right if they should go into judgment this day? Who taught these "drunken" Christians a one-minute prayer will sanctify them, and they go back to profanity with their drunken friends? Truly, amongst the sheep, there are wolves; a major majority that have hardened hearts and blinded eyes, who deceive and are being deceived.

But God always has a remnant. There are very few who love God in the midst of their situation or circumstance. When I see the ones that are so stout hearted—so strong willed, I see the potential once they are converted into a new creature in Christ. All the demons and devils had better tremble and leave this town in a hurry, because these will have a stout heart for the LORD, to build His kingdom on earth. Their will shall be stronger in the Spirit of Christ than it was in the spirit of the world.

They will become the mighty army of God in this City of Nashville. What is the 'Great Commission' about anyway? Nashville needs to know that She serves a God who delivers Her from such a hellish nightmare.

A TIME TO WITNESS

Many people are praying for revival in Nashville, but many *more* are not! Have you noticed that downtown is turning into a RED LIGHT DISTRICT? Where is the testimony of Jesus Christ in our city? Has "The fear of the LORD" left the church while a "fear" of the LORD has crept in? I say something is amiss. Our city is disintegrating within like a mighty oak that has been hollowed by insects.

"A true witness delivereth souls: but a deceitful witness speaketh lies. Doth not wisdom cry out and understanding put forth her voice? She crieth at the gates, at the entry of the city, at the coming in at the doors."
—PROVERBS 14:25

There is a *great* need for teaching on the streets, even more than preaching. I have found that people only believe what someone else has taught them. Many people rely on what someone else has told them and they count it as truth no matter how 'off' the doctrine. I realize that no one individual has complete truth, and yet I realize how that the church today has allowed anyone whom claims to be a Christian to be counted as a brother or sister in Christ. Those have made claims that they are a child of God, yet they walk in a cloud of darkness. They have no problem with smoking, drinking, profanities, and have pleasure with them who do such things. What sayeth the WORD OF THE LORD?? He who commits sin is a child of the devil!

"He that committeth sin is of the devil; for the devil sinneth from the beginning. For this purpose the Son of God was manifested, that he might destroy the works of the devil."
—I JOHN 3:8 (KJV)

I find that the LORD would draw a line in the dirt and challenge whosoever will step across to be holy and without blame—to be a witness for Jesus Christ, and His power, rather than to be a witness who has false claims of salvation without a change of heart, mind, will or spirit.

We must teach by example that our Christian testimony will truly testify for us, or it will testify against us!

"Then they that feared the LORD spake often one to another: and the LORD hearkened, and heard it, and a book of remembrance was written before him for them that feared the LORD, and that thought upon his name. And they shall be mine, saith the LORD of hosts, in that day when I make up my jewels; and I will spare them, as a man spareth his own son that serveth him. Then shall ye return, and discern between the righteous and the wicked, between him that serveth God and him that serveth him not."
—MALACHAI 3:16

"When the son of man shall come in his glory, and all the holy angels with him, then shall he sit upon the throne of his glory: And before him shall be gathered all nations; and he shall separate them one form another, as a shepherd divideth his sheep from the goats: And he shall set the sheep on his right hand, but the goats on the left. Then shall the King say unto them on his right hand, Come, ye blessed of my Father, inherit the kingdom prepared for you from the foundation of the world: For I was an hungred, and ye gave me meat: I was thirsty, and ye gave me drink: I was a stranger, and ye took me in: Naked, and ye clothed me: I was sick, and ye visited me: I was in prison, and ye came unto me."
—MATTHEW 25:31-36

"For I am not ashamed of the gospel of Christ: for it is the power of God unto salvation to every one that believeth; to the Jew first, and also to the Greek...all attributes of him from the creation of the world are clearly seen, being understood by the things that are made, even his eternal power and Godhead; so that they are without excuse."
—ROMANS 1:16,20

People on the street need the stability of Jesus in you! Being allowed to convince "Christians" that you shouldn't judge lest ye be judged is taken many times in the wrong spirit of mind:

"The LORD is known by the judgment which he executeth."
—PSALMS 9:16

"I beheld, and the same horn made war with the saints, and prevailed against them; Until the Ancient of days came, and judgment was given to the saints of the most High; and the time came that the saints possessed the kingdom."
—DANIEL 7:21-22

"Judge not according to the appearance, but judge righteous judgment."
—JOHN 7:24

But we are sure that the judgment of God is according to truth against them which commit such things.
—Romans 1:28

TEACH SOUND DOCTRINE

Are you one to uphold the Law of Righteousness in the Kingdom of God? Do you exercise the mindset that Jesus has or the mindset of the Pharisees? Does the love of Jesus look at the lost through your eyes while putting forth sound doctrine, or does your own zeal stare at people with a religious spirit because they don't serve God the way you want them to. There is a difference. Sound doctrine must be taught not preached. When people get understanding with the heart and mind of God it's like the timely rain...

"My doctrine shall drop as the rain, my speech shall distil as the dew, as the small rain upon the tender herb, and as the showers upon the grass."
—Deuteronomy 32:2

Every man of God believes if you seek the LORD GOD ALMIGHTY with *all of your heart* you will be found of Him. So I say there is a fault among those who teach not by example. I am convinced that the more you come into Gods presence, the more His presence comes into you. Remember how Moses' face shone after 40 days on the mount with the LORD?! Those who are identified as Gods children must have the gratitude to be true to His complete Lordship, if we don't have a sincere gratitude, there will be a lack of desire to pray and seek God's face in order to continue in repentance and grow in "His" grace.

NO GRATITUDE SMELLS OF ATTITUDE

Most of the time when one has an attitude it is because of selfishness, a wantoness of desiring control. Some identify this as pride. Pride will take our vision to other things besides the essence of *building* His kingdom while here on earth. Pride makes no sacrifices to God. It is selfish in itself. God in His love gives us His divine law and then gives us a free choice, and makes it plain for even a child to see. If you obey His Word, then you'll receive blessings and covenants of life, peace and joy. On the other side of the scale, if you are disobedient to His Word (the Bible) then you find a condemnation for disobedience, anger, frustration—that curse of sin which brings spiritual death. According to the measure of disobedience, some have been so miserable they've taken their own lives—even when they had a right choice, and a wrong choice to make. Even so, many times we make choices when we don't make choices. What pleases God in your choices?

When we think of repentance in praying for revival, we think of fasting in order to bring our flesh in line with the Spirit. Fasting makes our spirit more sensitive to focus on repentance; all wrong doing; unveiled or veiled. We must search our hearts and mind before God allowing His Spirit to search us. Usually there is a brokeness of our lives in the presence of the LORD. We become as clay pots in the Potter's presence. Then we begin to receive forgiveness of our sins:

"But if we walk in the light, as he is in the light, we have fellowship one with another, and the blood of Jesus Christ his Son cleanseth us from all sin. If we say that we have no sin, we deceive ourselves, and the truth is not in us. If we confess our sins, he is faithful and just to forgive us our sins, and to cleanse us from all unrighteousness."
—I JOHN 1:7-9

Once we have received fresh atonement then we have access to make war on our spiritual enemies. True repentance allows one to make amends, with any one we may have hurt. God loves restoration. It is beautiful, and it is His Divine design when we walk in the light as He is in the light. True fellowship. True communion. True life!!

"He who can hear, let him listen to and heed what the Spirit says to the assemblies (churches)... For you say, I am rich; I have prospered and grown wealthy, and I am in need of nothing; and you do not realize and understand that you are wretched, pitiable, poor, blind, and naked.
Therefore I counsel you to purchase from Me gold refined and tested by fire, that you may be (truly) wealthy, and white clothes to clothe you and to keep the shame of your nudity from being seen, and salve to put on your eyes, that you may see."
—REVELATION 3:13, 22 (AMPLIFIED BIBLE)

ANOINT YOUR EYES!

When you think of anointing your eyes with eye salve, what would you use? Anointing oil? 100% pure olive oil? Do you think of putting a little smear on your eyelids??

Well guess what!!!??? After searching out about anointing your eyes with eye salve, the word refers to the word, "stibium stibnate; tartar emetic." It is commonly used in cough syrups as an expectorant. You see, it is a poison that induces vomiting. It is so toxic it can cause death! However, used in cough syrup, it is just enough to help you get up a strong enough cough to break up the congestion in you chest or lungs...

So what is the word trying to say...anoint thine eyes with eye salve, that thou mayest see. Anoint your eyes with a healthy amount of this expectorant, rub it as an ointment all over and around your eyes, and let the expectorant draw out any self-righteousness, pride, lack of gratitude, bitterness, hate, envy, strife, backbiting, murmuring, griping, and complaining. Let it draw out the poison and death of sin, and then you prayers can be heard through a true repentance worked by Godly sorrow. The Word tells us..."as many as I love I rebuke, and chasten; be zealous therefore and repent. He that hath an ear to hear, let him hear what the Spirit is saying to the churches."

Perhaps you have always wanted to see more in the kingdom of God; especially those signs, miracles, deliverance, healing, the dead being raised, and so much more that Gods word promises. But maybe your eyes; your imagination; your faith, are *sin sick*. Maybe we should obey Gods word and start dealing with our eyes — spirit, soul and body. If you weren't seeing so well in the natural, and you were able and had the means to afford it, wouldn't you get your eyes tested to see if you needed glasses to improve your vision?? Most people do and they make eye appointments. Well we have a great physician, his name is Jehovah Rapha (The LORD our healer).

"If thou will diligently hearken to the voice of the LORD thy God, and wilt do that which is right in his sight, and wilt give ear to his commandments, and keep all his statutes, I will put none of these diseases upon thee, which I have brought upon the Egyptians: for I am the LORD that healeth thee. And they came to Elim, where were twelve wells of water, and threescore and ten palm trees: and they encamped there by the waters."
—EXODUS 15:26-27

AN INVITATION

God hates lukewarmness! You know—people of God who think everything will get done by God or the preacher. Don't you realize that God does not call us to sit in churches, but to go out into the world to counsel the lost to come into relationship and communion with him? After three years, or even two years, we should have been discipled enough to be fishers of men! Yet our eyes must be sick with some kind of self-righteous deception called Laodecia.

I *invite you* to hit the streets in Nashville, and get to know God's heartbeat on the streets. It won't take long to see who it is He still wants to save and deliver; or maybe you can sit in church on Sunday, and act like you're exempt from reaching the world with *your* personal testimony.

"Beloved, think it not strange concerning the fiery trial which is to try you, as though some strange thing happened unto you: But rejoice, inasmuch as ye are partakers of Christ's sufferings; that, when his glory shall be revealed, ye may be glad also with exceeding joy. If ye be reproached for the name of Christ, happy are ye: for the spirit of glory and of God resteth upon you; on their part he is evil spoken of, but on your part he is glorified. But let none of you suffer as a murderer, or as a thief, or as an evildoers, or as a busybody in other men's matters. Yet if any man suffer as a Christian, let him not be ashamed; but let him glorify God on this behalf. For the time is come that judgment must begin at the house of God."
—I PETER 4:12-19

I'll see you downtown in Nashville, doing His bidding to win the lost. No one will ever turn to God unless you relate and convince them by your testimony. That's how you overcome the world—by the *Blood* of the Lamb, and the *word* of your testimony! *Glory to God!*

About the Author

Mark and Brenda Goad reside in Chapmansborough, TN. with their son, and daughter. Open Your Eyes Ministry gathers downtown on Thursday nights at 7:00pm at the "old" hospital near First Street to feed the homeless and preach the good news.

A Man With a Mission

Nashville Rescue Mission interview with:
Gary Bougeois: President of The Nashville Rescue Mission
Bruce Newport: Public Relations and Chief Fundraiser
Hosted by: Jeffrey M. Richfield

Jeff: One of the visions of this book is to encapsulate a message that will catapult people into Christ-like action. That is why I chose The Mission as one of the authors—because down here you are *living out* the vision of Christ-like compassion, taking it to the streets, not being a spectator. So if you have anything to throw in on that...What is your vision for the Rescue Mission and how is it evolving?

Gary: The grand view and vision here at the Mission in a nutshell is rescuing people from a life in the street, and offering them Jesus. Our goal is helping those who have life defeating issues, and providing "the way" for them to overcome those issues. Basically, this breaks down into three parts. First, the Rescue Mission helps in preventing homelessness from happening. Part two, which we are starting now, is helping people who have fallen into hard times, and helping them deal with those issues. And finally, the third part will be helping those people from relapsing back into that way of life.

We have an agenda on how to achieve those things. Oftentimes, the people we deal with are people often forgotten. They are often viewed as people who "made their bed now let them sleep in it," or "this is a land of opportunity here in America, and if they messed up, it's their own fault—it's not my responsibility to help them. When we look at Christ and what He has done for us—He came down to help people and He could've said the same thing about those sinners, "He made his bed, now let him sleep in it. Look at what I done for them already. They've messed it up it's their fault." Yet, He loved us in spite of ourselves.

Often people who end up on the street are people who are not clean. They are people who have rough edges about them—people that many times, the average person might find offensive. But, there again, Christ did not find mankind too offensive that He did not come down and become one of us and dwell amongst us. He was a stone carpenter, and He dwelt and worked with men who were dirty, sweaty, and not smelling really good. I'm sure it was not pleasant for God to do that but he did because He loved us. He saw beyond our faults and frailties, and saw beyond us as being people that were messed up. He saw us as people He loved that were created in His image. People that He gave value, meaning and purpose, and He wanted to redeem them and rescue them. He wanted to help them overcome through His shed blood, and be able to be called joint heirs of His. He called them friends and that's our goal—to see beyond this person's dirt in a sense—to see beyond the sin of their life—to see in them what God sees in all of us—to help them to know the redemption of Christ so they can become all that He has designed them to be—that they can know Jesus themselves, and live as joint heirs with Christ—to be called a friend of God, fulfilling the potential God gave them.

Jeff: You talk about the values that Jesus displayed. What do you think are some of the core values in the Mission's purpose?

Gary: One of the core values of this mission is to let the less fortunate know that God loves them. Therefore, we are helping people that are often overlooked—the downcast. We explain that God loves him or her—that no one should be abandoned—that God does not walk away from mankind, but it is mankind who walks away from God. We're helping people that God loves and is reaching out to. Until a person has drawn his last breath, God is giving him opportunities. God is reaching out to them, and so should we. So, we do not abandon people simply because they are dirty and have problems. We believe that if you really want people to change, then you have to offer them something to help them change. You can't just walk up to somebody and say, "Change—get over it—deal with it", and expect it to happen. That is why we have various programs. We have one for younger men in Pleasant View, Tennessee, that's for the 8-25 age group. We have the women and children's programs, and we have the downtown ministry.

We believe that compassion is part of the Christian life. Christ brings compassion to us and so should we to others. The concept of grace, mercy, and compassion requires understanding coupled with action. What I mean by that is if we say we really care about these people, then we should understand what their situation is, and what we can do to help. That is what our mentoring programs are all about. That is what our "safety net" side is all about. All the people see is the "safety net" part of the division. It is our reaching out to the person on the street, offering food, shelter, and clothing and minor medical care. We are the largest "safety net" in town helping people to get back on their feet, but that's not our only goal. Our goal is to be a spiritual hospital built on that "safety net" to help them overcome these life-defeating issues. So they can look in the mirror some day, and know that they are fulfilling God's purpose for their life—so that they can be pleased with what they see.

Jeff: As I listen to what you are talking about, I think about the mainline churches out there right now, and it seems like you're actually doing something a lot of churches aren't—saving lost souls. You are producing results many churches just don't get a chance to see. Where can church participators plug into the Mission to help extend a hand of compassion?

Gary: There are a lot of areas a Christian can volunteer their time to help individuals who have fallen on hard times or are dealing with the issues of life issues, and hopeless scenarios. As far as the church itself goes, I believe the Mission fulfills a role that God has intended churches to be a part of to fulfill. It's not our purpose to shoot holes at churches, but it's easy I think, for churches to get the suburban mindset—that we reach out to a certain type of individual who we're comfortable with that's like us. That's human nature. But when we do that, we often exclude others that may not fit that mindset or economic class, or the suburban goals. Those that don't fit, sometimes are forgotten. The average church might say "They are welcome to come and worship with us," but we know that often times, that person knows they're not really welcome in feeling. A person might shake their hand and say, "It's good to see you this morning," but that's about the extent of the relationship. At that point, those people drift away.

Jeff: Do you think fear has a part of it? Because, see, you're in the mindset of doing it. You're hands on with these people every day. You have overcome "the fears." So fear is probably a contributing factor—fear of the unknown.

Gary: Yes, fear is a major factor with a lot of people on the street too. They are fearful of their own existence. They may not sleep well. They sleep with one eye open, so to speak. But also how other people perceive them, and what they think of them creates a fear factor. They wonder if passers by will accept them or reject them. Those issues are important. I think churches that want reach out to them have to let these people know, "Hey, we love you, we care about you, and welcome you." It is not saying that a church has to all of a sudden forsake itself. I'm not saying they have to become something that they are not. I'm saying they have to open the door and allow people to be loved.

Jeff: We have talked about some of the needs of mentoring and pastoring. What other opportunities are open for churches to participate in? Is there any other ways the Body of Christ can help?

Gary: There's a whole host of areas from mentoring, tutoring, and teaching. Whatever skills a person has can be contributed here. A lawyer can help with legal issues; an accountant can help with teaching a finance class. There is a whole host of areas where a person can use their skills or gifts in reaching out to people.

Jeff: Gary, you've been at the Mission 2-1/2 years now, where were you before that?

Gary: Before the Mission, I've been a pastor and also a prison Chaplin. The jail ministry prepared me for this type of work because I dealt with these same types of issues that often arise within a homeless setting of people who have life defeating issues and addictions. People that may have had a dysfunctional background—like maybe not knowing what it is to be loved—or maybe they have never seen what it is to be a man or a lady modeled well before them—or what is expected from them by society. We often assume people have had the same type of upbringing we've had or the same type of opportunities we've had because we're in "America"—and that's not necessarily true. Not everybody has seen what it's like to have a good role model in a father or mother. Some just haven't had the same backgrounds as us. I'm not saying that everybody who is homeless has come out of a dysfunctional poverty-stricken background. We have seen all walks of life come to us in need of our aid, but there again, it goes back to *compassion* and *understanding.* It is important that we understand what it is they are going through, and what are their needs are and what ways we can help.

Jeff: Right, I see it now. This is most definitely a spiritual hospital, a safe refuge. As a church member thinking about approaching the needy and the homeless for a minute....what is the method you might use in reaching out to someone on the street? What do you suppose might be a typical question or response one would expect in reaching out? I think this is where Bruce's testimony comes in. Bruce, can you tell me, once being homeless yourself, why is it that all the homeless just don't come down to the Mission to get help?

Bruce Newport: I think the main reason they're not all down here is it's more of an excuse than a protection. Sometimes they'll come up with, "We are spying on them up here," or "They take your money," and some even say, "They charge up there." The bottom line is they know when they come into our facilities *accountability* remains for the whole format. You have to answer to a higher authority here. When you come in it's about recovery; it's about getting off the street. When they're confronted with their problems it's very uncomfortable for them to face their issues. For example, for some it's uncomfortable to get up there at chapel services and mention the program—that they want to break their addiction problems or whatever. That's the main excuse. The underlying excuse is some just don't want to face their issues.

Jeff: When you came in did you have any fears?

Bruce: No, realistically, I messed up long enough. I came in the later part of '96. I had been floating around since January of that year—so I was just sick and tired of being sick and tired.

Jeff: So now, what roles do you play in the Mission?

Bruce: I'm the head of Public relations and fundraising. At times you want to pull your hair out, and other times—when you see the life changes—you're just ecstatic!

Jeff: Well, you're the proof in the pudding, so to speak.

Bruce: I guess the downside is when you talk to people on the streets—especially young guys—I say, "Look you don't want to be like me." They say, "Why not, now you're fine. I can blow it out five or six more years, and nothing is going to happen to me and I can turn my life around like you." But you never know when God is going to pull that rug out from underneath you, and take your life. I tell them, "You're playing with His life not your own." So realistically, He makes that decision—not you. You see they're living *their* will and their life...and that's sad.

Jeff: I agree. Obviously, there must first be an inward brokeness before God will deal with someone to bring about a life change. Now, to enter the Rescue Mission program are there any fees? If a homeless person comes in tomorrow and makes a decision to enter, what are the steps?

Gary: If a person says they want to get on the program, first, they go through what we call a "seeker phase." This is a design of the program we have where for 30-45 days they come to understand what their problem is; how bad is that problem; what is change; and do they really want to endure the day to day "discomfort" that comes from any level of change. It asks them the questions, "What does the new man or lady look like?" And, "Do they want to become that person?" They need to understand these things first. When they come to say, "I understand and I do want change", then they go into a 6-9 month program that's broken up into five phases. At the beginning of each phase they establish goals and at the end of each phase they evaluate goals. A counselor who tracks them through the phases may say, "Well, Bob, you're doing good with listening and anger-management, etc., but maybe you're not doing so hot in this other area. It seems that we're struggling a little bit with this. Maybe we need to deal with that a little more efficiently before we go to phase two."

That's why we say 6 to 9 months—however long it takes to "get it." It's not a magic formula that says in 90 days or 6 months you're going to be fine. It's, "Have you achieved the goals you've come to establish to make a life change?" So to finish it, they deal with those life-defeating issues. Once they finish that, then they can be interviewed. It's not guaranteed, but they can be interviewed to go into our transitional housing program, which is another 6-9 months or even up to one year. At that point, there is a high level of accountability and responsibility, and they need to have a job. We will do a financial plan with them based on how much money they are making. We require seeing a savings slip each week based on that financial plan. The goal here is that they are now practicing being this new man. They are working on the rough edges. It's not that they have been infused with knowledge and say, "O.k. God, now provide and do", no—it's helping them practice and *do for themselves.* As they discover those rough edges, we help them shave them off and deal with them.

The bible studies, the individual counseling, and group counseling are continued throughout as they are practicing and learning. We also look for mentors during the last two or three months of the program. That mentor simply becomes a source of encouragement and a friend that we train on how to do this. The goal there is not to become a behavioral therapist or a trained psychologist, rather, a *friend.* What happens to a lot of people that maybe get clean and sober for six, nine months, or a year—and doing well, but not totally 100% on their feet, is they go out into the community and look for friends. If the churches do not accept them with open arms or they don't find good Christian friends, they gravitate back to their old friends who are doing drugs and up to no good. Of course, they end up falling back into the same predicament that brought them to the Mission, and the cycle continues. The mentors help them break that cycle. The mentor is one person who cares—a person who wants to see them succeed, and give them at least one friend. Also, that mentor can introduce them into their church of like-mind and religious background where this person will feel comfortable. It may be that they have never been to church before or felt comfortable with church. That is what the mentor is there for.

A typical problem is, they get stressed, their job is stretched, and they want to drink. Then the mentor can say, "I see you're struggling, why don't you come back to the Mission for more counseling." This helps them through that time to help prevent relapse. That's the overall structure of what were trying to do here. The program is free until they get into the transitional housing program. At that point, it is a very modest fee for what they are receiving. They get an efficiency apartment and are still able to eat at the Mission, and receive clothing and things. The point is, they have to learn to pay rent and they have to learn responsibility. They also have to learn to maintain their room as we do room inspections. It's not a flophouse here, and they have to treat it like it's their home.

Jeff: It sounds like tough love.

Bruce: Yes. It would be nice to say that everybody who goes through the program does well, but we have seen enough do well to keep us going and we're doing what God wants us to do, and seeing *good* results!

Jeff: Now that you mentioned the mentoring needs that leads me to my next question. If you were on a citywide platform speaking to the churches of Nashville, what would be the most important heart issue that would want to get across to them? You see here at the Mission there is an opportunity, not just the mentorship, but also newfound spiritual awareness and prayer opportunities. This is nothing less than a gathering place where God's promises and His covenant are being fulfilled. In the Bible, part of 2 Chronicles 7:14 says, "If we seek His face *and* turn from our evil ways, that there will be a healing in our land." What, in your eyes, is the reason why there hasn't been a revival like the 1700's and 1800's and what can we do to play a part in it? I know it's not man's decision to "make revival happen" or "put God in a box," but we're definitely to be playing a role.

Gary: That's a burden of mine. I think there is a real need for revival in Nashville in the area of *compassion* towards others. It's not so much the area to argue "tit for tat," and who is theologically more accurate than the other group, but on the basics that we agree on—faith in Christ, love for man, and reaching out to others in love. Revival can be as simple as this—that we genuinely show that *love* for each other as Christians. That in itself can be a struggle many times. But, also to show love for all mankind all over the world—every individual; not just the clean; not just the wealthy; not just the well-dressed and educated, but for *any* individual. If we could come to understand that God loves us all equally, and we're all sinners in the eyes of God who need redemption, grace and mercy. If we could truly love others as God loves us, then I think we could see more of that revival happen. Then people would see we are genuine in our faith, and not just people of doctrine.

Jeff: What would bring about that change as far as true compassion, true Christ-like love in action in the people of Nashville? I'm burdened with a prayer of *aggravation* on this issue, but I know it's going to be the breath of God that is going to change our hearts. First, we have to allow God to bring us true change. That's what this book is all about. Guys, would you consider being a part of a citywide concerted prayer effort to help bring that change in seeking holiness and calling upon God for *His* spiritual awakening for Nashville in our lifetime?

Gary: Yes, prayer is obviously an important part of it. When we pray to God to have that communion and fellowship with Him. That's where we find God. We seek Him for who He is, and see who we are, and our great need for Him. Obviously prayer, bible studies, and worship is very important in our relationship with God. There are a lot of good churches with a lot of good things in them. I am not trying to bad mouth churches in any way, but I think it's easy for people to get comfortable into certain things. For example, if I'm going to a church and they offered me youth programs for the kids, and have a nice worship service—"all" for this and "all" for that. I can eat cake and feel satisfied. But do I see church as a place where I also serve and give back. Using our spiritual gifts honors God. I think Christians need to see church as not only a place where they receive, but also as a place to go *to give.*

Usually, my spiritual gifts honor God. I think people; Christians in our community need to see church as beyond a place where I go to receive but also a place where I go to give. Through the church, their involvement in places like the mission, where they can use those gifts as a body; as a group of believers, to reach out to everyone, will make a difference.

Every once in awhile, I will have a pastor come to me and say, "Yeah, I sent some guys down to you". I know what he means(that someone has been asking him for a dime, or a buck, or they have problems. Maybe a guy that's inebriated that came to their doorstep, and he wants to send him to us because we're prepared to deal with that. But, sometimes, and they don't even think about it, I think some guys may communicate that this is not the type of person my church is set up to reach out to. He needs to go somewhere else, out of sight, out of mind. I don't want to go so far as to say they don't see the homeless as human, but if a wealthy man was on the doorstep, who was cleanly dressed and said, "I need something maybe you can help me." They would probably spend the time. But, if they know it is a poor person who is dirty, and it was about "money, money, money," it's easy for them to close the door.

It's not bashing the Pastor who does this because often times they are not prepared to deal with that. I think they need to stop and say, "Well, how can we be involved in helping that individual."

A church needs to think how they can fully meet the needs of everyone in their community, not just the type that typically fill the pews. Some churches are seeking to do that. We have several churches that come down now to do chapel service. I'm not saying all churches don't, there is a lot of good effort. But when you look at 1,500 churches in Nashville, and if 1,500 churches were fulfilling this, then it would be a much different scene.

Jeff: Please give me a run down on the history of the mission.

Gary: The history of this Mission started out of a revival back in 1953 or 1954. Charles Fuller was holding a revival here in Nashville at the Ryman Auditorium. At the end of his week of meeting, they gave him $1,000 check for his services, which back then was a healthy amount of money. He said, "No, you keep the money and do something to help these people that are on the street." The reason why he said that was because he was staying at the James Robinson apartments, and he walked from there to the Ryman Auditorium. In the evening he would always get some man asking if he could spare a dime. He felt that money should be used to do something to help that individual. As a result of that, a group of concerned Christians that were a part of that revival accepted that challenge, and they started what is now called the Nashville Rescue Mission. It has just grown over the years. The year, 1954, was when the Mission actually started.

Jeff: Who was the original founder?

Gary: There wasn't any one individual, but it was a group. A board of director's that had this burden and desire to help the poor of Nashville had a vision. But, it wasn't the vision of just one man. It was the vision of "The Man."

Jeff: Ultimately, "A City On Its Knees," is a vision for cities all across America—that through kneeling in prayer is where God speaks. Then we arise, and walk to take this idea not to just ministries, but to show how Christian's can plug in, and where they can be a light in a dark world, and salt to the earth.

Gary: I want to reiterate that I believe that most churches would get involved in helping if they *knew* how or they *understood.* So what I would want to communicate is not a negative towards the Body of Christ in Nashville. You can't expect somebody to do something they don't know about, and you can't expect them to get involved in an area they don't know where to get involved. You can't expect someone to do something that they're fearful of or unfamiliar with. Most of the church today simply doesn't know how to help these people, so it's easier to just withdraw.

That's what we want to communicate here—to help them to understand how they can reach out to the less fortunate, and help them to know what these people are going through. To give them the opportunity through a structure like the Mission that they can reach out to these individuals, where honestly, most churches cannot. Unless it's a large church they may not have the staff needed to deal with an individual that has these types of problems. I'm not saying that every church has to start its own homeless ministry because they may not have the required skills necessary, but I believe they should be willing to be a part of something that helps the poor.

Jeff: What is your estimate of how many homeless there are in Nashville?

Bruce: We have heard numbers of like 3,000 but that's an old number. That number incorporates the person that may be staying on grandma's couch or 1,000 other places. It may not be that there are 3,000 on the street, but I've heard there are 2,000 or 2,500.

Jeff: Of most of the graduates, do some of them continue working in the Mission?

Gary: Right, 40% of our staff are people who were formally in the program. There again, we could share stories of people who stereotypically think that some guy is a high school dropout coming out of the projects, but it's not. Like I shared with you, there's an Auburn graduate who came from a wealthy family. Right now, we have a fellow who is formerly with GM as a mid-level executive at General Motors. We had a lawyer who recently went through the program. I remember meeting with a guy who was a Navy Seal. We've had small business owners and all walks of life, people with Masters Degrees and such. I remember sitting here a couple of weeks ago chatting with a homeless man who has been on the streets for years, but very well educated. If you were to start talking philosophy, he would start talking philosophers, and start talking about theories and what not because he's been to college. You find all kinds. Right now I know a man who is at our Mission who was a former physics teacher who just mentally snapped. He is a very quite man, but snapped somewhere.

Roughly 40% of the homeless have some kind of mental illness and that's another thing that the people don't understand how to deal with it. What we're doing here is partnering with the Mental Health Co-op. When that individual comes our way, the Mental Health Co-op can help get them to a psychiatrist to be evaluated, and so forth. If it were a person we can work with in our program, our goal would be to help them here. If the diagnosis is paranoia, or they are having severe problems where there is harm to himself or someone else, then Mental Health Co-op will have about 60 days to get him into the right kind of facility like

Middle Tennessee Health Center, to get the right kind of care. Mental illness is a big issue as well as drug addiction on the street.

Jeff: Can you give me your statistical information such as, how many rooms will there be, and how many apartments will be built? Things like that.

Bruce: I have that information. With this building we are really ramping up. Eventually, we will be able to have an admission of 700 people bed capacity. That's not right now, we don't have the staffing for that big of a facility. Last night we had 437 people and we are running 450-500 average.

Jeff: I really appreciate what you are doing here at The Mission. Is there anything you want to say in closing?

Gary: I think what I communicated is the core values of the Mission. I think, as people understand they will say, "That's my values too", and they will come into agreement with us. They will say, "How can we work together to fulfill those values?" We want to communicate those core values and communicate to people who we are and what we're doing because there is a misconception. A lot of people don't know; it's just rumors in the wind. We want to communicate who we are; what is the Mission; what are we doing; and how are we doing it well.
    That's what we're trying to do now. How can the Mission do that in a better way? We can go out to churches, go out to pastor fellowships, and meet with people to explain these things to overcome the misconception they have; the ignorance such as, "What does the Mission do? Oh, they feed them and let them sleep in beds. I don't know, what do they do."

Jeff: So you're willing to send some people out to tell the churches?

Gary: Definitely, we're trying to do that kind of thing. That's what I would really like to communicate. These are the core values of the Mission; this is how we're seeking to fulfill them; and here are opportunities that churches have to be involved with us.
    The doors of The Nashville Rescue Mission are always here. And they remain open to the poor, the hungry, the lost, the hurting, *and* the Body of Christ. Christ is knocking on the doors of individuals and the heart of the city of Nashville. Who will come, open them and let Him in? Who will come partner with us, and join us in rebuilding this CITY, and help establish it to be a safe refuge for the Lord's sake and the sake of the people?

WHAT THE NASHVILLE UNION MISSION OFFERS:

Homeless and Program facilities:
Sleeping up to 750 men, women and children a night.

Soup Kitchens:
Serving an average of 1400 meals a day for breakfast, lunch, and dinner.

Education and Training:
G.E.D, reading, Bible Study, computers, basic life skills, finance, college prep.

Anchor Home for Young Men:
2nd chance and recovery for ages 18-26.

Men's Program:
Adult recovery center for men 26 and older.

Family Life Center:
Shelter for women and children.

Hope Center:
Recovery center for women.

Traveler's Aid:
Help for the stranded, battered, run away and mentally-ill by giving counsel, travel assistance, food and clothing.

Lodging Place:
Over 40 new apartments available for committed individuals that have successfully completed one of our programs.

Mission Clinic:
Providing basic healthcare by volunteer doctors from local hospitals.

**The Nashville Union Mission receives no Government funding. All funding comes from individuals, businesses and organizations.

DID YOU KNOW...?

- The Nashville Metropolitan Area has a homeless population of approximately 3000 men, women and children

- Based on the same estimates 600 are veterans and about 360 are children under the age of 18. Approximately 144 of the children on the streets are under the age of 5

- Approximately 40% of the homeless in Middle Tennessee have a mental illness

- 85% of the homeless abuse drugs, alcohol or are involved in some other form of addictive behavior

DID YOU KNOW
THAT THE NASHVILLE UNION RESCUE MISSION...?

- Is the largest homeless provider in Tennessee and one of the largest in the United States averaging 1200 meals a day and provides rest for over 450 men women and children a night

- Offers several recovery and educational programs to help the homeless return to society as productive citizens – Over 33% of the people they assist daily are enrolled in a recovery program

- Offers a Travelers Aid program that assisted over 1,100 homeless and indigent individuals with relocation or emergency assistance

THE URGENT NEED

- Immediate action is needed to respond to the growing number of homeless in our community. The Mission is currently exceeding its holding capacity. Recovery facilities are dated and overcrowded.

- A new facility is urgently needed to accommodate current numbers.

- The Mission is currently building a new Mission facility. The new facility will allow for a capacity of up to 750 needy men, women and children.

- To get involved in one of our ministries please call (615) 255-2475 or write: PO Box 333229, Nashville, TN 37203-7535 website: www.NASHVILLERESCUEMISSION.ORG

Capture His Beauty

by Alicia Griffin

LONG BEFORE THE world was created, God decided that humankind would be His dwelling place. Our Lord chose to place His glorious presence in the hearts and bodies of His people, but because of man's sinful nature, rebelliousness, and opposition to Godliness, man's heart—the Temple of God—was defiled.

God's unconditional love for us does not manipulate behavioral changes in us to remove our sins. Instead, we are free to walk in either rebelliousness or obedience to God. However, God won't allow His presence and glory to abide in a place where corruption is present. He has to remove his glorious presence from us when there are sinful issues in our lives that we try to ignore. That's just what sin does: it holds back and thwarts God's plan and destiny for us, and He won't be able to reveal Himself to us, as He desires.

God permitted Christ to be disgraced and punished in our place for this very reason: to allow for the creation of free, moral children that are purged of all unrighteousness. It is through God's Son that we can be liberated from Satan's captivity and live a life that is worthy of our calling. This was and is God's eternal purpose for us.

When God spoke to Moses from the burning bush (Ex. 3:4-6; Acts 7:32) and introduced Himself as "the God of thy fathers, the God of Abraham, Isaac, and the God of Jacob," Moses hid his face from God and trembled with fear, for he was afraid to look upon God's Glory (Ex. 33:18-23; Num12:6-8). Amazingly, God and Moses spoke to each other with audible voices just as men do, without the aid of a mediator. This is the way God wants to communicate and have intimacy with us. He says to us, "Come, My bride, come and sit by My side. Let Me hold you close and speak My words of love to you."

The Lord acknowledged to Moses that He had seen the afflictions of His people. He had heard their cry, known their sorrows, and seen their oppression. God sees our failures and knows our feelings. He sees us during our life's journey; when distance has lost its enchantment for us, and when we tend to sloth and slumber and become lukewarm. He knows our hearts and our works.

Just as the Lord revealed His glory to Moses and saw his potential, He wants to infuse us with a passion to capture His character, His beauty, and to lean on Him, abandoning ourselves into His arms and spread through us the fragrance of the knowledge of Him. If we would turn to the Lord and acknowledge our iniquities, if we would turn back from our wicked ways, He would heal our wounds and revive our spirits.

God wants to restore to us the essence of life as He floods our soul with His presence. He wants this day to be a day of a new beginning. *God wants us to capture His beauty!*

We were fashioned within as well as without by Him to manifest His nature. We were designed to have God on the throne of our hearts, but we have chosen to forfeit our inheritance by letting self occupy that that throne instead. If we are totally available to Him, He will reveal His mighty power through us to change our lives, our families, our neighborhoods, and even the nations!

Since the beginning of time, we have tried to regain our initial intimacy with God by our own works. This is what the Bible calls "dead works". It is the desire to ease a guilty conscience or to promote ourselves before man, but our hearts cannot be made clean by religious activities, or by our attempts to make ourselves appear to be righteous. We can only be cleansed and renewed by the blood of the covenant made with God through Jesus Christ.

When we experience salvation, we receive a new nature and the old man is crucified. When we present ourselves before the Lord in true repentance and brokenheartedness, He will forgive us and place in us the desire to seek His face, listen to His word, and give our lives to Him in worship (Jer. 29:12-13,14 & Heb.10:16-18).

God is often pictured in the scriptures as the source of living water for the refreshment of the spiritually thirsty (Ps. 36:8,9 & 42:1, 2). When God's healing waters begin to flow

(Eze. 47:8), we will start bearing fruit and growing in Christ. We can be His habitation, learn His secrets, and receive His revelations. In Isaiah 41:18 the Lord says, "I will open rivers in high places, and fountains in the midst of the valleys: I will make the wilderness a pool of water, and the dry land springs of water."

Let's take an honest inventory of our lives. Let's look at our trials and intense testings we've been through. God wants to pour more of His Glory on us. He wants us to have a ravenous appetite for more of Him and consequently, He wants to fill us with His inexhaustible wonder beyond anything we've experienced in our lifetime. God wants to mete out to us glory and revelation beyond any previous measure (Eph. 1:8, 9)!

When our hearts open up and are tender to God's overtures of love, He will create in us a hunger to seek Him and to know Him. Imagine the angelic hosts surrounding Him in His regal Throne, declaring His Majesty with unrelenting crescendo! Let's come to Him with a thankful heart and proclaim His righteousness! God would take great pleasure in that.

"The Lord thy God in the midst of thee is mighty; He will save, he will rejoice over thee with joy; he will rest in his love, he will joy over thee with singing."
—ZEPH. 3:17

Sounds like we've never heard before will continue to reverberate throughout eternity, peal after peal of praise surrounding us with songs of deliverance (Ps. 32:7). For dominion belongs to the Lord and He rules over the nations!

Let's proclaim our destiny! We are redeemed children of God working hand in hand with Him towards the realization of His redemptive purposes on earth. God allows us, as His children, to make decisions that will influence history. Our inaction can make the atonement ineffective for lost people, and our fervent prayers will release cumulative amounts of God's power until enough has been released to accomplish His will. We are carriers of His powerful Holy Spirit. We are ambassadors of the High and Lofty One, The Great I Am; the One who inhabits eternity, whose name is Holy, and whose counsel shall stand.

HE LIVES! HE FULFILLS! HE IS OUR ALMIGHTY FRIEND!
That we should weak or heartless be,
Anxious of troubled when He's within?
We will sing unto our Lord
Glorious in holiness
We purpose to serve you, Lord!
The lover of our soul!!!

About the Author
Alicia Griffin hails from Mexico and attends Belmont Church. She has two boys, one girl, and is happily married. Alicia is simply a worshipper and intercessor who thirsts for God!

A Lighthouse City

by Betsy Headden

I love Nashville, Tennessee! As a native Nashvillian, this love is growing as I sense the Lord's love for it! I believe NASHVILLE IS DESTINED TO BE A LIGHTHOUSE CITY, humbly pointing the way for many cities in our nation and around the world for the kingdom of God. The new sound of worship and anointed music will be heard across the globe as our Redeemer infuses His Holy Spirit into all the incredible talents and abilities which He has given—releasing them for the glory of God!

Yes, there is an awesome call upon the musicians and upon the whole citywide area! Back in the early nineties we were struck by this fact, as we met several different individuals who had seen an amazing vision, none of them knowing each other. In each of their separate visions, angels were encircling Nashville, facing outward with trumpets to their mouths. They were calling for people to come here from all directions! They called for teachers and musicians. It was exciting to watch as this vision unfolded before our eyes. The anointed teachers and musicians have come! Reinforcements have arrived! Light is shining in the darkness!

As a gradual maturing process has taken place in the Body of Christ here, I can see how the Lord has been building a foundation upon which His revival can rest! There is now such EXPECTANCY. There is a sense of the desperate need for revival! The newspaper reports of violence and murder are unbearable on most days now. But God's plan is for righteousness to increase at the same time! Awaken us; revive us, O Lord!

It has been a long time since our nation has seen a whole city affected by the true gospel in action, stopping crime, closing nightclubs, and causing the name of Jesus to be discussed on every street! Though pastors are meeting together to pray and unite, and prayers have gone up for years...we wait...Now is the time for us, the Church of Nashville, to prepare our NEW WINESKINS! If a Great Awakening is indeed coming, His new wine cannot be contained in old wineskins. There has always been an entirely new and radical lifestyle empowered by the Holy Spirit which has come with every Biblical and historical revival. Will we be ready? The time is ripe for the answers to those hundreds of thousands of prayers that have gone up from this place. Now we must MOBILIZE on a larger scale!

The Lord has more for us! The greater works are yet to come. Though ministries to the poor are plowing up the hard ground of oppression and injustice, the workers are too few! And there is a multitude of people in greater Nashville who does not know the Lord Jesus Christ as Savior and Lord! How can this be with a church building on every corner? Yes, it is time to cry out TOGETHER for the harvest of Nashville! As reports of dozens of city transformations come before us, WE ARE HUNGRY and GREATLY DESIRE TO SEE OUR OWN CITY TRANSFORMED! There is a rallying cry as never before being sounded right here in Nashville. Jesus said that a kingdom divided would fall. It follows that a city divided will also fall. But we are encouraged! We CAN be united in Christ! The promise of God is that He will command His BLESSING when we come together in unity!

Some of the *new wineskins* being prepared have to do with a JOINING of the NASHVILLE BODY OF CHRIST with a FOCUS ON THE CITY.

There must be:

1. *A coming together of those who have been praying in their own congregations.* We learn in scripture that a city must have walls of protection, otherwise it is too vulnerable to enemy attack. So put on the new wineskin of citywide prayer gatherings! They are coming soon! Spirit-led prayer will be the wall of fire around our city.
2. *A joining of the city's church leaders with a citywide focus.* A fresh move of the Spirit upon them, not just in one accord, but together in one accord, will change the spiritual atmosphere over the city, and the balance of power will shift toward the Church, as it was meant to be.
3. *A joining of congregations for massive worship and prayer.* This unity in prayer and worship will PREPARE THE WAY FOR REVIVAL!

As in Nehemiah's day, let's come against that prevailing evil spirit that has worked hard to keep us apart, by COMING TOGETHER as ONE CHURCH whenever the trumpet sounds! "The work is extensive and spread out, and we are widely separated from each other along the wall. Wherever you hear the sound of the trumpet, come and JOIN us there. Our God will fight for us" (Neh. 4:19-20)! This is when the gates of hell will not prevail against us! Some have perceived that the enemy's scheme is to cause our ears to be deaf to the voice of the Spirit as He woos the Church toward oneness. That evil plan includes muting the Church so that the anointed word does not go out from Nashville! It would mute the praying Church as well! Our voice must be heard in heaven! His sound must be heard through the music of "Worship City USA!" As Jesus cast the deaf and dumb spirit out of the young boy, let us come together as His Body casting out that spirit from Nashville, Tennessee! Let His great light go up from among us and displace that darkness! Large nets will be put in place for the harvest—we have a little NETworking to do!

A Lighthouse City

"I pray also for them who will believe in Me...that all of them may be one....as we are one...May they be brought to complete unity to let the world know that you sent Me and have loved them even as you have loved Me"

—JN. 17:20,22,23

About the Author

Betsy Headden has been a diligent intercessor for uncountable years over Nashville. She has been prayer coordinator and has a heart for unity and networking within the Body of Christ. She has been to Israel six times. Betsy and her husband, Henry, attend Belmont Church and have two wonderful children.

CAN I GET A WITNESS?

by Jeff Deyo
Worship City Ministries

TONIGHT WAS MY first time to sing for the band Zilch. Zilch was a band on Gotee Records that was formed in 1997 by the touring band for dc Talk. They had asked me to fill in for a few nights since their singer had left the group. This particular night we were in Michigan doing a concert for about 700 kids at a Youth for Christ rally. I remember being somewhat apprehensive because of all the new songs I had to sing. The other guys in Zilch asked me if I could share the Gospel and then lead some worship songs toward the end (after the concert part). With all the new songs I had to learn in such a short time, I knew if I could just get to the worship part I would be OK since I had done that many times before.

I had always seen worship as a stepping-stone to *real* music. Singing in church had always seemed more like practice for the big leagues. But time and time again, I found myself at youth camps, retreats and church services singing songs from a stage that lyrically were directed *to* God and cried out for the audience to sing along—songs I honestly didn't care to lead at that point in my life. In my earlier years, I had led "worship" songs like, "Lean On Me", and "Pharaoh, Pharaoh," that really only existed to entertain the audience and to tire out high energy summer campers. In this way the staff all hoped to make it through camp without a serious incident. But over the months and years, I was gradually being drawn along with my audiences toward songs that spoke more of the greatness and beauty of God, and how incredible it is to have relationship with Him. These songs seemed to directly attune our senses to His wonderful and unmistakable frequency of love—something we all desired.

But tonight was different. God had planned for something very special to happen—something I really didn't see coming. As I spoke and shared, God's awesome power arose in me. I shared with a passion that came from deep within—deeper than all the other times before. I poured my heart out with a "life or death" intensity. I shared as if the message I brought was the most important thing these people would ever hear! That night, for 71 young people it was just that. As we sang "Awesome God" and some other worship songs around 200 kids made their way to the front. Seventy-one of those did a one-eighty in their hearts, and raced toward God for the very first time. Praise the Lord!

We worshipped God together through songs directed to *Him* for a little while longer. As we did, everyone seemed to disappear except God. The band was no longer the focus. The light show was no longer important. The stunning outfits we wore paled in the light of Jesus, and the atmosphere of Heaven literally descended into that school auditorium. We were dramatically transformed—each heart. Nothing else mattered but God.

That night radically altered my course in many ways. I went on to join the band Zilch, but more importantly, I resolved to join God's band of radical worshippers even though I didn't completely understand what that meant. Jesus talks about these worshippers with the woman at the well in John, chapter four—a group of people the Father is *seeking* who worship Him in spirit *and* in truth.

One might assume this change in me happened on the stage that night, but it had really happened during the many months before our concert in Michigan. See I had been meeting with Jesus more regularly. In fact, my "quiet time" seemed to be taking on a new life. I had been challenged to add the element of worship through song to my "quiet time"—something that had never occurred to me to do. All my life I had been taught to simply read my Bible and pray, but now, as I cranked up the volume on my CD player to sing along in worship to God, I found myself having to rename this time to my "loud time".

Like many, I had found it difficult to remain consistent in spending time with God and even a greater challenge to have passion to *want* to seek the Lord. Two years before my first Zilch concert I had started praying to God for something to change in my heart. I recognized after being a Christian for over 20 years, I still never really longed to spend time with God like David did. In fact, I felt far from being a man *after* God's own heart. Yes, I was a Christian, and a strong one at that, but I never woke up in the morning, opened my eyes and bounded out of bed to go read my Bible. I never anticipated the time I would spend with Jesus the way I anticipated other things in life, like going to a good movie, or kissing my wife or simply eating a bowl of chocolate, caramel ice cream with crunchy stuff on top! I began to pray to God that my passion and desire for Him would increase beyond all the other passions in my life. I began to ask that He would cause me supernaturally to hunger for His Word and to thirst deeper for relationship with Him. I knew this was not a natural thing for me, and I knew it was going to take a miracle for it to happen—fortunately I had come to the right person—to the God of all miracles with whom all things are possible!

THE REAL DEAL

I believe one of the main ways God began developing a longing in my heart for Him was through the worship songs I sang in my time with Him. I had always thought this type of worship was reserved only for church on Sundays. It had never entered my mind that I could sing to God by myself. It wasn't that I didn't want to—I had just never thought of it before.

What began to happen was the strengthening of a three-strand cord. I had honestly found my prayer life somewhat boring, with very little life. I had found my Bible study times to be lacking in excitement and without much understanding or revelation of what I was reading. But now, it seemed that I had discovered the missing ingredient. It wasn't as if the worship songs were more important than reading my Bible or praying. It was as if worshipping and singing to God had suddenly unlocked a cavernous reservoir in my heart and mind, revealing a void in me that I longed to have filled by God—one that I really hadn't known existed. As I worshipped, I hungered for His Word more. When I read His Word, I desired to pray more. When I prayed, I longed to express my love to God through song more. Around and around it went like a tightly wrapped three-strand cord that could not and would not be broken. I went from barely being able to spend 10 minutes with God (and never consistently) to watching 60-90 minutes go by without even noticing! God was beginning to answer my prayer!

I suppose I shouldn't have been surprised when my passion for God began to shine more brilliantly on the stage. I found myself completely unashamed about showing my love for God in front of others. Before, I had found it a little embarrassing to "let myself go" in worship in front of people, but now it really didn't seem to matter as much what people thought. The main reason I could do this publicly was I was drawing from a well that had been dug with God in private—a well that had fresh water in it *from just that morning*—not stagnant and lifeless from several days ago, but pure and clean. These were rivers of Living Water that were stirring up in me, filling me, not just to the top, but to overflowing. This was the REAL deal!

A short time after our night in Michigan, those of us in Zilch decided to add one worship song to the middle of our non-worship set. I don't think we grasped the magnitude of this decision, but nevertheless, we agreed we really wanted to give God at least one direct "nod" during our Christian "show".

As a result of this one song, we found ourselves amazed by the results. We watched as people in the crowd transformed before our very eyes. They didn't so much look or act different. They still jumped and danced. They still raised their hands. They still sang, and they still worshipped. I guess it was really the focus that changed. Though we hadn't realized it or even desired it, we had begun creating little worshippers and followers of the band Zilch. The people in the audience lifted their hands toward us, sang our songs and admired our great musical abilities. All the while we moved cleverly on stage and danced in the light of our own songs, loudly and boldly with the aid of a mammoth sound system.

Our goal had not been for people to idolize us, but simply to be cool enough that people would listen to what we had to say about God. We figured if we impressed them and gained their favor that they would listen as we attempted to point them to Jesus. This was a good and honest philosophy, but God desired to show us an easier, more fruitful way to draw people to Him—His way. He wanted us to understand that He didn't need us to make Him cool and He didn't need us to impress people. He was cool enough on His own, and if anyone were going to do any impressing, it would be Him. All we needed to do was worship Him.

Amazingly, as we led that one worship song, the atmosphere of the place began to change. People began to focus their attention directly on God. In fact, at first, we found ourselves a little uncomfortable, because everyone seemed to be forgetting about us on the stage. But, as this happened night after night, we began to enjoy it. No longer did we need to worry about being cool or making just the right moves to impress the crowd. No longer did we have to fight to keep the audience's attention with the hope that someone would see Jesus in our message. Suddenly the middleman was taken out of the equation and people were simply being drawn directly to Jesus as we worshipped Him. As we lifted Him up from the earth, He was drawing them—all of them—to Himself (John 12:32). Our job suddenly became much easier. In fact we found ourselves able to just relax and enjoy God for ourselves—right on the stage!

As this went on night after night, we couldn't help but begin asking the obvious question—what if we did a whole concert like this instead of just one song? Would the impact be magnified? What if we recorded a CD that was totally worship in the same style of music we loved (different than what we understood to be the accepted "worship" style)? What if all we did was provide an atmosphere for people to seek God and be drawn to Him? What if instead of giving them hype, we pointed them to Hope. The answer seemed to be just as obvious and just as poignant as the question. God was definitely leading us. That was undeniable.

FROM GLORY TO GLORY

One year later we found ourselves with a new CD, and new band name (SONICFLOOd) and a new passion—turning people into worshippers of Jesus Christ. Our concerts had completely changed. The philosophy had been turned upside down, and people were getting healed and saved without us even leading them in a direct prayer of salvation. They were simply coming into God's presence and God, Himself, was convicting them and leading them in these prayers as we worshipped together. Even more exciting were the people who were for the first time seeing Jesus as more than just a guy who keeps us from going to Hell. They were becoming people who no longer only believed in the Lord but who truly knew Him—people who walked and talked with Him and spent time in His presence—people who were so blown away by Jesus' sacrifice on the cross that they couldn't help but go around telling everyone they knew about their awesome Savior! What an incredible thing was happening as we simply exalted Jesus and let Him do the rest!

Early on in SONICFLOOd we received a preaching video from Ray Hughes, a man who became quite a mentor to us. We sat down as a band and watched this video (strange, in and of itself), and we sat with our mouths hanging on the floor as Ray preached about how God uses sound in the Bible to move many things. Ray showed us biblically how powerful sound is and how God moves mightily in it. All of creation was actually SPOKEN into existence. God used a simple SHOUT to topple the walls of Jericho. In Israel's day, God used sound to win many battles—like when the people surrounded the enemy's camp and broke their jars and blew their trumpets. Those sounds alone caused the enemy to turn on itself, giving Israel the victory. Or like the time when the worshippers and singers marched in front of the warriors, worshipping God and singing allowing a great victory.

Ray spoke about how Revelation 4 and 5 describes all of creation—all of heaven and earth and everything under the earth praising God, singing, "Holy, holy, holy." Imagine all the angels and EVERYTHING that ever lived or was created joining together in one mass choir to praise and honor God. This would NOT be a small sound. Many people think that in order to worship God you have to be quiet. I don't think this great multitude of billions and billions were very quiet. I can only imagine a HUGE, LOUD, sound! Revelation 19:6 describes this sound as the sound of many mighty rushing waters! If you've ever been to Niagara Falls, you know what I'm talking about. If you get close to falls you can hear how loud they are, but if you take the tour down below and behind the falls, you will find that you can barely hear yourself think. If you take that sound and multiply it by a billion, you might register the sound that all of creation is going to make on the first day in heaven—let alone on the ten thousandth day.

When we heard the description of worship in Revelation 19:6 we were absolutely speechless. You see, up to this point we hadn't fully understood the meaning of our name, SONICFLOOd. Suddenly, when

Ray showed us the passage that describes the sound of worship in heaven as the sound of many rushing waters we realized it was speaking of a SONICFLOOd. A sound so great it was a flood of thunderous waters—a sound of intense, heartfelt worship, pounding the shores of the devil's sand-castle over and over again. It was the sound of heaven coming to earth to join together people of all ages, cultures and backgrounds to worship the King of kings! This was our destiny—to bring a piece of the beauty of heaven to earth so people could find their way to Jesus. WOW!

IT'S ALL ABOUT JESUS

About this time, God led us to start a monthly worship gathering for people in Nashville to seek God together. Our city is full of people with dreams. THEIR dream to be someone important, to be famous, to do something great, or maybe simply to touch someone with their gifts. Many of these dreams and their dreamers are unused or unfulfilled since only one in so very many gets to sing or do music for a career. So many of those who do achieve their dreams in Nashville, on a tour bus, on the radio or on the big stage, somehow still find themselves alone, lost or just as empty as when they came. These people found like so many others that the dreams they finally fulfilled were still in and of themselves unfulfilling. As a result, we have broken dreams, broken hearts and broken people in Nashville—lots of them.

We thought worshipping God might be something these people could use to receive some healing. After all, we had experienced the same thing. After five years of trying to "make it" in Nashville, I found myself broken and beat up from the pain of constantly laying my creations before men only to have them chewed up and spit out again. Even though I began singing with a band with a record deal, there was still no true or lasting fulfillment. It was only when I worshipped God that everything changed. Being in His presence was sort of like a drug, only the sole side affects were things like peace, love, and forgiveness. We thought that maybe some others in Nashville could use some of that stuff also.

So, in March of 1999 we had a CD release party for SONICFLOOd. However we didn't celebrate our CD as normal. We simply invited all our friends and industry buddies to come celebrate the King of kings with us as we worshipped God together. We called it SONICPRAISe, and it was a smash hit! We found this a little surprising since everyone knows playing to a Nashville audience as a Christian Contemporary Artist can be one of the worst possible experiences. The crowds can come across very jaded toward the performers because there are so many musicians, and so many people who know people, who know people, who know famous people. They seem to sit there and look at you like, "show me something I haven't already seen. I dare you!"

But at SONICPRAISe, we didn't seem to have this problem. I guess it was because we were presenting something that blew the best of all light shows away. We were showing them the One who created the light. At SONICPRAISe they weren't necessarily impressed by our awesome sound, because they were too busy honoring the One whom made our ears. And they didn't seem to care about our melodies or infectious rhythms because they were enveloped in the song of the Holy One—attuned to the beat of His heart. This was something far beyond anything man could do. In fact, the very people who had become bored with what man could do were suddenly overwhelmed, and utterly drawn into what God could do and was doing in them!

Though we had no idea of the significance of this, we reasoned we should keep meeting on a monthly basis. That first gathering was the first of many very special nights to come. The word spread and people began to come out of the woodwork to join us. We started meeting in a little building that used to be a Baptist church but that was turned into a risqué nightclub called "The Church." Month after month, we would pack out that place, take communion together, pray for our city and worship our guts out. I was personally healed of 10 years of allergies and shared it publicly at one of the gatherings. Many people were set free and it was all because of Jesus. He was making us worshippers that would worship Him in both truth and in spirit.

Slowly but surely the vision began to develop. We honestly didn't start with any real agenda but just to come and worship. It was almost as if God had us on a need to know basis and that we (nor any of the demons in hell) didn't need to know. We just needed to trust and obey. So we did.

God began placing the purpose for our meeting together in my heart a step at a time. This gathering was actually something He had long desired. He started showing me a picture of what it might look like to see people of all types shapes, sizes, backgrounds and colors come together to seek Him and how that would please Him. He started showing us verses like John 17:21 where Jesus specifically prays that we (Christians) would be One just like He and the Father—so that all people might know that He was sent to the earth. He started showing us verses like Amos 9:11 and Acts 15:16-17 where God declares His passionate desire to restore the Kingdom of David, the most worshipping kingdom of all time—a King and a kingdom *after* God's own heart. In verse 17, God says He wants to restore David's Kingdom for one reason—so that *all of humanity might find the Lord.* This is God's heart. He recently showed me Ephesians 3:10 that reveals God's secret plan for all time. It says, *"God's purpose was to show his wisdom in all its rich variety to all the rulers and authorities in the heavenly realms. They will see this when Jews and Gentiles are joined together in his church. This was his plan from all eternity, and it has now been carried out through Christ Jesus our Lord."* God's heart is for ALL people to come to Him—together!

MY EYES NOW ANOINTED

As I chased after His heart desiring His purpose and plan for my life, I found my heart longing for the things His heart longed for. I found myself burning with a passion for His church, as Jesus did. In John 2:17, the Bible reminds us that Jesus had a deep passion for God's house that burned within Him. I started becoming consumed with seeing His Body (those who have received salvation) fulfill their destiny and go on to become worshippers of our Lord, making disciples all along the way. I saw so many people repent (turn away) from their old natures and to depend solely on the Holy Spirit working within them accomplishing greater things than they could have ever imagined.

Through all of this God was showing me the true importance of UNITY within His church. When I say, "He was showing me", I don't mean He was telling me anything brand new or apart from His Word. In fact these scriptures have been in the Bible for centuries. It wasn't that I needed God to speak them any louder. It was that I needed God to take off my blinders so I could see and understand His truth that was there all along.

God has an order to things. All things happen for a reason and for a purpose. I was beginning to understand that if we Christians wanted "B" to happen then we would have to pray specifically for "A" to happen. He was using verses like Psalm 40:3 to drive home His point. It reads, "He has given me a new song to sing, a hymn of praise to our God. Many will see what He has done and be astounded. They will put their trust in the Lord." If we want people to trust the Lord and be astounded by what He has done, there needs to be a profound exchange between God and us. Not necessarily of music, but of our hearts exalting God from deep within—of us sincerely recognizing that God is God, and that there is NO other like Him. This is the supernatural song within each of us that will draw others to Jesus.

Furthermore, I don't think this verse is suggesting we have to become popular singers who can write new songs to see people trust in the Lord. It does suggest however that God is going to be the One and ONLY giver of the "song." This song is not going to be initiated from within us or be a result of our skills and talents. It's not even going to come to us from some other human through their gifting. The verse specifically says that God Himself is the giver of the song. It is clear through this that we are incapable of having the results we want (people putting their trust in the Lord) without God giving us the tools we need to draw our hearts to His, and their hearts to His.

Psalm 40 tells us that the song is specifically and expressly for "me." This isn't just any old song that God flings down from heaven to whomever catches it. It isn't like the lottery where the lucky man wins the prize. This song we're talking about is given directly to *me* from God. It is a special song that God designed for me that is full of purpose for my life in order that I touch those around me for the Kingdom of God. It suggests that when we discover the new song deep within us—the song of love, hope and peace—that we are going to see fruit from this song in our daily lives. This will in turn cause others to discover what trusting God is all about. David says, "The Lord is my strength. *He is my song*" (Psalm 33).

If we want to see people fall in love with Jesus we must FIRST deepen our walk and relationship with Him. We must KNOW this Jesus if we want others to know Him through us. We are going to have to aim to live lives of worship. We have to ask God to make us more like Peter and John when they went before the council. In Acts 4:13, the council saw them as regular men with no special training, yet they recognized them as having been with Jesus. This is the key. People need to recognize us as people who have been with Jesus. When we are around someone enough we generally begin to take on their characteristics. We say things the way they do. We do things the way they do. When we are close enough we even walk away smelling as they do.

We need to ask God to make us holy. Then we need to walk out holiness. We need to seek God to help us be obedient to His commands showing our genuine love for Him. We must understand that though being truly good is NOT achievable on our own, to seek God to make us good is certainly an important thing. Seeking good is NOT legalism. It's something we are going to need to do if we want to see ALL PEOPLE come to know the Lord. The Bible tells us to pursue godliness. Pursue is a word we use when we speak of a lion going after a zebra or gazelle. The lion is hot on the trail of dinner. The Bible says we need to be that way concerning pursuing righteous and holy. The key here is NOT seeking goodness but seeking God to make us good. It becomes legalism only when we seek goodness for goodness' sake.

When we know God the good news is that God is working righteousness in us to help us be good. Philippians 2:13 says it this way: "For God is working in you, giving you the *desire* to obey Him and *power* to do what pleases Him." That blows me away! You mean to tell me, all this time I've spent struggling to be good could have been used instead for seeking God while letting Him make me good? Yep. I think there's a verse somewhere that says something about seeking God first.

We should seek God and allow Him to make us righteous. We don't need to seek to be holy. We need to seek God and allow Him to fill us with His holiness. In fact, the bad news is that we CAN'T do enough work to be good enough. The good news is Jesus already did all the work for us. It is finished! Again, it says that God is WORKING in us to help us obey—that means we don't have to work at obeying. We just need to seek Him!

We all struggle so much with certain sins that seem to continue to plague us, but this verse in Philippians seems to show us that putting many of these struggles to rest is actually possible. It lets us know that we can no longer lean on the excuse of our old sinful nature. We should be leaning on His power for strength to obey. Romans 6:15-23 tells us that we are FREE from our old sinful nature. Verse 22 tells us we are FREE from the power of sin. Verse 16b tells us we can either CHOOSE sin, which leads to death or CHOOSE to obey and receive God's approval. Romans 8:12-13 is the clearest however: *"... you have no obligation whatsoever to do what your sinful nature urges you to do. For if you keep on following it, you will perish. But if through the POWER of the Holy Spirit you turn from it and its evil deeds, you will live."* Maybe we should read that again. It doesn't get much clearer!

In this way we are given the POWER to live lives of worship unto our God. We can now tap into His power to live lives of honesty and humility in front of this world that God loves so much. In fact, we MUST tap into the power of God or we risk making a mockery of Him and His plan for His children by continually saying one thing while doing another. When we tap into His power we honor God and show the world we are nothing WITHOUT Him! I am not suggesting that we can be perfect, but we must allow God to be in the process of perfecting us by His power. The only thing we have to "do" is allow God to "do" whatever He wants in us and through us! When we live by the Spirit people notice, and they want to know where they can get what we have. That is "worship" evangelism!

So, in order to reach the world for Christ, we're going to need a significant amount of unity among the congregations in our city. And, in order to have unity between our congregations, we are going to have to become more deeply unified with Jesus. This requires that we worship Him at a whole new level—with our songs AND our lives! This is what God has been working out in me, and what I have been challenging others with at our monthly gatherings. As we went deeper and deeper with SONICFLOOd, I began to realize how real and powerful this WORSHIP was. I began to understand how important it was that we REALLY live our lives in such a way that our own actions and lifestyles didn't disqualify our worship on stage and our words about unity.

WORSHIP IS A LIFESTYLE NOT A SONG

I remember one of the special days I experienced in the studio, recording the SONICFLOOd CD. We were near completion on the project during the summer of 1999, but I still had one more song to sing on. The song I was scheduled to sing that day was a song I didn't know very well. I had sung it once or twice in a worship service, but still hadn't really learned the words. I picked up the lyric sheet and pressed RECORD and began to work on learning the song. I had no idea that this particular song was going to touch a nerve in me that would cause my heart to almost jump out of my chest! As I sang the words, tears began to roll down my cheeks. My voice began to quiver as I choked out the lyrics of this song written by Matt Redman. It has changed the face of the church all over the world:

When the music fades
And all is stripped away
And I simply come
Longing just to bring
Something that's of worth
That will bless Your heart

I'll bring You more than a song
For a song in itself
Is not what you have required?
You search much deeper within
Through the way things appear
You're looking into my heart

CHORUS
I'm coming back to the heart of worship
And it's all about You
It's all about You, Jesus
I'm sorry, Lord for the thing I've made it
When it's all about You
It's all about You, Jesus

King of endless worth
No one could express
How much You deserve
Though I'm week and poor
All I have is Yours
Every single breath

This song was born out of a very unique story. Apparently the pastor of Matt Redman's church felt at one point that the church was beginning to "worship" worship. He felt that with their great worship band and all the great songs, that people were beginning to enjoy singing and listening to the music more than being with the One who made the music. It seemed that it was becoming more about the experience and the feeling we get when we sing than about the One whom made those feelings. It's so easy to seek the feeling rather than seek the One who gives you real joy. It's just as easy to seek the healing instead of seeking the Healer or to seek the gift rather than the Giver.

Matt's pastor felt led by the Lord to call the church to a music fast—a time where the church would not sing or play music at all but where they would just pray and cry out to the Lord with their voices and hearts. I'm sure this was a challenge at first. But if I have the story correct, I understand that some of the most powerful times of worship in that church came during this music fast. I suppose this might happen as your mind experiences something it is not used to. It would force a person to refocus. There would be no music to hide behind. If you were going to worship you would have determine to do so and you would have to decide not to be embarrassed with any music to cover up your voice.

As I understand it, Heart of Worship was the first song written and sung after the fast was finally over. I suppose the song begs the question, "What happens in YOU when the music fades?" If we had no more music or fancy musicians would that keep you from worshipping God? If you could not sing any more, would you cease to exalt the King?

As SONICFLOOd, we had put together a slickly produced album with lots of big sounds, huge guitars, thick background vocals, powerful drum loops, clever effects and singable melodies. But with Heart of Worship being the last song on the record we wanted to make a statement. We wanted the song to represent something different outwardly than the rest of the songs. Instead of beefing up the production, we actually scaled back the production on the song. In fact, I believe we even used less production than Matt did on the original recording. We weren't trying to be more spiritual than anyone else was, but we wanted to make a point. We wanted the song and its message to be ALL the focus.

We love huge production and believe it is a part of the flood of sound God called us to. We wanted the worship experience to be as big and incredible as any other musical experience. But with this one song, we simply wanted to give a clear reminder to our listeners (and to ourselves) not to get caught up in the beautiful sound more than the beautiful Savior—not to enjoy the incredible blending of instruments more than the incredible knowledge of God's presence. We wanted to remind everyone that we weren't just bringing sounds, songs and rhythms, but that we were bringing much MORE than a song, more than slick production, more than skillful playing, more than fancy chords and melodies. We were bringing our HEARTS—which was the bottom line!

God is calling us back to His heart. Maybe we have made something of worship that it's not supposed to be. Maybe with our worship industry, and our worship record labels, and our new worship churches we too have fallen in love with the music instead of with the God of music, Jesus. The Father sent His Son to die for us that we might worship Jesus and KNOW Him! There is nothing wrong with having a worship industry, having worship churches or even having worship record labels. It becomes wrong when we begin to exploit the act of worship just to sell our products, to win new church attendees, and to create new Dove Award categories.

A NEW DENOMINATION

Worship is affecting many things. Many denominations are beginning to meld together in some ways. You may have heard the term "Bapticostle." Or you may have gone to a church that is referred to as a Spirit-filled Episcopal Church. These days, we are less likely to see a particular church's denomination affiliation listed on their church sign. When it comes to denominations it seems we have come a long way in the church. We've come away from thinking our way is the *only* way. In our church there are people from so many different denominations it's difficult to keep track. People don't seem to be as worried about joining or attending churches where the doctrine is perfectly fit to our tastes right down to the color of the carpet. But, there is a new denomination forming.

The new denomination is founded on worship style. What I mean is that so many of us around the United States are now basing where we attend church on the music style and/or intensity of the worship. Does a church worship with a piano and an organ or with a full band? Does the church have a praise band or praise team? Do they have a choir, praise singers, or a combination of both? Does the church sing hymns, choruses, or some Christian versions of popular secular songs? Is there a person who stands at the front directing the congregation or is there a lead worshipper? Does the church spend several minutes worshipping or close to an hour or more? Is there more of a formula with two songs an offering, one song where we sit down, a special number and a sermon, or is there a block of time dedicated to seeking God through song? Does the preaching come before or after the worship?

These are all questions the "modern" churchgoer is asking before they decide to pile their family into the car to go to church. As good as it is to be intently interested in worshipping God, we have begun to believe that worship is a certain song style or music style. This is not healthy. In Isaiah 58, God gets on Israel's case because they continually come to Him making a show of worship all the while continuing to cheat their employees. God is frustrated as the people come tearing their clothes and wearing sackcloth while ignoring their needy neighbors.

Many times we do the same thing. Even with a renewed worship focus in our churches and homes it is easy to make it about how good we felt this time when we worshipped or how many tears we cried this week during the song service. He wants us to understand that worship is an attitude. It is a world-view. It is the foundation. It should encompass every millisecond of our lives. Every action either is or is NOT an act of worship. Every thought either is or is NOT something that gives God glory. Every word either is or is NOT something that shows off how AWESOME God is.

God is trying to help us understand that worship is not a song style or a music style. It is a LIFESTYLE. Every time we think a thought, make a move, speak a word, or sing a song, we have a direct opportunity to worship our God. God has placed us on this planet to bring Him glory. He didn't put us here so we could just give Him glory on Sunday morning, Sunday night, and Wednesday night. He didn't give us breath so we could simply lift Him up during our quiet time. He didn't form us with His hands so we could only please Him during our prayer before a meal.

Jesus wants more than a song. You may say, "Then what does He want?" That is a great question. What does God want? The answer, I'm afraid, is too basic for some. In fact, it is one of those answers that will confound even the wise. It is too simple for the intellectual to grasp. It may even go right over the scholar's head. The answer? All God wants is YOU—every part, every word, every thought, every deed, every minute of every hour of every day of every year. He wants everything you are and everything you've got—all of YOU! God wants and deserves all of you—all the time!

A NEW NAME

As people continued to pour into the SONICPRAISe gatherings, it became clear that God wanted to change the name of our gathering. For some, it was becoming more about the band than it was about God. So, after my time with SONICFLOOd, I felt it was time to change the name to WorshipCityPraise. Nashville is known around the world as Music City USA. This is the name it has held for some time. We are a city that is full of music. Country Music and Christian Music headquarters are located here, as well as hundreds and hundreds of recording studios. Most of the industry's recording artists from Country and Christian Music live in the Nashville district. We are a city of music.

But a few years ago, God began to put it on some people's hearts to begin praying for our city to have a new name. Just like Saul to Paul and Abram to Abraham, they were asking God to rename our city. The name God laid upon us was the name Worship City USA. This is a name that refocuses the "glory" where it is due—back to God. Music didn't start out being a man-focused term, but over the years it has been used to exalt man instead of the One who created both the man and the music.

As a result of this, we decided to rename SONICPRAISe to WorshipCityPraise denoting it as a gathering of praise in Worship City. We wanted to go ahead and begin calling the city by its new name even though the nations of the world did not recognize this name. We began calling Nashville "Worship City USA" by faith. We decided to begin calling things that weren't as if they were until they ARE! Many in the city have joined with us, passionately praying to God to change the characteristics of our city so we would become known as Worship City. We realize that in order for this to happen around the world, our city is going to have to look different, smell different, feel different, taste different, and sound different. So we're not praying for God to let people know about the name change He's given us, we're praying for Him to change us until we come into line with the new name He has given us!

We are excited because we are on the way to seeing this change take place. In fact, we know it will happen because God is the One who has changed our name—not us. He desires this MORE than we do! Its neat after a few months to hear some of the local Christian radio station DJ's referring to Nashville as Worship City as they announce the weather or tell the time. God is doing it! We simply want to join in where He is working!

We are not satisfied anymore with a sign in front of the church that reads "Revival This Week." We don't want a special week where people focus on God just to turn around and see no change in their families in the way they treat their employees or in the way they seek Him. We've got to see TRUE transformation, REAL revival, and ACTUAL awakening! We've got to see it. All of creation weeps and groans for it! Our hearts ache for it not so we can give glory to the change, but so we can give glory to the Changer. Not so we can witness what we prayed for coming to pass, but so we can see families restored, and people flipped upside down with the realization that God is REAL!!

Isn't anyone tired of what man can do? I'm soooooooooooooo bored with man's attempt to impress me with his knowledge and his abilities! I'm so sick of man's devices, campaigns and strategies. Isn't there anyone who would simply point me to Jesus without first skimming a little of the glory off the top for themselves like Ananias and Sapphira? Isn't there anyone who will stop trying to hustle me for a big offering and simply trust God to supply their need according to His riches and glory as they do what God has called them to do? (I'm all for offerings and teaching on this, but not when we have to beg for it). I know God works in spite of us. I know He works in spite of me — and I praise Him for that! That is His grace. But couldn't we just GET REAL for a minute? Couldn't we just throw out our agendas and our need to be the one who thought of the idea? Couldn't we just stop acting so pious and fake? Couldn't we stop saying "I'm fine" when really our marriage is falling apart? Couldn't we just be REAL?

Doesn't anyone want to see what God can do? It seems we're absolutely so self sufficient that we're satisfied with simply hearing ABOUT all God can do. Thankfully, God is raising up a generation that is dying to KNOW Him. They're not young and they're not old. They're just alive! And their cry is, "I want to know You! I want to hear Your voice. I want to know You more! I want to touch You. I want to see Your face. I want to know You more!" In his song "In The Secret", Andy Park captures the heartbeat of those who aren't satisfied with anything less than all of God. But like Andy, we aren't even satisfied with just singing this song! We only want to see Jesus! We want to jump into his lap! We want to hear Him say, "I love you, my child"! There is something inside us that longs to be physically in His presence—to look into His eyes and to embrace Him!

We may not even realize what we're asking for, but we do know that nothing else has satisfied us yet. We've tasted just a little of Him and there's nothing like it! There's no drug, or food, or earthly relationship, or material thing, or movie, or savory slice of knowledge that can fulfill us like our God can! It's like we've tasted real meat and vegetables for the first time after eating a steady diet of candy for years and years. Suddenly we've come alive to all that is available for enjoyment! Yes, candy is OK for a special treat every once in a while, but the buffet table is what has now been laid before us! How could we ever go back? Yet there are so many hurdles and roadblocks, but we fight on. We must have more of Jesus. We must know this God who risked it all to have us as His! We must stop at nothing—even death—to be with Him forever. And before we die we must walk and talk with Him as much as is humanly possible. And we must tell everyone we know about Him.

Is that you? Is that me? Well, I know that is the me I want to be! And I won't stop dropping to my knees asking God to make me more like Him until the day I feel His heavenly arms wrapped around my glorified body!

See the REAL vision of WorshipCityPraise is not to fill stadiums with people praising God or to show what great city leaders we are. It's not to sell ten million copies of the live CD recorded at our gathering (though I'm certainly not against this <smile>) or to be known throughout history as the one who brought Nashville together.

The REAL goal is to have people go home from these gatherings convinced that being with Jesus is going to make them better fathers and better mothers. We want them to realize that God can produce in them better sisters and brothers, better sons and daughters, better neighbors and better relatives. We pray fervently for people to return to their homes and workplaces determined to seek God to make them better employers and employees, better churchgoers and better Christians.

As He answers these prayers (and He will), there is no question that He is making us better witnesses. If we are better friends we are better witnesses. If we are better teachers we are better witnesses. If we are better elders, we are better witnesses. If we are better child-care workers, we are better witnesses. If we are better government officials, we are better witnesses. If we are better pastors, we are better witnesses. If we are better grandmas, we are better witnesses. When we are better people, we are much better witnesses.

What is better? Better is being like Jesus.

How can we be like Jesus? Be with Him.

Do we want to be better? Of course we do!

Just ask Him for help.

Sing to Him in your time with Him. Allow Him to stir up your heart with the things that stir His. Read His Word. Hide it in your heart so you won't sin against Him. Pray hard. If you don't know what to say, ask Him for the words. He's got plenty. Consider what you would pray for if you were Him. Then start all over again. Worship. Word. Prayer. Worship. Word. Prayer. Worship. Word. Prayer.

Can I get a witness?

About the Author

Jeff and Martha Deyo attend Cornerstone Church. Jeff's hungry heart is likened to Joshua and Caleb as there is no dream too big for him in pursuit of God. We as Nashvillian's are proud to have this team who continue to lead us into the Promised Land taking out the 'giants' with Christ. See www.WorshipCityPraise.com for more information.

EPILOGUE

In active participation with Christ...

BECOME A FIRESTARTER!

by Jeffrey M. Richfield

HENRY T. BLACKABY said, *"The heart of God and the heart of the one God chooses must beat as one! The heart of God must not only be revealed, but received for true transformation."*

God revealed Himself mightily to Elijah because he *submitted* himself humbly to God's will. Through prayer, Elijah was transformed into a man who knew his God. He was confident and willing to "risk it all" in receiving God's fire from heaven. He believed God. It is said that the Spirit of Elijah will return in the latter days. *Oh, rain on us Lord!* James claimed that Elijah was *"a man of like flesh"* (James 5:17). Therefore, we are no different today from the Elijah of yesterday. Are we not to carry the many diversities, examples, and reflections of who Jesus is to the people in our day with confidence? God is still displayed through His chosen ones—people willing to "risk it all." One's who will sacrifice this world for intimacy with Jesus. One's who will submit humbly in prayer and worship, walking with God. Our God is the *firebringer*. And these fearless ones are the *firestarter's* of our generation. They are the builders, seekers, reformers and warriors of God's kingdom today.

It could start right now—right here with you. Become a firestarter with Jesus! Channel the fire of the Holy Spirit towards this city! For example, ask God where you can be a light in the city—believing God to draw business executives together for an hour of prayer for families, neighborhoods, schools, government leaders, the town, the city, and the State. Ask God to birth in you a new desire, burning from coals deep in your heart and soul, to see revival swoop down upon Nashville and ignite Worship City into an unquenchable spiritual fire!

As the beachhead of Christian publishing and Christian music, Nashville carries the mantle of God's presence *to the nations!* And as the Southern Gateway to the inner courts of God, this Volunteer State carries the weight of God's Ark *to the world!*

The seed for revival has been planted and is rooting in fertile soil. Father God is on the move watering His garden (His Bride). The vine will soon emerge and blossom. All the climate conditions are ripe for a great spiritual harvest. The light of the Son is bearing down upon us even now as we reflect His glory ever so bright here in Worship City, USA. I say to you fearless ones, "Arise now, you faithful witnesses—awaken from sleep!"

Can you feel the heat? The trumpets are sounding! God has already delivered Nashville into our hands! (Joshua 6:2) To God be the glory forever and ever!

> *"Arise, shine; for your light has come, and the glory of the Lord has risen upon you. Lift up your eyes and look around; then you shall see and be radiant; your heart shall thrill and rejoice…"*
> —ISAIAH 60:1,4,5

{Top quote reference "Created to be God's Friend" page 41, copyright 2000, by Henry Blackaby Ministries, Thomas Nelson Publishers}

SALVATION†

IF YOU have never confessed Jesus Christ as your personal Savior and made Him Lord of your life, it's time to do so right now. The gift of salvation is free but at such a great cost. Call upon Jesus right now and make Him Lord of your life. Jesus is the way, the truth, and the light. The Bible says that no one can come to the Father but through Jesus. Let Jesus fill you with His spirit of joy through intimately knowing Him! God wishes that none should perish but that all receive eternal life through believing and acting upon the Holy Spirit's call. God the Father may be drawing you now. You have heard the Word, and so faith has risen inside your heart. The Holy Spirit may have brought deep conviction to your soul. The Bible declares that, "All have sinned and fall short of the glory of God" (Romans 3:23). We all need forgiveness for our sins. Life is in the blood. Jesus' blood was spilled out for you as the final offering for your sins at the cross. Take away the cross and we are all hopeless. Acknowledge His sacrifice. Submit to His Lordship. Confirm it through prayer.

Ask Jesus into your life right now. Say, "Jesus, I come to You in humbleness and in brokenness. I realize I am a sinner and that I need Your eternal salvation. I recognize that You, Jesus Christ, paid my penalty of sin by dying on the cross at Calvary over two thousand years ago. I believe You died and were buried and that You rose again in fulfillment of the Holy scriptures. I want to live in eternity with You! I need Your mercy and grace to cover my sin. I know my soul lives eternally, and through faith I accept You right now into my heart. I ask you, Lord, to cleanse me and wash away my sin with Your precious atoning blood. Release me, Lord, from all bondage and set me free! I will commit to seek Your face, call upon You through prayer, and walk in daily repentance. I thank you, Lord, for Your gift of salvation! Thank You for what You have already done and what You are about to do. Thank You for rescuing me! Thank You for my victory in Jesus!

If you have declared this prayer *in your heart* through faith, then you are a new creature in Christ Jesus! Begin your walk with God by asking Him to bring you new relationships that will lead you closer to the way of Christ. Your walk with Christ is a walk of active faith, expressed by your obedience to His call. You will hear His voice by reading of His word daily, through prayer, and through relationships with His people. Find other God-fearing people and start learning about the Lord God Almighty, who created the universe but wants an intimate relationship with you. May God richly bless you.

"Now to Him who is able to keep you from falling, and to make you stand without blemish in the presence of His glory with rejoicing, to the only God our Savior, through Jesus Christ our Lord, be glory, majesty, power, and authority, before all time and now and forever. Amen."

—JUDE 3:24-25

SELF EVALUATION:
PREPARING FOR PERSONAL REVIVAL

by Life Action Ministries

GOD IS EAGER to manifest His reviving presence and power in every generation. But we must take steps to prepare for the release of His in our midst.

On the eve of their passage over Jordan into the Promised Land, Joshua charged the children of Israel to prepare their hearts:

> *"...Sanctify yourselves: for tomorrow the Lord will do wonders among you."*
> —JOSHUA 3:5

The psalmist understood the importance of spiritual preparation for revival:

> *"Righteousness shall go before Him and shall set us in the way of His steps"*
> —PSALM 85:13

The questions on the following pages are designed to reveal specific areas of spiritual need in our lives. These areas must be dealt with in preparation for personal and corporate revival.

STEPS OF ACTION

1. *Pray* the prayer of the psalmist: "Search me, O God, and know my heart: try me, and know my thoughts: and see if there is any wicked way in me, and lead me in the way everlasting." (Psalm 139:23,24).

2. *Be totally honest* as you answer each question.

3. *Agree with God* about each need He reveals in your life. Confess each sin, with the willingness to make it right and forsake it.

4. *Praise God* for His cleansing and forgiveness.

5. *Renew your mind* and rebuild your life through meditation and practical application of the Word of God.

6. *Review* these questions periodically to remain sensitive to your need for ongoing revival.

1. Genuine Salvation (II Corinthians 5:17)   Yes   No

   a. Was there ever a time in my life that I genuinely repented of my sin?   — —

   b. Was there ever a time in my life that I placed all my trust in Jesus Christ alone to save me?   — —

   c. Was there ever a time in my life that I completely surrendered to Jesus Christ as the Master and Lord of my life?   — —

2. God's Word (Psalm 119:97; 119:140)

   a. Do I love to read and meditate on the Word of God?   — —

   b. Are my personal devotions consistent and meaningful?   — —

   c. Do I practically apply God's Word to my everyday life?   — —

3. Humility (Isaiah 57:15)

   a. Am I quick to recognize and agree with God in confession when I have sinned?   — —

   b. Am I quick to admit to others when I am wrong?   — —

   c. Do I rejoice when others are praised and recognized and my accomplishments go unnoticed by men?   — —

   d. Do I esteem all others as better than myself?   — —

4. Obedience (Hebrews 13:17; I Samuel 15:22)

   a. Do I consistently obey what I know God wants me to do?   — —

   b. Do I consistently obey the human authorities God has placed over my life?   — —

5. Pure Heart (I John 1:9)

   a. Do I confess my sin by name?   — —

   b. Do I keep "sort sin" accounts with God (confess as he convicts)?   — —

   c. Am I willing to give up all sin for God?   — —

6. Clear Conscience (Acts 24:16)
   a. Do I consistently seek forgiveness from those
      I wrong or offend?   — —
   b. Is my conscience clear with every man?
      (Can I honestly say,"There is no one I have
      ever wronged or offended in any way and not
      gone back to them and sought forgiveness?)   — —

7. Priorities (Matthew 6:33)
   a. Does my schedule reveal that God is first in my life? — —
   b. Does my checkbook reveal that God is first in my life? — —
   c. Next to my relationship with God, is my relationship
      with my family my highest priority?   — —

8. Values (Colossians 3:12)
   a. Do I love what God loves and hate what God hates?   — —
   b. Do I value highly the things that please God?   — —
   c. Are my affections and goals fixed on eternal values? — —

9. Sacrifice (Philippians 3:7,8)
   a. Am I willing to sacrifice whatever is necessary to see
      God move in my life and church (time, convenience,
      comfort, reputation)?   — —
   b. Is my life characterized by genuine sacrifice for
      the cause of Christ?   — —

10. Spirit Control (Galatians 5:22-25, Ephesians 5:18-21)
    a. Am I allowing Jesus to be Lord of my life in every area? — —
    b. Am I allowing the Holy Spirit to fill my life each day?   — —
    c. Is there consistent evidence of the fruit of the Spirit
       produced in my life?   — —

11. First Love (Philippians 1:21,23)
    a. Am I as much in love with Jesus as I have ever been? — —
    b. Am I thrilled with Jesus, filled with His joy and peace,
       and making Him the continual object of my love?   — —

12. Motives (Acts 5:29; Matthew 10:28)
    a. Am I more concerned about what God thinks then
       what others think?   — —
    b. Would I pray, read my Bible, give, and serve as much
       if nobody but God ever noticed?   — —
    c. Am I more concerned about pleasing men than God?   — —

13. Moral Purity (Ephesians 5:3,4)
    a. Do I keep my mind free from books, magazines, or entertainment that could stimulate fantasizing or immoral thoughts? — —
    b. Are my conversation and behavior pure and above reproach? — —

14. Forgiveness (Colossians 3:12, 13)
    a. Do I seek to resolve conflicts in relationships as soon as possible? — —
    b. Am I quick to forgive those who wrong me or hurt me? — —

15. Sensitivity (Matthew 5:23,24)
    a. Am I sensitive to the conviction and prompting of God's Spirit? — —
    b. Am I quick to respond in humility and obedience to the Conviction of God's Spirit? — —

16. Evangelism (Romans 9:3, Luke 24:46,48)
    a. Do I have a burden for lost souls? — —
    b. Do I consistently witness for Christ? — —

17. Prayer (I Timothy 2:1)
    a. Am I faithful in praying for the needs of others? — —
    b. Do I pray specifically , fervently, and faithfully for revival in my life, my church, and our nation? — —

These questions are credited to:
Life Action Ministries
PO Box 31
Buchanan, MI 49107-0031
(616) 684-5905
Used by permission.

METROPOLITAN GOVERNMENT OF NASHVILLE
AND DAVIDSON COUNTY
102 Metro Courthouse
Nashville, Tennessee 37201

Jason Alexander
Councilman, 28th District

To ministry partners:

I wanted to write and inform you of the event that took place April 3rd, at the Courthouse; as well as, the event that will place May 1st.

My goal within the Nashville City Council legislature has always been to see Christ exalted at the government level. On April 3rd, Jeff Deyo, Jesse Richardson, Jim Freedman, myself, and a few others, prayed outside the Courthouse for the soul of our city. The number of people present were few. Yet—I felt the Spirit of God as strong as I have ever felt. As we prayed and walked around the Courthouse proclaiming this city for Christ—I knew that this is not about our desire to see Nashville changed - we are simply part of God's great desire to see it changed. He is the One who sets apart. He is the One Who will exalt this city if we will only "humble ourselves and pray."

On May 1st - I will through a city resolution proclaim June 9th as Worship City USA Day in Nashville—honoring the work of Jeff and everyone who has seen the vision God has placed on his heart. Please come and be a part of that night. Again, it is not about anything we have planned or goals we have set for the kingdom—I truly feel this is an avenue that God has chosen to show Himself and we are simply the bearers of the message.

Things in this country are changing and shifting. Our new president is showing more than anyone in recent history that Godly people and principles still have a role in America's future. Lets begin to proclaim what God is going to do in Nashville. If we do not—He said the rocks will cry out. See you May 1st.

In His Time and Love,
Jason Alexander
Metropolitan Government of Nashville
Councilman, 28th District

About the Author
Jason is the youngest councilman in the Metro government office. He and his newlywed, formerly Jennifer Brown, attend Cornerstone church. From the city's political leadership, the new "youngblood" he offers our city adds immeasurably toward the doors opening wide for a spiritual rebirth of a city! God, we bless you for blessing us!

A resolution recognizing June 9, 2001, as "Worship City USA Day" in Nashville.

WHEREAS, on June 9, 2001, WorshipCityPraise will celebrate with prayer, fasting and worship on the hill below the State Capital Building in downtown Nashville to celebrate the unity of faith in Nashville, and to mark the one-year anniversary of the Billy Graham Crusade; and

WHEREAS, WorshipCityPraise is a faith based ministry whose purpose is to gather people of all races, ages, denominations and backgrounds in Nashville to seek transformation of our nation, city and surrounding areas through worship, spiritual healings and prayer; and

WHEREAS, not only does WorshipCityPraise meet monthly at various churches around Nashville, ministering to various communities, but they meet monthly with church and government leaders in a gathering called WorshipCityPrayer; and

WHEREAS, WorshipCityPraise is organized in cooperation with a local coalition, Nashville Bridges; and

WHEREAS, WorshipCityPraise (formerly SONICPRAISe) was started in March of 1999, by worship leader Jeff Deyo and others; and

WHEREAS, it is fitting and proper that the Metropolitan Council recognize WorshipCityPraise for their goal in spreading the word.

NOW, THEREFORE, BE IT RESOLVED BY THE COUNCIL OF THE METROPOLITAN GOVERNMENT OF NASHVILLE AND DAVIDSON COUNTY:

SECTION 1.   The Metropolitan Council hereby goes on record as recognizing the SECOND Saturday of June each year (Starting June 9, 2001), as "Worship City USA Day" in Nashville.

SECTION 2.   The Metropolitan Council Staff Office is directed to prepare a copy of this Resolution to be presented to Mr. Jeff Deyo and Mr. Jim Freedman on behalf of WorshipCityPraise and Nashville Bridges Coalition.

SECTION 3.   This Resolution shall take effect from and after its adoption, the welfare of The Metropolitan Government of Nashville and Davidson County requiring it.

INTRODUCED BY:

Members of Council and passed on May 1, 2001!!

Epilogue

CONSTITUTIONAL COVENANT RENEWAL & REVIVAL PRIMER
—Sign, date, tear out and place this on your bathroom mirror—

Father God, Here I am, this day, _____of the year, _____ .
Here *am I,* in the *presence* of the Lord God Almighty, the God of Israel, my
Savior Jesus Christ, on holy ground;

Lord, *as a sinner,* I come *humbly* this day and *plead* Your mercy and
forgiveness for my vile thoughts, profane deeds, and sinful actions. I
plead the Blood of Jesus over my soul. I ask you to purge me from my
sins, transgressions, and inequities, *and* my family's also. Oh God, bring
joy in Jesus' name into my life, my family, and my house. As for me, and
my house—WE WILL serve the Lord! Father God, cloak me and my family
with the whole Armor of God this day, to prevail in humility, by seeking
Your grace for victory!
    —JOSH.24:15 / EPH. 6:10

I come with no sacrifice, but only that of a poor and contrite
spirit. I come humbly realizing you desire obedience more than sacrifice.
Lord, from this moment on I sense the urgency of Your calling upon my
life and now make a new covenant and *commitment* to love You Lord, with
all my heart, soul, and mind and to love my neighbor as myself.
    MATT.22:37-39

I vow today to return to You, Lord Jesus, with my *whole* heart, and I
will *pursue* holiness and a *renewed* intimate relationship with You through the
daily study of Your word, giving myself daily to prevailing *prayer* in my secret
place, *seeking* Your face through *exhorbitant worship, turning* from my wicked ways
through *consecration* and *repentance,* cleansing myself from all unrighteousness.
    —JOEL 2:12 / 2COR.7:1

I am now ready to embrace the hope of revival *individually* through
my walk of serving in obedience, faithfulness, and loyalty ministering to
you. I will submit to *whatever* You desire for my life, my family, and our
future because You Lord know the end from the beginning. I know you
have called me by name and have plans of blessing for my family, prosperity
and hope for our future. Oh Lord, restore to me the *fear* of the Lord!
    —JER.29-11 / PSALM 1 / GEN.39:3

Almighty God, as I prepare for Your outpouring of the Holy Spirit in total abandonment, I trust Your grace Jesus, and ask for its empowerment. I now cleanse *myself* of all unrighteousness and shameful lusts. You have commissioned me to go out to bear the good news. Send me, Lord! Send me! I shall begin this day to change the spiritual climate around me. Lead me this day to serve Your Divine purpose being fulfilled that You may bring forth the "renewal of all things," in gathering all things under heaven and earth into subjection to Christ Jesus' authority.
—Heb.12:28-29 / Eph.1

In my *perceiving* Your desires for me, I will *prioritize* time in Your word to renew the Spirit of my mind, *purify* myself from all filth, *pray* with unceasing passion, *proclaim* my faith boldly to others, *prepare* the way before You, and *partner* with like-minded people and organizations. I will stand in the gap, as a living sacrifice, and ask for Your indwelling Holy Spirit to abide in my heart through faith.
—Rom. 12:1 / Matt.3:3 / Ezek.22:30

Oh Lord, *bless* me indeed, *enlarge* my ministry opportunities to lead others to Christ. Make *me* a sanctuary for You, keep Your *hand* before me, keep temptation away from me this day I pray(for Your glory eternally!
—1Chron.4:10

I pray these things in the *mighty* and *precious* name of Jesus Christ, my rock and my redeemer! AMEN!

SIGNED   DATED

"When you make a vow to God, do not delay in fulfilling it; for He has no pleasure in fools. Fulfill what you vow. It is better that you should not vow than that you should vow and not fulfill it...fear God!"
—Eccl. 5:4-7

Epilogue

PROCLAMATION FOR CITYWIDE GATES

FOR THE (area) GATE IN (City or County).

We the people of (City), (State), gather this day, (Day), (Date), in the year (   ), in the presence of our Lord, the God of Israel, and our Savior, Jesus Christ, to make proclamation in preparation for the conquest of this city, land, and this territory, and this establishment, on behalf of all its people, to return to the Lord thy God with our whole heart (Joel 2:12), and that the lost shall be saved, that this land will be healed (2 Chron. 7:14).

FATHER GOD, we declare, standing at the Northwest Gate of Nashville Tennessee, that at the mighty name of our blessed Prince, Jesus Christ, that ALL DEMONIC POWERS, at this city gate MUST FLEE AND SCATTER, away from Nashville.

FATHER GOD, we declare that this city and surrounding territories will have a change of 'spiritual climate' as we put our hands on the thermostat of God's power, to bring the lost and unsaved, to the knowledge of Jesus Christ, that they will be saved.

FATHER GOD, we declare that Your perimeter shall be established here, by our faithfulness to prayer, establishing a beachhead of godliness, removing all spiritual darkness; providing a tangible setting for the kingdom of God.

FATHER GOD, we secure this perimeter by abstaining from the clutches of sin, seeking a life of holiness, toppling over the realm of darkness, through repentance, reconciliation, and restitution.

FATHER GOD, we expand Your perimeter by using Your Biblical models, to win this city for Christ, by building up an army of saints, that launch an attack on the forces of darkness.

FATHER GOD, we infiltrate satan's base of operations, by dropping bombs of prayer, praying peace, and speaking blessings to this city, by touching and caring for the lost and unsaved, and being sent out by the power of God (Acts 1:8).

FATHER GOD, we attack and destroy satan's perimeter by force, sounding the trumpets, to signal an end to his destructive powers, by preaching the good news to every creature in this city, and nurturing new believers, to become spiritual pillars in this community.

FATHER GOD, the laborers are few, and the harvest is ripe. We implore the Lord of the harvest, to send more laborer's into the fields, that more souls can be saved, to further advance the Kingdom of God in this city.

GOD ALMIGHTY, we speak blessings to this city; we speak peace to this city; and we speak unity to this city. Hear our cry O Lord our Savior! In Jesus' Name.

ABOUT THE COMPILER

Jeffrey M. Richfield is called to prayer as "one crying in the wilderness" for all to repent and return to the Lord with all their heart, soul, might and spirit. Born a drummer, he has a heart and desire to worship in spirit and in truth. He served as a team leader in WorshipCityPrayer and is intimately involved with When Men Pray, Open Your Eyes Street Ministry, as Nashville becomes a City on its Knees.

Presently, he and his wife Jodi have two dear sons, James and Jacob. They are stewards of 120 acres of land in Joelton, TN (just 20 minutes from Nashville), called Eagles Landing. The perimeter of the property takes the shape of an eagle. They have dedicated the land to the Lord as a spiritual haven & retreat for prayer and multi-ministry functions, and as a place "just to get away from it all" to find peace with God.

As Isaiah 40:31 reads:

"Yet those who wait on the Lord will gain new strength; they will mount up with wings like eagles, they will run and not get tired, they will walk and no grow weary."

Eagles Landing is open for development as a multi-ministry type of nesting grounds for events, youth camp, prayer cabins, and church picnics. Future plans include a lake with "water falls of healing." The Spirit of the Lord rests on Eagles Landing. We need your help!

To receive information or if you feel you are called to partner with us in any way please contact:

Eagles Landing Mission
Jeffrey M. Richfield
P.O. Box 121
Joelton, TN. 37080
Tel: 615-299-8100 fax: 615-299-8685
Email: Jeff@acityonitsknees.org

In closing, we have to allow God to bring us true lasting change. But we all have a part to play. That's what this book is all about. This is a Maxidonian call to the people of the city to come together for prayer of revival intercession for Nashville. Would you prayerfully consider being a part of a citywide concerted effort of prevailing prayer to help bring revival to this city, spreading to the nation? A spark has begun, but we need more youth, government officials and church leaders. For such a time and place as this, email me or call the number above. God Bless You.

A
CITY
ON ITS
K N E E S®

A state of prayer to a city of revival

Order/ partner form:

Quantity of books:_____ (Call for multiple quantity rates)

Name: _____

Address: _____

City:_____ St:_____ Zip: _____

Home #: (__) _____

Work #: (__) _____

EMAIL:_____

Please charge my gifts and any materials ordered to:
☐ VISA   ☐ Mastercard   ☐ AMEX   ☐ Discover

Card #: _____

Name on Card: _____

Exp. Date ____/____

Signature: _____

Return to:Jeffrey Richfield
ACITYonitsKNEES
P.O. Box 121 Joelton, TN 37080
Order Line: 615-299-8100 / www.aCityonitsKnees.org

Yes, Jeffrey, I would like to support the ministry of ACityonitsKnees and Eagle's Landing Mission with a gift of: (*see note at bottom)
☐ $40.00 ☐ $50.00 ☐ $60.00 ☐ $___
☐ My seed gift is $30 or more. Please send me:
A City on its Knees, Worship City Champions CD, and a Worship City USA Day T-shirt.
(Tshirts alone are $10.00)

Monthly Seed/Prayer Partners
☐ I am (or wish to become) ACITYonitsKNEES seed partner. My monthly seed gift of $____ is enclosed. Please send me the monthly partner audiocassette and/or keep me updated on your weekly email citywide prayerinfogram.
*NOTE: All purchases and donations accepted are split into citywide ministries and Bridges Network ministries pool to visit prisoners, help the fatherless, to feed the poor, clothe the naked, preach to the lost and worship in city parks.
All donations are tax deductible.